SOLDIERS OF THE WAR OF 1812 BURIED IN TENNESSEE

NAMES ABSTRACTED FROM COLONEL DAVID HENLEY'S "WASTEBOOK" REGULAR AND MILITIA PERSONNEL FOR PERIOD 1793-1798 IN SOUTHWEST TERRITORY (TENNESSEE)

PETITION FROM OVERTON COUNTY - 1813

HENDERSON & McGHEE, STOREKEEPERS MARYVILLE, TENNESSEE ACCOUNT OCTOBER 1814 TO DECEMBER 1815

Compiled by
Mary Hardin McCown
Colonel David Henley Chapter

Inez E. Burns
Major James Houston Chapter

Southern Historical Press, Inc.
Greenville, South Carolina

This volume was reproduced from
an 1959 edition located in the
Publisher's private Library

All rights reserved. No part of this publication may be reproduced, stored in a retrieval system or transmitted in any form or by any means without the prior written permission of the publisher.

Please Direct All Correspondence and Book Orders to:

Southern Historical Press, Inc.
1071 Park West Blvd.
Greenville, SC 29611

Copyright 1959 by: Mary Hardin McCown & Inez W. Burns
ISBN #978-1-63914-613-0
Printed in the United States of America

NATIONAL SOCIETY UNITED STATES DAUGHTERS OF 1812

NATIONAL HEADQUARTERS:
1461 RHODE ISLAND AVENUE, N. W., WASHINGTON, D. C.

President National -- 1958-61 Mrs. Uel Stephens, 2714 Greene Ave., Forth Worth, 9 Texas

Honorary Vice President National -- Mrs. Robert P. Armistead, Blair Blvd., Nashville, Tennessee

TENNESSEE SOCIETY - Organized May 7, 1909 by Mrs. Thomas Buford, at her residence, 120 Twenty Fourth Ave., S., Nashville, Tennessee

HONORARY STATE PRESIDENTS

Mrs. Thomas Buford, Nashville - deceased	1909-12
Mrs. Louise M. Spencer, Nashville - deceased	1914-15
Mrs. Mary C. Dorris, Nashville - deceased	1915-16
Mrs. Thomas Day, Memphis - deceased	1923-25
Mrs. William Vaught, Elizabethton - deceased	1926-27
Mrs. William Hitzing, Memphis	1927-29
Mrs. Fred W. Kelsey, Chattanooga - deceased	1929-31
Mrs. Robert P. Armistead, Nashville	1931-33
Mrs. Leonidas W. McCown, Johnson City	1933-35
Mrs. J. D. Howley, Nashville	1935-36
Mrs. Walter M. Berry, Memphis	1936-37
Mrs. Albert W. Craig, Knoxville - deceased	1937-40
Mrs. Rutledge Smith, Nashville - deceased	1941-43
Mrs. Cyrus Griffin Martin, Chattanooga	1943-47
Mrs. Reubin Hayes, Knoxville	1947-49
Mrs. J. Culpepper Brooks, Chattanooga	1949-52
Mrs. Penelope J. Allen, Chattanooga	1952-55
Mrs. Frank L. Weiland, Nashville - deceased	1955-56
Mrs. C. O. McNamee, Nashville	1956-58

OFFICERS

Tennessee Society - 1958-61

President - Mrs. L. D. Bejach, 43 Belleair Drive, Memphis 4
First Vice President - Mrs. Cecil T. Hays, 1603 Dodds Avenue, Chattanooga
Second Vice President - Mrs. A. B. Neil, Sr., 624 Enquirer Avenue, Nashville
Third Vice President - Mrs. Sam D. Harris, 310 Gardner Street, Chattanooga
Fourth Vice President - Mrs. Henry Brackin, 401 Hillwood Drive, Nashville
Chaplain - Mrs. Willard Steele, 250 N. Crest Road, Chattanooga 4
Recording Secretary - Mrs. Hillyard Paschall, 117 Woodmont Blvd., Nashville
Corresponding Secretary - Mrs. Homer Jones, 1100 Greenwood Road, Chattanooga
Treasurer - Mrs. W. K. Page, 786 N. McNeil, Memphis
Registrar - Mrs. Hugh McCain, 1513 Linden Avenue, Memphis
Historian - Mrs. F. D. Gwinn, 709 Mt. Vernon Avenue, Chattanooga
Librarian - Mrs. Thomas Shockley, 2102 25th Avenue, S., Nashville
Curator - Mrs. C. R. Eaves, Louise Terrace Apartments, Chattanooga
Parliamentarian - Mrs. L. B. Gardiner, 1863 Cowden Avenue, Memphis

CHAPTERS

Col. Thomas Hart Benton, Nashville	Mrs. John D. Lewis, President
Alexander Doran, Cleveland	Mrs. Will H. Fillauer, President
Old Hickory, Nashville	Mrs. Thomas Shckley, President
Star Spangled Banner, Memphis	Mrs. R. Seth McCallen, President
Volunteer, Chattanooga	Mrs. Charles C. Moore, President
Chief Wauhatchie, Chattanooga	Mrs. Clifton P. Wright, President
Gen. James Winchester, Nashville	Mrs. Henry Brackin, President

UNITED STATES DAUGHTERS OF 1812
TENNESSEE SOCIETY - 1909--1959
CHAPTERS AND ORGANIZATION DATES

COL THOMAS HART BENTON #1 - - Franklin - - - - - June 1, 1914
   By Miss Susie Gentry*   (Disb 1919)

HERO OF NEW ORLEANS - - - - - Nashville - - - - Oct 19, 1915
   By Mrs Mary C Dorris*   (Inactive)

OLD HICKORY #1 - - - - - - - Memphis - - - - March 17, 1916
   By Mrs L E Goldwire*   (Inactive)

WATAUGA - - - - - - - - - - - Elizabethton - - - - Oct 11, 1923
   By Mrs W M Vaught*   (Inactive)

PRESIDENT JAMES MADISON - - - Jackson - - - - - 1925
   By Miss Laura Bishop   (Inactive c 1930)

GENERAL NATHANIEL TAYLOR - - Bristol - - - - - 1925
   By Mrs John I Cox*   (Disb 1930)

COL DAVID HENLEY - - - - - - Johnson City - - - March 30, 1925
   By Mrs Sidney G Gilbreath*   (Inactive)

CAPT WEITZEL-McBRIDE - - - Mountain City - - - 1925
   By Mrs George A Oster*   (Inactive)

MAJOR JAMES HOUSTON - - - - - Maryville - - - - July 24, 1925
   By Mrs Isaac Messler*   (Inactive)

VOLUNTEER - - - - - - - - - - Chattanooga - - - - - Oct 7, 1925
   By Mrs Frederick W Kelsey*

ALEXANDER DORAN - - - - - - - - Cleveland - - - - Oct 15, 1927
   By Mrs E F Campbell*

GIDEON PILLOW - - - - - - - - Nashville - - - April 10, 1928
   By Mrs West H Morton*   (Inactive)

COL THOMAS HART BENTON #2 - - Nashville - - - March 30, 1929
   By Miss Susie Gentry*

EDWARD SWANSON - - - - - - - - Franklin - - - - - Dec 29, 1929
   By Miss Susie Gentry*   (Inactive)

TOHOPEKA - - - - - - - - - - Knoxville - - - - Feb 28, 1935
   By Mrs Albert L Craig*   (Inactive)

STAR SPANGLED BANNER - - - - Memphis - - - - - - April 8, 1948
   By Mrs Berry B Brooks

CHIEF WAUHATCHIE - - - - - Chattanooga - - - - May 25, 1954
   By Mrs Cecil T Hayes

OLD HICKORY #2 - - - - - - - Nashville - - - - Feb 20, 1957
   By Mrs Thomas Shockley

GEN JAMES WINCHESTER - - - - Nashville - - - - Sept 26, 1957
   By Mrs Charles C Forehand

*Deceased

TABLE OF CONTENTS

Foreword and Acknowledgements — v

Soldiers of War of 1812
    Buried in Tennessee — 1

Soldiers of War of 1812
    Buried in Other States — 126

Prisoners of War from Tennessee
    Held at Quebec, Canada — 135

Abstracts from Col David Henley's "Waste Book" — 136

Petition from Overton County, 1813 — 152

Henderson and McGhee (Maryville, Tenn) Accounts
    Oct 1814 - Dec 1815 — 154

Addenda — 155

SOLDIERS OF WAR OF 1812 BURIED IN TENNESSEE

"People will not look forward to posterity who do not look backward to their ancestors." -Edmund Burke

FOREWORD

The compilation of these records has covered a period of more than thirty years, during which time some research has been made into the history of the heroic deeds of those who helped to mould this nation between the close of the American Revolution and the close of the War of 1812-15. After the Second War of Independence was fought to establish the freedom of the seas, those men who won this victory vowed never to disband, so on Sept 14, 1814 was founded the General Society of the War of 1812. Then near the end of the century - on Jan 8, 1892 (the anniversary of the Battle of New Orleans) - Mrs Flora Adams Darling, a seventh generation descendant from Henry Adams of Baintree, Mass, organized in the city of New York the National Society of the United States Daughters of 1776-1814, which was later called "United States Daughters of 1812". Incorporated by an Act of Congress in 1901, the signing of this Bill was one of the last official acts of the late President William McKinley.

A member of this Society must furnish proof of lineal descent from an ancestor who gave service in one of the early Indian Wars, or Insurrections, or of the Creek Indian War of 1813-14, or of the War of 1812-15, which culminated in the Battle of New Orleans, Jan 8, 1815.

When war was declared against England in June 1812, Gov Willie (Wylie) Blount of Tennessee immediately tendered to President James Madison, 2500 Volunteers under the command of Gen Andrew Jackson. That following August, after the Massacre at Ft Mimms, the Legislature of Tennessee passed an Act (on Sept 25, 1813) raising 2500 men and authorizing the banks to lend a sum not exceeding $300,000 for their arms and equipment. Then both young and old came forward to enlist, proving our claim to the name - VOLUNTEER. These first Volunteers were three months men, but later the militia and the drafted regiments were for a six months term.

When the Capitol was burned by the British in 1814, a great many records were destroyed, so it has always been difficult to obtain complete records of service in the War of 1812. It is of interest to note that the British Archives of the War of 1812 are at Ottawa, Canada. During the term of Mrs Clarence W Jenne as president of the National Society, working through Sec of War Weeks and Sen Henry Cabot Lodge, two large volumes of some 2000 to 3000 folios were discovered in Ottawa, namely (1) the General Entry Book of the Prisoners of War at Quebec, Canada and (2) Correspondence re their Keeping and Exchange. These were copied and a copy filed with the War Department at Washington and another in our National Archives of U S D of 1812. Later, in 1910, a window in St Michael's Church at Dartmoor, Devonshire, England, memorialized those American prisoners who built this church while imprisoned there; and again, in 1929 a Memorial

Gateway at Princetown, Dartmoor, Devonshire, England was dedicated to the 218 prisoners buried there in the cemetery. This tragedy of Dartmoor has been graphically depicted in several novels - "The American Prisoner" by Eden Philpotts, "The Story of Dartmoor Prison" by Sir Basil Thompson, and in the 1930s "The Lively Lady" and "Captain Caution" by Kenneth Roberts.

One of the principal objectives of the National Society is research and preservation of all data re this conflict. So, from its organization in 1925, the Colonel David Henley Chapter of Tennessee Society U S D of 1812 in Johnson City has endeavored to collect and transcribe records. A list of those pensioners living in Washington County in 1883 (the last published list) was obtained from the Pension Office. Of the nineteen, four were survivors in 1883. Of course by 1925, when we began, all of these were deceased, so our task was to locate their graves and collect data concerning them. The first grave located in Washington County was that of a Virginian, Adam Radar, who had served in Virginia and later moved to Washington County, and lived about half way between Johnson City and Jonesboro. His old home still stands just south of the main line of the Southern Railway, which was built several years after his death.

A suitable chart or record blank was formulated to record this data gathered on each Veteran. During a National meeting in Washington contact was made with a member from a distant state who had similar ideas, and that blank now used by the National Society is the evolution of those two blanks.

During my term as State President of the Tennessee Society, 1933-35, a contest was conducted throughout the twelve chapters then extant and 185 records were collected on Soldiers Buried in Tennessee. The Abstract of these was published in the Tennessee Society's Year Book in 1935, and a copy of the completed blanks was bound and filed with both the Tennessee State and National U S D of 1812 libraries. It was the repeated use and the inquiries about these records which gave me the urge and the inspiration to gather all available records and publish them. It is hoped that this collection will prove a storehouse of valuable information and will assist in obtaining members for the National Society. Therefore, since then (1935) a continuing attempt has been made to search county and local histories, biographies, genealogies, files of old newspapers, Bible and tombstone records, church records, the Court minutes and deeds in various counties of Tennessee and adjoining sister states. Repeated trips have been made to consult the Tennessee State Archives in Nashville, as well as trips to and repeated inquiries to the War Department files in Washington for verification of data. Every available record which might reveal some data has been consulted. In addition to research in published and manuscript materials in many private and public libraries and court records, a great amount of data has been gathered from people - from those interested folk who remember the stories handed down by word of mouth from one generation to the following ones - It is they who do much to preserve the history of our great nation.

Our aim has been to list: "Soldiers of the War of 1812 Buried in Tennessee".

ACKNOWLEDGEMENTS:

Material for this volume has been found in the libraries of the National Society U S D of 1812 and the N S D A R in Washington, D C; the Tennessee State Library and Tennessee State Archives in Nashville, which also house the Tennessee Society's books; the Chattanooga Public Library; the McClung Collection in the Lawson McGhee Library in Knoxville; the Mayne Williams Public Library in Johnson City, and the East Tennessee State College Library, also in Johnson City, where the file of the Johnson City Comet, 1883-1905, is kept; the County Court records in various Virginia and North Carolina counties, as well as those in many Tennessee counties; the North Carolina State Archives in Raleigh; the Virginia State Archives in Richmond; many Church records, both published and manuscripts, including those owned by the Baptist Society of Historic Research in Johnson City (this Society owns the Holston Association of Baptist records, 1786-1959); the members of the different chapters of Tennessee Society of 1812 who have sent in data during the contest years and since then; and my own large list of correspondents 1925-1959 who have responded to my call for War of 1812 data. References have been given in the abstracts of each soldier where data was found.

It would be impossible to mention every one who has helped in some way, including those rural friends who have helped locate graveyards, who possessed treasured family Bibles, and who knew personally many of these Veterans of 1812. They have been most generous with their time and information. To all I am deeply grateful. Without your help the goal could not have been reached. But I cannot refrain from paying a silent tribute to some who worked with me during the early years and who are now gone. "Their names, their years are with us yet on the silent shores of memory." Among them were; Mr J Fain Anderson, Washington College, one of my very first consultants, who knew several of these Veterans, attended their funerals, and helped me locate the graves where I placed Government markers; Miss Augusta Bradford, Librarian, Mes Fred W Kelsey and A S Bowen, Chattanooga, the last named served as State Chairman of Grave Locations during the contest years, 1933-35; Mes Isaac Messler and Thos F Broady and Mr Wm A Parham, Maryville, all of whom knew well Blount County and its neighbors and had gathered much data which they shared with me; Mes George A Oster and James I Wagner, Mountain City; Mrs Thomas Buford, Nashville, Organizing President of Tennessee Society, whom I met only once, but whose enthusiastic letters gave me moral courage and wholehearted support. It is especially fitting that this publication commemorates the 50th Anniversary of the birth date of Tennessee Society in 1909; Miss Susie Gentry, that dear little lady from Franklin, the first Secretary and who organized three chapters herself, was a constant source of help as well as stimulation, always urging me to go farther in research and endeavor; Mes Fred W Millspaugh, W H Hollingshead, West Morton and Miss Louise Lindsley, and Mrs Joseph H Acklen, compiler of Tennessee's Bible Records and

Tombstone Inscriptions, all of these gave from their collections; Mr Fillauer and his two Elizabeths, who introduced me to Mr J M Wooten, the Bradley County historian and the Edwards Account Book; Mrs W M Vaught, Elizabethton; Mrs Sidney G Gilbreath, the organizing Regent of Col David Henley Chapter, who owned the "WASTE BOOK", and Verne Fisher Miller, whose stay was all too short but whose inspiration follows me yet; Mr and Mrs Albert L Craig, Knoxville, who took us traipsing to far-off cemeteries, no matter how rough the roads; Judge Samuel C Williams, my fellow-townsman, who encouraged me and to whose library I had free access; Mrs L L McIntyre, Erwin, a member of Col David Henley, whose work as State Chairman of Real Daughters was a real contribution, and her sister, Mrs Bowen of Bluefield, who sent me Virginia records; Mr and Mrs John Trotwood Moore, each one State Archivist and Librarian, who were always ready with willing assistance whenever I sought it; Mr William T Johnson, Elizabethton, a dear uncle, who apparently knew every one and their connections in Carter County; Mrs George W Hardin, my beloved mother, who went on treks with me and baby sat with my young son, Hardin, while I copied tombstones and Bible records and talked with folks. I feel confident that all are watching from the heavenly shores and must be as thankful as we are for the finished task.

Among those collaborators who shall be privileged to view the volume about to appear are: Mrs Nancy Jones Stickley, Sweetwater and Madisonville, a beloved preceptor and teacher of research, without whose guidance and help I would never have had confidence to begin the work; Miss Laura E Luttrell, Knoxville Librarian and Historian, whose Knox County Census of 1850 was so helpful; Roscoe C D'Armand, Knoxville, who was generous with Knox County data; Mrs Penelope J Allen, with her Leaves From the Family Tree, and her inexhaustible supply of Tennesseeana, and Miss Zella Armstrong, with her Twenty-four Hundred Pensioners of the Revolution and War of 1812, both of Chattanooga, whose collections were of immeasurable aid; Mes Cecil T Hayes and John Kain, also Chattanooga, ready to answer letters with help; Prentiss Price, Rogersville, who supplied Hawkins County records; Ferol Frost Hubbs and Richard Doughty, Greeneville, who sent data from their Greene County files; Joseph A Sharp, Sevierville, whose Sevier County data yielded many records; Mrs Elizabeth Cass Bailey, Johnson City and Col David Henley, who served as Co-Chairman for the 1933-35 list; Mrs C A Brown, also of Col David Henley, who trekked with me for data and helped to set grave markers; Robert T Nave and Mrs J Frank Seiler, Elizabethton, who shared their data with me; Mes B D Jackson, Homer F Sloan, Willis Hitzing, Ruth Henley Duncan and Lillian Johnson Gardiner, all of Memphis; Mes Robert P Armistead and J F Draughon Nashville; Belle Lyle Tilden, Johnson City, who has become a willing pupil these past years; Mr Robert T Quarles, Jr, Director of Tennessee Archives, always alert with an answer to my every question, one, who, in my opinion, knows more than any living historian about Tennessee's part in the War of 1812; Inez E Burns, the Blount County Historian, who came into the picture about five years ago, and who, with her tireless zeal, has helped untangle and complete many unfinished records left by earlier historians, and who agreed to go along with me to the final completion of the task. Probably without her efficient cooperation, it might not have been realized. So it is with grateful recognition of her help, and with real affection for Inez, that I include her name with that of my own; lastly, but by no means least, my husband L W McCown, and son Wallace Hardin McCown, who both have, all through the years, not only tolerated, but have helped me to accomplish that which has fascinated and thrilled me and which I have enjoyed - this recording and preserving in a permanent form, incomplete though it may be, the story of some of those men who served during this important period of our country's history. They lived during times which surely tried men's souls - but they bequeathed to us a part of the rich heritage which we enjoy today.

So, it is with humble recognition and gratitude to all who have had some part in this volume, and in dependence on that Divine Providence who daily has guided our steps, that it is presented as my contribution to the Tennessee Society, U S D of 1812, Mrs L D Bejach, President, on the Fiftieth Anniversary, 1909-1959.

June 20, 1959
Johnson City, Tennessee

Mary Hardin McCown (Mrs L W)

Key to data: Name of soldier; birth and death dates with county at death; name of wife with marriage date and her dates; service; reference for service; grave location in cemetery and county; whether marked or unmarked.

Abbreviations besides those generally used include:

B L Wt - Bounty Land Warrant	mos - months
c - circa; about	P D - Pension Dept
Cem - Cemetery	T S A - Tenn State Archives
E T V - East Tenn Volunteers	U S A - U S Archives
Fam - Family	N C S A - N C State Archives
Govt - Government	Va S A - Virginia State Archives
hist - history	unkn - unknown
m - mile	unmkd - unmarked
md - married	W D - War Dept
Mil - Militia	W T V - West Tenn Volunteers
mkd - marked	

The list is arranged in alphabetical order.

SOLDIERS OF THE WAR OF 1812 BURIED IN TENNESSEE

ADAIR, JOHN (1732--2-24-1827 Knox Co); Md Ellen Crawford (   ); J P 1792-Constitutional Convention 1796; T S A; Fam Cem now Lynnhurst Cem, Knoxville, Knox Co; Mkd by D A R. (Also Rev War)

ADAMS, NATH. M Sr. (1795-- 1872 Trousdale Co); Md Nancy Holliday (1798--1872); Pvt, Capt Carter's Co; Goodspeed Trousdale Co; likely in Trousdale Co; Pvt mkr.

ADAMS, RADFORD (--c 1880 Greene Co); Md--several times; War of 1812; T S A; Mt Carmel Meth Cem, Andrew Johnson Hiway near Painter's Creek, Greene Co; Unmkd. (One Radford Adams bur Liberty Free Will Bapt Cem on 190 N E Telford, Washington Co- Co L 5th Tenn Inf Mex War.)

ADAMS, SIMON (--c 1830 Hamilton Co); Md Nelly Lovelady 1-1-1816 (c 1795--aft 1855); Musician Capt Isaac Williams' Co, Col Sam Bunch's Regt Mtd Gunmen 4 mos; W D & P D; Cem Hamilton Co; Unkn.

ADAMS, WILLIAM (--d Johnson Co); Md Susannah Adams (   ); Pvt 7th U S Inf; W D & Nelson Papers in McClung Archives; likely in Johnson Co; Unkn.

AGEE, JAMES (1789-- 1844 Campbell Co); Md Elizabeth Tudor (1792--1865); Servd in Gen John Cocke's Regt; W D & B L Wt; likely in Campbell Co; Unkn.

ALEXANDER, ANDREW MILLER (--killed 12-23-1814 N O); Md Nancy Doran (4-19-1794--4-25-1865); Pvt, Capt Robt Moore's Co, 2nd Regt Mtd Gunmen, transfrd 10-29-1814 to Lieut Jesse Been's Co Spies, Gen John Coffee; W D; Old St Louis Cem N O, La; Unkn.

ALEXANDER, DICKS (8-17-1790--7-23-1875 Hawkins Co); Md Sarah Ann Graham 3-26-1828 (12-21-1805--1-6-1882); Ensign 39th Regt U S Inf, 3-17-1814, 3rd Lieut 5-20-1814--6-15-1815; T S A & Obt, Press & Messenger, Knoxville 7-28-1875; Old Pres Cem Rogersville, Hawkins Co; Pvt Mkr.

ALEXANDER, JOHN (--6-18-1831 Washington Co); Md Martha Ferguson (   ); Pvt, Capt Henry McCray's Co, Col Ewen Allison's Regt E T Mil, 1-5-1814--1-14-1814 when he furnished a Sub-W B Stringer; W D; Fairview Meth Cem 2 m SW Jonesboro, Washington Co; Govt mkr.

ALEXANDER, OLIVER (1732--1812-15 likely Blount Co); Md Margaret Paul (1735--1812-3); J P Blount Co; Blount Co Records; likely Blount Co; Unkn.

ALEXANDER, STEPHEN K (--c 1860 Greene Co); Md   (   ); Srgt, Capt Jacob Hoyal's Co, Col Ewen Allison's Regt E T Mil, 1-10-1814--5-23-1814; W D; Camp Creek Cem, Greene Co; Unmkd.

ALLEN, Dr DANIEL (--d Davidson Co); Md   (   );
War of 1812;   ; Old City Cem, Nashville,
Davidson Co; Pvt mkr.

ALLEN, ISAAC (--d Cocke Co); Md   (   ); 2nd
Sheriff, Cocke Co 1797, 2nd Maj, Col Wm Lillard's 2nd Regt,
E T V, 10-13-1813--2-8-1814; Cocke Co Hist & W D & T S A;
Allen Fam Cem, Cocke Co; Unkn.

ALLEN, JOHN (Long John) (12-30-1772--1-6-1849 Cocke Co); Md
Peggy Huff 1810 (--4-21-1849); Capt at Raisin River 1812 &
Tohopeka 1814; W D & T S A; Allen Fam Cem, Cocke Co; Pvt mkr.

ALLEN, REUBEN (--11-7-1825 Cocke Co); Md Mary Jones 2-26-1805
(4-2-1788--11-13-1864); Pvt, Capt Joseph Hale's Co, Col Sam
Bayless' 4th Regt E T Drftd Mil, 11-8-1814--5-16-1815; also
Lieut 4-5-1798 Cocke Co Mil; W D & T S A & P D; Allen Fam Cem
on Wolfe Creek, Cocke Co; Pvt mkr. (Reuben Allen Pension
#6,948 War of 1812, Wd Mary Allen W#31,562, living in
Tucheleeche Cove, Blount Co.)

ALLEN, ROBERT (6-19-1778--8-19-1844 Smith Co); Md
(   ); Col under Andrew Jackson; W D; Greenwood Cem
Carthage, Smith Co; Pvt mkr.

ALLEN, THOMAS (6-23-1787--1-16-1848 Shelby Co); Md Betsy
Ecklen 1807 (10-24-1789--12-27-1858); Corp, Capt J W Godley's
Co N C Mil, Beaufort Regt, Lathan's N C Mil, 7-15-1813--7-18-
1813; W D & N C A; Cem near Cordova, Shelby Co; Pvt mkr.

ALLISON, ROBERT (1795-- 1861 Washington Co); Md 1--Hodge
(   ), 2-Mary Chester Gammon 1810 (--1887); Pvt,
Capt Allen S Bacon's Co Drftd Mil, Maj Thomas C Clark's Regt
1-10-1814--7-21-1814; W D & T S A; Hodge Fam Cem near
Watauga River, Washington Co; Pvt mkr.

ALLISON, URIAH (1782-- 182- Roane Co); Md Nancy Clark Cox
1-29-1820 (1800--); 2nd Lieut 8th U S Inf, 3-15-1813, recruited the first co in Roane Co; W D & Roane Co Hist, Wells;
Bethel Pres Cem, Kingston, Roane Co; Pvt mkr.

ALLSTATT, NICHOLAS (--d Ft Williams, 3-2-1814); single; Pvt,
Capt Child's Co, Col John Brown's 2nd Regt 1-10-1814; T S A;
Ft Williams, Talladega Co, Ala; Unmkd.

ALMONY, JOHN (1782--liv 1840 Sullivan Co); Md
(   ); War of 1812; P D & 2400 Pensioners, Armstrong;
likely in Sullivan Co; Unkn.

ANDERSON, Gen ALEXANDER OUTLAW (11-10-1795--5-23-1869 Knox
Co); Md 1-Maria Hamilton of Washington (   ), 2-a coz
Eliza Rosa Deaderick 6-7-1825 (--d 10-15-1886); Pvt, Capt
Henry Stephen's Co, Col Sam Bunch's Regt, 10-17-1813--1-3-
1814, wounded in battle; W D & French Broad-Holston Hist &
Anderson-Deaderick-Shelby-McDowell Hist; Old Gray Cem in
Knoxville, Knox Co; Pvt mkr.

ANDERSON, INSLEE (4-1753--11-4-1791 St Clair's Defeat); Md Miss McDonough (   ); killed at St Clair's Defeat; W D & Letter-Gen Henry Knox to Gen Washington; likely where killed; Unkn.

ANDERSON, ISAAC (3-26-1780--1-28-1857 Blount Co); Md Flora McCampbell 10-19-1802 (6-3-1782--11-18-1852); Chaplain, Brigade under Gen James White in Creek War; Century of Maryville College-Wilson; 1st, New Providence Pres Cem, now Maryville College Cem, Maryville, Blount Co; Pvt mkr and monument.

ANDERSON, JAMES (2-18-1790--1-6-1858 Perry Co); Md Sarah Hughes 9-26-1817 (6-24-1793--8-4-1850); Pvt, Capt Patterson's Co, Col N T Perkins Regt Mtd Vol Riflemen; T S A; Perry Co; Unkn.

ANDERSON, JAMES (1791-- d Knox Co); Md Anne Ford (c 1795--); Pvt, Capt Perry's Co, Col Sam Wear's 1st Regt E T V; W D & T S A; Anderson-Ford Fam Cem near Meridian Bapt Ch, Knox Co; Pvt mkr.

ANDERSON, JOHN Jr (10-5-1778--10-27-1814 Ft Strother, Ala); Md Betsy McNair 11-12-1805 (3-31-1783--8-13-1859); Lieut Col, under Col Wm Johnson's 3rd Regt E T Drftd Mil, 9-17-1814--d at Ft Strother, 10-27-1814; W D & T S A & Goodspeed E T; likely Ft Strother, Ala; Unkn.

ANDERSON, JOHN (--d Tenn); Md   (   ); served as Lieut Col War of 1812; Armstrong's Hamilton Co Hist; likely in Tenn; Unkn. (This may be same as one preceding.)

ANDERSON, JONATHAN (--d Blount Co); Md Julia Famer 1819 (   ); War of 1812; P D (W #31,217); likely Blount Co; Unkn.

ANDERSON, Maj NATHANIEL (1796--3-9-1867 Shelby Co); Md (   ); served at Fight in Craney Island at Norfolk; W D & Elmwood Cem Record Book; Elmwood Cem in Memphis, Shelby Co; Govt mkr.

ANDERSON, ROBERT (--d South Pittsburg, Marion Co); Md (   ); War of 1812; W D; moved from Marion Co to National Cem, Chattanooga, Hamilton Co; Unkn.

ANDREWS, JAMES (1785-- 1850 Williamson Co); Md Jane McGuire 1805 (1787--1845); Creek War; Goodspeed Maury Co; likely Williamson Co; Unkn.

ANDREWS, JOHN (1788-- liv 1840 Henderson Co); Md (   ); War of 1812; P D & 2400 Pensioners, Armstrong; likely Henderson Co; Unkn.

ANDREWS, JONES (1791-- 1843 Marshall Co); Md Lucy Lanier (1803--1861); War of 1812; Goodspeed Marshall Co; likely Marshall Co; Unkn.

ARMSTRONG, JAMES (Trooper) (1736--9-28-1813 Knox Co); Md Susan Wells 1782 (   ); Holston Treaty at White's Fort, 1791; T S A; Armstrong Fam Cem on Flat Creek, Knox Co; Pvt mkr.

ARMSTRONG, ROBERT (Surveyor) (12-13-1774--2-3-1849 Knoxville Knox Co); Md 1-Elizabeth Wear 10-19-1798 (--d 1820), 2-Charlotte Perry (   ); Pvt, Capt Hugh Beard's Mil, 1792, D Sheriff Knox Co, 1793-4, Pvt, Capt Nath Evans' Co Cav, U S A 1793, Surveyor, 1807, 1817-1849, 5th Distr; T S A & Knox Co; Knoxville Cem, Knox Co; Pvt mkr.

ARMSTRONG, ROBERT (1791--2-23-1854 Nashville, Davidson Co); Md   (   ); Lieut in Artillery Co under Gen Jackson in Creek War-Aide-de-camp at N O; T S A & Acklen; Old City Cem at Nashville, Davidson Co; Pvt mkr. (Andrew Jackson bequeathed his sword to him.)

ARNOLD, THOMAS DICKENS (5-3-1798--5-26-1870 Greene Co); Md (   ); Drummer Boy aged 14 yrs-Pvt, Capt John L Jennings' Co, Col Saunders' 7th Regt Va Mil, 8-11-1814--11-15-1814; Va A & Congressional Dir; Oak Grove Cem, Greene Co; Pvt mkr.

ATCHLEY, ISAAC (--c 1788-8-4-1854 Sevier Co); Md Mary Bowers 2-4-1830 (1800-- liv 4-2-1855); Corp, Capt Andrew Lawson's Co, Col Wm Johnson's 3rd Regt E T Drftd Mil, 9-20-1814--5-3-1815; T S A & P D; likely in Sevier Co; Unkn.

ATCHLEY, JESSE (-- liv 4-11-1855 aged 67 yrs Bradley Co); Md   (   ); Pvt, Capt Andrew Lawson's Co, Col Wm Johnson's 3rd Regt E T Drftd Mil, 9-20-1814--5-3-1815; W D & T S A & P D; Cem 6 m W Cleveland, Bradley Co; Unkn.

ATKINSON, THOMAS WALTON (1777--2-7-1862 Montgomery Co); Md Lizzie Hunley (--d 1809); Srgt, Capt Butler's Co Ky Mil, 9-18-1812--10-12-1812 & Capt Ky Vol Mil, 8-24-1813 for 3 mos at Battle of Thames; W D & Ky S A & P D; Clarksville, Montgomery Co; Pvt mkr.

ATKINSON, WILTON (--d 1853 Washington Co); Md Martha B Machen 2-17-1817 (   ); War of 1812 in Gen Jackson's Troops; Masengill Hist; likely Old Cem Jonesboro, Washington Co; Unmkd.

ATKINSON, PLEASANT (--d Marshall co); Md 1-Saphronia Holmes (--d 1835), 2-Emily Woods (   ); War of 1812; Goodspeed Marshall Co; likely Marshall Co; Unkn.

BADGETT, RANSON (1772-- 1862 Blount Co); Md Sophira Hunter (1794--1865); War of 1812; Goodspeed Knox Co; likely Fam Cem near Knox-Blount Co line; Unkn.

BAILEY, JOHN (--d 7-4-1814); Md   (   ); Pvt, 1st Regt U S Inf, d in service; 2400 Pensioners, Armstrong; likely where died; Unkn.

BAKER, JOHN E (1-8-1781-10-23-1866 Wilson Co); Md Elizabeth Bensby (2-2-1804--9-9-1829); at Battle of N O, 1815; Goodspeed Wilson Co; likely in Wilson Co; Pvt mkr.

BAKER, WILLIAM (--d in Tenn); Md   (   ); 1st Lieut, Capt Wm Hamilton's Co, Col Wm Lillard's 2nd Regt, E T V, 10-12-1813--2-8-1814, & Pvt, Capt Reuben Tipton's Co Mtd Gunmen, Maj John Child's Regt; W D; in Tenn; Unkn.

BALEY, JOHN (--killed 11-3-1813 Tallushatchee, Ala); Md (   ); Corp, Capt Wm Locke's Co, Col John Allcorn's Regt W T V Cav, 9-24-1813--11-3-1813 killed; W D & T S A; likely in Ala; Unkn.

BALL, JOSEPH (1787-- Inv 1867 Washington Co); Md   (15 children); Pvt, Capt Andrew Lawson's Co, Col Wm Johnson's 3rd Regt E T Drftd Mil, 9-20-1814--5-3-1815; W D & T S A; likely in Washington Co; Unkn.

BANDY, EPPERSON (--liv 1828 Pension Wilson Co); Md (   ); War of 1812; P D & 2400 Pensioners, Armstrong; likely Wilson Co; Unkn.

BANDY, JAMESON (9-16-1788--1-16-1873 Perry Co); Md (   ); Lieut, Capt George Smith's Co Spies, Col Robt Dyer's Regt Cav & Mtd Riflemen, 9-24-1813--4-30-1814, promoted 1st Lieut 12-24-1813; W D & T S A; Cem at Denson's Landing, Perry Co; Pvt mkr. (He was an M D.)

BANKS, Maj Gen JAMES (1765-- 1828 Memphis, Shelby Co); Md Catherine Nelson 1789 (   ); Capt Penn Regt, 1793 & Maj Gen 11th Div Pa Mil, 8-3-1811; Penn State Archives; Memphis, Shelby Co; Unkn.

BANTON, JOAB (--d in Tenn); Md   (   ); Capt, W T Mil, 1813; T S A; likely in Tenn; Unkn.

BARFIELD, JAMES (--c 1782-- liv 1840 aged 58 yrs Lauderdale Co); Md   (   ); Pvt Tenn Mil, 1828 in Carroll Co, 1840 Lauderdale Co; P D & 2400 Pensioners, Armstrong; likely Lauderdale Co; Unkn.

BARKER, LEWIS (-- Camden, Benton Co); Md   (   ); War of 1812; B L Wt; Cem at Camden, Benton Co; Unkn. (Bur at Camden on land granted father Zachary Barker or brother Needham Barker for Rev War services.)

BARLOW, HENSON (--9-3-1828 Jefferson Co); Md
(   ); Pvt 7th U S Inf; W D & P D; likely Jefferson
Co; Unkn.

BARNES, HENRY (--killed 11-9-1813 Talledega, Ala); Md
(   ); Trumpeter, Capt John W Byrn's Co, Col John
Allcorn's Regt Mtd W T Mil, 9-24-1813--11-9-1813 killed;
W D & T S A; likely Ala; Unkn.

BARR, JAMES (--d Sumner Co); Md   (   );
served in Tenn Rangers; W D & P D & 2400 Pensioners, Armstrong; likely in Sumner Co; Unkn.

BARRY, ASA (1787-- 1870 Robertson Co); Md
(   ); War of 1812; W D; likely in Robertson Co; Unkn.

BARRY, JOHN (b Ireland --d Mobile Ala in service); Md
(   ); War of 1812; Goodspeed E T Hist; likely in Ala;
Unkn.

BARTON, DAVID (3-15-1744--7-15-1815 Wilson Co); Md Hannah
Hill 6-9-1771 (3-25-1754--   ); Pvt, Capt Thomas
Bradley's Co, Col John Allcorn W T Vol Cav, 9-24-1813--
12-10-1813, pd to 12-26-1813; W D & T S A; Fam Cem in Wilson
Co; Pvt mkr. (Also Lieut in Rev War.)

BASSFORD, JAMES (--d Madison Co); Md   (   );
Pvt 39th U S Inf, Col John Williams Regt; P D & 2400 Pensioners, Armstrong; likely in Madison Co; Unkn.

BATES, ISAAC (--d Shelby Co); Md   (   );
Pvt, Col Armstrong's Regt; Pension 1828 List & 2400 Pensioners, Armstrong; likely in Shelby Co; Unkn.

BATES, WILLIAM (--d in Tenn); Md   (   );
Ensign Capt Jehu Stephens Co, Col Sam Wear's 1st Regt E T V,
Gen John Coffee, 10-6-1814--4-6-1815; W D; likely in Tenn;
Unkn.

BAYLESS, JOHN (6-13-1773--11-30-1858 Knox Co now Union Co);
Md 1-Elizabeth Jones 1792 (1775--1848), 2-Rebecca Jackson
(   ); Capt, Col Sam Wear's 1st Regt E T V, 9-23-1813--
12-22-1813; W D & T S A; Bayless Fam Cem in Union Co; Pvt mkr.

BAYLESS, REES (8-22-1787--10-29-1864 Washington Co); Md 1-
Margaret Young 1804 (--10-5-1828), 2-Elizabeth McFerrin 1829
(5-17-1804--1829); Pvt, Capt Sam Bayless' Co, Mtd Vol, Col
John Williams Regt E T Vol 12-1-1812--3-25-1813; W D;
Cherokee Bapt Cem in Washington Co; Pvt mkr.

BAYLESS, REUBEN (6-7-1854--11-7-1826 Washington Co); Md
Margaret   (1-31-1751--3-1-1828); Pvt, Capt David G.
Vance's Co Mtd Inf, Col Sam Bunch's Regt E T Mil, 10-16-1813
--1-22-1814; W D & T S A; Cherokee Bapt Cem in Washington Co;
Pvt mkr.

BAYLESS, Col SAMUEL (--d Monroe Co); Md Mary (1784--3-31-1843); Col 4th E T Drftd Mil, 11-13-1814--5-18-1815; W D & T S A; likely in Madisonville Cem, Monroe Co; Unkn.

BEAL, GEORGE (--d Bradley Co); Md ( ); Pvt, Capt Welch's Co ---Regt; Edwards' Acct Bk & P D; likely in Bradley Co; Unkn.

BEAN, WILLIAM (1784-- 1815 in Miss); Md Nancy Blevins 1802 (1770--aft 1815); Courier in Capt Samuel Thompson's Co, Col Edwin Boothe's 5th Regt, 11-13-1814--5-19-1815; T S A; near Natchez in unkn grave; Unmkd.

BEASLEY, JAMES (1790-- 1848 Rutherford Co); Md Mrs Eliza E Henderson Simmons 1832 (3-3-1812--1853); Pvt, Capt Wm Walker's Co, 2nd Regt Ga Mil, 10-12-1814--12-12-1814; W D & Ga S A; Rutherford Co Cem; Pvt mkr.

BEDFORD, WILLIAM F (--d Nashville, Davidson Co); Md ( ); War of 1812; Acklen's Records; Old City Cem Nashville, Davidson Co; Pvt mkr.

BEELER, Capt BENJAMIN (2-16-1794--7-10-1877 Sullivan Co); Md Anna (3-1-1803--4-14-1879); War of 1812; T S A; Beeler (Buehler) Lutheran Cem in Sullivan Co; Pvt mkr.

BELL, Lieut JOHN (--d Madison Co); Md ( ); Lieut in Col Wm Russell's Spies; Pension 1828 List & 2400 Pensioners, Armstrong; likely in Madison Co; Unkn.

BELL, JOSEPH EDWARDS (8-22-1789--2-7-1871 Greene Co); Md 1-Nancy White 10-22-1809 (2-20-1791--9-7-1831), 2-Mary Ann Farnsworth 2-7-1832 (7-27-1793--8-1-1854), 3-Hephzibah Woolsey 1-17-1855 (7-8-1803--6-30-1872); Pvt, Capt Andrew Lawson's Co, Col Wm Johnson's 3rd Regt E T Drftd Mil, 9-20-1814--left in Camp Bell sick, never disch; W D & T S A & P D; Solomon's Lutheran Cem on Cove Creek, Greene Co; Pvt mkr. (Inscription-"Rev Joseph E Bell, M D 8-22-1789--2-7-1871, aged 81-6-15".)

BELL, Dr PULASKI BOTTS (1793--10-9-1862 Weakley Co); Md Sarah Lacey Nailling 9-26-1827 (2-29-1804--); Srgt, Capt Wm Wood's Co Va Mil; Va S A; Cem in Weakley Co; Pvt mkr.

BERRY, JAMES (5-11-1788-6-18-1856 Bradley Co); Md Elizabeth Shawn 5-12-1812 (1795--2-4-1863); Corp, Capt Henry Dix's Co 105th Regt Va Mil, disch 7-5-1814; W D & Va S A; Fort Hill Cem in Cleveland, Bradley Co; Pvt mkr.

BERRY, JOHN (9-22-1793--4-2-1874 Sullivan Co); Md Kitty Shryrock 6-16-1816 (11-9-1796--1-12-1889); Pvt, Capt H St George Tucker's Va Cav; W D & Va S A; East Hill Cem, Bristol, Va-Tenn; Pvt mkr.

BEWLEY, JACOB M (1787-- 1867 Jefferson Co); Md 1-Sarah Maroney
(   ), 2-Malinda Moore Lyle (   ); Pvt, War of
1812; Goodspeed Hamblen Co;. Cem in Jefferson Co; Unkn.

BIBLE, JOHN (1776 --d Greene Co); Md   (   );
2nd Lieut, Capt Jones' Co; Goodspeed Greene Co & W D; Cem on
Little Chucky River in Greene Co; Unkn.

BIDWELL, Maj CHARLES (9-10-1787--10-23-1848 Robertson Co); Md
Martha Binkley 12-6-1828 (1-14-1801--4-24-1855); Major in W T
Mil; T S A; Cem in Robertson Co; Pvt mkr.

BIGGS, JOHN (1752--12-1-1838 Blount Co); Md Isabella Wilson
(--d 1838); Pvt, Capt James Craig's Co, Col Lowry's 2nd Regt
W T Mil, 9-20-1814--4-29-1815; W D & T S A; Blount Co; Pvt mkr.

BILES, JIM (--d Davidson Co); Md   (   );
War of 1812; data from Robt J Bandy, V A, Mountain Home, Tenn;
Unkn Cem in Davidson Co; Unkn.

BITNER, SAMUEL (--killed at Ft Montgomery, Ala, 1814-15);
Md Margaret Grayham (--d aft 1816); Pvt, Capt Andrew Lawson's
Co, Col Wm Johnson's 3rd Regt E T Drftd Mil, Gen Nath Taylor's
Brigade; W D & T S A & Washington Co Court Minutes, Oct 23,
1816, says-"Samuel Bitner was killed on duty Ft Montgomery
during late war - he married Margaret Grayham in Greene Co...";
likely at Ft Montgomery, Ala; Unkn.

BLACK, JOSEPH (1781-- 1864 Anderson Co); Md Catherine Henry
(8-8-1784--7-24-1849); Lieut in Co---; Goodspeed Anderson Co;
likely in Cem in Anderson Co; Unkn.

BLACKBURN, JOHN (9-29-1747--4-20-1818 Jefferson Co); Md Janey
Mathes 4-2-1765 (   ); Member Jefferson Co Court;
Jefferson Co record; Dandridge Cem, Jefferson Co; Pvt mkr.

BLAIR, JOHN (9-13-1790--7-9-1863 Washington Co); Md
(   ); Member House Representatives, 1815-1817; Congressional Dir; Old Cem in Jonesboro, Washington Co; Pvt mkr.

BLAIR, JOHN B (1-12-1794--4-9-1876 Greene Co); Md Levica
Shields 1-31-1815 (10-11-1794--2-18-1886); Pvt, Capt Henry
McCray's Co, Col Ewen Allison's Regt E T Mil, 1-5-1814--5-23-
1814; W D & P D; New Providence Pres Cem near Millbrook,
Greene Co near Washington Co line; Pvt mkr.

BLAIR, SAMUEL (--likely Davidson Co); Md   (   );
in Buchanan's Fort, 1792; Davidson Co Hist; Cem in Davidson
Co; Unkn.

BLAIR, THOMAS (6-6-1790--10-28-1866 Georgetown, Hamilton Co);
Md Hanna Stone 1805 (8-14-1786--1-16-1856); Pvt, Capt John
Trimble's Co E T Mil, Maj Wm Russell, disch 4-5-1815; W D &
T S A; Old Blair Fam Cem 3 m S Georgetown, Hamilton Co; Pvt mkr.

BLEVINS, JOHNSON (--d 1863 Scott Co); Md   (   );
settled on No Business Creek 1815, with Jackson at N O; Scott
Co Hist-Sanderson; Station Camp Cem in Scott Co; Unkn.

BLOUNT, WILLIAM (3-26-1749--3-20-1800 Knoxville, Knox Co); Md
Mary Grainger 2-12-1778 (1761--10-7-1802); Governor S W Terr,
1790-96; T S A; First Pres Cem, Knoxville, Knox Co; Pvt mkr.
(Also Rev War)

BLOUNT, WILLIAM GRAINGER (1784--5-21-1827 Paris, Henry Co);
single; Sec State Tenn, 1812-15; T S A; Cem in Paris, Henry
Co; Pvt mkr.

BLOUNT, WILLIE (WYLIE) (4-18-1768--9-10-1835 Montgomery Co);
Md Lucinda Baker (   ); Sec to Gov Wm Blount 1790-96,
Gov of Tenn, 1809-15 throughout War of 1812; W D & T S A;
Clarksville Cem in Montgomery Co; Mkd by State of Tenn, 1878.

BOAZ, JAMES (--d 5-17-1814 Ft Williams, Ala); single; Pvt,
Capt Edward Buchanan's Co, Col Sam Bunch's Regt Drftd Mil,
1-10-1814--5-17-1814; W D & T S A; at Ft Williams, Talledega
Co, Ala; Unmkd.

BOGLE, ANDREW (4-29-1753--11-29-1813 Blount Co); Md Elizabeth
Campbell 5-24-1774 (4-4-1748--9-4-1845); J P of Blount Co 1795;
T S A; Eusebia Pres Cem, Blount Co; Pvt mkr. ("First owner of
the soil which now covers his remains.")

BOGLE, JAMES (10-8-1792--d aft 1820 Monroe Co); Md
(   ); 1st Corp, Capt Jehu Stephens' Co, Mtd Gunmen,
under Brig Gen John Coffee, 10-6-1814--4-6-1815; W D & T S A;
Unkn Cem in Monroe Co; Unkn.

BONDURANT, JACOB M (2-4-1795--12-25-1858 Davidson Co); Md
Elizabeth C Reed 2-17-1824 (   ); Pvt under Gen Jackson
where he acquired title of Major; Hist of Davidson Co-Clayton
p 482; Fam Cem (Old Hickory Golf Club) in Davidson Co; Pvt mkr.

BOOTHE, CHARLES (1785-90--6-24-1845 Limestone Co, Ala (bur in
Tenn); Md Lucy Ann Abernathy 6-24-1811 (1787--1870); Q M in
Capt Fisher's Co, Col Jesse Reid's Regt Va Vol, 7-21-1812--
8-26-1814; Va S A; Bethel Cem (Widow Legge) in Giles Co, near
Minor Hill; Pvt mkr.

BOOTHE, EDWIN (1774--11-17-1824 in Knox Co); Md Mrs Alice
Murphy Dennis 10-16-1808 (   ); Col 5th Drftd E T Mil,
11-13-1814--5-15-1815; W D & T S A; First Pres Cem, Knoxville,
Knox Co; Pvt mkr (broken).

BOOTHE, JOSEPH (1786--6-7-1849 Washington Co); Md Sarah
(--12-5-1828 aged 48 yrs); Corp, Capt John Hampton's Co, Col
Ewen Allison's Regt E T Mil 1-5-1814--7-26-1814; W D & T S A;
Cherokee Bapt Cem in Washington Co; Pvt mkr.

BORING, GREENBERRY (1762--1-7-1874 Washington Co); Md Mary Ruble 10-11-1807 (6-26-1790--aft 1883); Pvt, Capt Andrew Lawson's Co, Col Wm Johnson's 3rd Regt E T Drftd Mil, 9-14-1814 --5-9-1815; W D & T S A; Hodge Fam Cem on Watauga River, Washington Co; Pvt mkr.

BORDEN, AUGUSTEN (--c 1783-- liv 5-14-1852 aged 69 yrs in Monroe Co); Md ( ); Pvt, Capt Andrew Lawson's Co, Col Wm Johnson's 3rd Regt E T Mil, 9-8-1814--5-1-1815, marched 1200 miles; W D & T S A & P D; likely in Monroe Co; Unkn.

BOSLEY, JOHN (--d Davidson Co); Md Delilah Robertson ( ); War of 1812; T S A; Cem on Robertson Hiway off Charlotte Pike, Davidson Co; Pvt mkr. (Also Rev War)

BOWEN, JOHN (7-1766--4-1823 Grainger Co); Md Sarah Bean c 1790 (1768--1853); J P of Grainger Co; Co Records; Hammer Fam Cem near Rutledge, Grainger Co; Unmkd.

BOWERS, VALENTINE (9-23-1788--4-12-1867 Carter Co); Md Abigail Buck 10-1-1808 (1793--7-16-1878); Pvt, Capt Adam Winsell's Co, Col Ewen Allison's Regt E T Drftd Mil, 1-10-1814--5-26-1814; W D & P D; Bowers Fam Cem near Siam, Carter Co; Pvt mkr.

BOWMAN, SAMUEL (6-8-1783-- 1874 Knox Co); Md Elizabeth Green ( ); Pvt so named in Capt David McKamy's Co, Col Wm Johnson's 3rd Regt E T Drftd Mil, 9-8-1814--5-1-1815; W D & T S A; Cem in Knox Co; Unkn.

BOYD, JAMES (10-18-1780--d Blount Co); Md Hannah McMurray 9-3-1799 (1779-1868); Pvt, Capt John Trimble's Co Mtd Inf, Maj Wm Russell's Battln, 10-5-1814--4-5-1815; W D & T S A; Eusebia Pres Cem in Blount Co; Pvt mkr.

BOYD, JOHN (8-10-1776--d Blount Co); Md Katy Holloway 1799 ( ); Pvt, Capt John Trimble's Co Mtd Inf, Maj Wm Russell's Battln, 10-5-1814--4-5-1815; W D & T S A; Unkn Cem in Blount Co; Unkn.

BOYD, JOSEPH (1797--8-18-1874 Monroe Co); Md 1-Anne Martin 1798 ( ), 2-Margaret Lilburn 2-22-1822 ( ); Pvt, Capt David Yarnell's Co, Col Regt, 1-13-1814--5-1-1815, transfrd Capt James Berry's Co 5-2-1814--7-17-1814; W D & T S A; Mt Vernon Cem in Monroe Co; Pvt mkr.

BRADFORD, Maj HENRY (1757--7-1815 Sumner Co); Md Elizabeth Paine Blakemore 7-1785 (1769--aft 1801); Revenue Off in Adams & Jefferson's Admr, & Brig Major of Mero Distr 1791; W D & T S A; Fam Cem at Hendersonville, Sumner Co; Pvt mkr. (Also Rev War)

BRADFORD, Col HENRY (12-25-1776--4-16-1871 Polk Co); Md Rachel (1786--); War of 1812; ; Old Columbus Cem in Polk Co; Pvt mkr.

BRADFORD, PRIESTLY (2-7-1795--5-7-1854 Sumner Co); Md Elizabeth Genette (3-26-1799--9-14-1853); War of 1812; T S A; Fam Cem at Hendersonville, Sumner Co; Pvt mkr.

BRADFUTE, ARCHIBALD (1786--7-24-1865 Jefferson Co); Md Louiza Moore 10-28-1834 (1806--1884); Pvt, Capt James Leftwich's Co Cav, Maj J T Woodford's Va Mil, 9-3-1814--11-29-1814; W D & Va S A; Leadville Meth Cem, 1 m from White Pine, Jefferson Co; Unmkd.

BRADSHAW, RICHARD HARDIN (1-15-1788--10-3-1872 Jefferson Co); Md Lydia Prigmore 8-4-1809 (10-10-1778--11-27-1853); Pvt, Capt Thomas McQuiston's Co, Col Wm Lillard's 2nd Regt E T V, 10-13-1813--2-8-1814; W D & T S A; Mt Horeb Cem in Jefferson Co; Pvt mkr.

BRAMLEY, JOHN (--3-14-1833 Fayette Co); Md Sarah Ammonette 3-19-1812 (c 1797--liv 1855 Fayette Co); Pvt, Capt Simeon Perry's Co, Col Sam Wear's 1st Regt E T V, 9-23-1813--12-23-1813; W D & P D; likely in Fayette Co; Pvt mkr. (W T 67045 55-160 Pension Dept)

BRANDON, Capt GEORGE (8-2-1770--5-12-1844 Rutherford Co); Md Sidney McGuire 2-9-1797 (11-30-1794--2-22-1819); Capt, 2nd Regt Mtd Gunmen, Col Newton Cannon W T V, 9-24-1812--11-22-1813; W D & T S A; Rutherford Co; Pvt mkr.

BRANNER, CASPER (5-22-1788--11-22-1867 Jefferson Co); Md Mariah Doherty 1809 (1-8-1793--11-18-1847); 1st Corp, Capt John Roper's Co, Col Wm Lillard's 2nd Regt E T V, 10-13-1813--2-8-1814; W D & P D; Pres Cem in Dandridge, Jefferson Co; Pvt mkr.

BRAKEBILL, HENRY (1793--d Monroe Co); Md Anna Davis 1-30-1838 (   ); War of 1812;   ; likely in Monroe Co; Unkn.

BRAKEBILL, JOHN (4-17-1798--10-5-1859 Blount Co); Md Ann Thomas 2-17-1817 (10-16-1798--3-25-1877); Pvt, Capt David McKamey's Co, Col Wm Johnson's 3rd Regt Drftd Mil, 9-29-1814--5-18-1815; W D & T S A; Fam Cem in Blount Co near Cedar Grove Bapt Ch; Pvt mkr.

BRAKEBILL, PETER (--d Monroe Co); Md   (   ); 3rd Srgt, Capt David McKamey's Co, Col Wm Johnson's 3rd Regt Drftd Mil, 9-29-1814--5-18-1815; W D & T S A; likely in Monroe Co; Unkn.

BRECKINRIDGE, JOHN (1773--5-9-1858 Lincoln Co); Md Margaret Beatty (   ); Pvt, Capt Waller's Co, Col Wm Metcalf's 1st Regt W T Mil, 11-13-1814--5-13-1815; W D & T S A; likely Lincoln Co near Medium Pres Ch; Unkn.

BREGINS, JOHN (--liv 1840 aged 67 yrs Perry Co); Md (   ); War of 1812; 1840 Pension List & 2400 Pensioners, Armstrong; likely in Perry Co; Unkn.

BRICKEY, WILLIAM (1780-- 1856 Blount Co); Md Eleanor Dobkins (1781--1860); Pvt, Capt James Allen's Co, Col Ewen Allison's Regt E T Mil, 1-17-1814-- at Ft Williams 4-2-1814, transfrd to Capt Joseph Duncan's Co, Col Sam Bunch's Mtd Inf --7-21-1814; W D & Blount Co Hist-Burns; Myers Cem at Townsend, Blount Co; Pvt mkr.

BRIGANCE, CHARLES (1790-- 1885 Robertson Co); Md (   ); Pvt, Capt John W Byers Co, Tenn Mil, 13-1812; T S A; likely Robertson Co; Unkn.

BRITTON, JOHN (--d Greene Co); Md Elizabeth   (--2-18-1860 aged 70 yrs); War of 1812; P D; likely Greene Co; Unkn.

BRITTON, JOSEPH (1756--8-8-1823 Bedford Co); Md Dorothy Horner 3-8-1786 (1769--7-8-1844); Lieut, 28th Regt under Gen Andrew Jackson, 7-8-1813; T S A; Bedford, now Marshall Co; Pvt mkr.

BROCK, J W (-- Claiborne Co); Md   (   ); Pvt in Tenn Mil; T S A; Ferguson Fam Cem near Tazewell, Claiborne Co; Govt mkr.

BROOKS, JOSEPH (--liv 1828 Overton Co); Md (   ); served 2nd Regt U S Rifles; 1828 List & 2400 Pensioners, Armstrong; likely in Overton Co; Unkn.

BROOKS, LAWSON S (--d Knox Co); Md Catherine Myer (   ); War of 1812; Goodspeed Knox Co; likely in Knox Co; Unkn. (Also Rev War)

BROOKS, MOSES (4-1-1760--1-25-1830 Knox Co); Md Mrs Agnes Gamble Fowler 8-2-1785 (6-9-1765--8-2-1826); War of 1812; French Broad-Holston Hist; Brooks Fam Cem near Lebanon-in-the-Forks, Knox Co; now mkd. (Also Rev War)

BROWDER, JOSEPH (11-14-1789--4-13-1862 McMinn Co); Md (   ); War of 1812; data from Mrs D B Todd, Etowah; Clear Springs Cem near Englewood, McMinn Co; Pvt mkr.

BROWDER, WILLIAM (2-10-1792--6-29-1890 Meigs Co); Md Elizabeth Lackey 1814 (   ); Pvt, Brig Gen James White's Brig at Lookout Mt during War; Hist of Sweetwater Valley-Lenoir; Cem in Meigs Co; Pvt mkr.

BROWN, DAVID (--aft 1860 Washington Co); Md Betsy Gilleland (--bef husband); Pvt, Capt Jonathan Waddle's Co, Col Sam Bayless' 4th Regt E T Drftd Mil, 11-13-1814--5-18-1815; W D & T S A; Old Salem Pres Cem at Washington College, Washington Co; Govt mkr.

BROWN, GEORGE (4-12-1784--10-27-1873 Johnson Co); Md Sarah Roberts (6-13-1787--3-20-1869); Pvt, Capt Jesse Cole's Co, Col Sam Wear's 1st Regt E T V, 10-18-1813--1-18-1814, disch Fish Springs, Carter Co; W D & T S A; Brown Fam Cem in Johnson Co; Pvt mkr.

BROWN, JACOB II (8-3-1761-- 1838 Washington Co); Md Elizabeth Byrd 2-9-1786 (1767--1847); Pvt, Capt Andrew Lawson's Co, Col Wm Johnson's 3rd Regt E T Drftd Mil, 9-20-1813--5-9-1814; W D & T S A; Brown Fam Cem on Nolachucky River, Washington Co; Pvt mkr. (Tombstone gives death as 1841 - Error - Inv in Washington Co dated 1838.)

BROWN, JACOB (11-20-1789--5-20-1860 Bradley Co); Md Sarah Million 3-21-1811 (1793--1874); Pvt, Capt David G Vance's Co Mtd Inf, Col Sam Bunch's Regt E T V, 10-16-1813--1-22-1814; W D & T S A & P D; Cem near Cleveland, Bradley Co; Pvt mkr.

BROWN, Col JOHN (9-15-1779-- 1845 Roane Co); Md 1-Mary M Allison (   ), 2-Nancy Cox Allison (wid Uriah Allison) (1800--); Col, 2nd Regt E T V under Gen George Doherty, Mtd Gunmen, 1-1-1814--5-20-1814; W D & T S A; Bethel Pres Cem at Kingston, Roane Co; large pvt mkr.

BROWN, JOHN G (--d Washington Co); Md   (   ); War of 1812, apptd 5-10-1805 Capt 1st Regt Washington Co Mil; John Sevier Commission Bk & Nelson's Papers, McClung Room, Knoxville; Unkn Cem in Washington Co; Unkn.

BROWN, JOHN WESLEY (1-22-1788--11-18-1849 Washington Co); Md Margaret Kincheloe 1-7-1817 (1801--7-8-1883); Pvt, Capt Jacob Hartsell's Co, Col Wm Lillard's 2nd Regt E T V, 10-12-1813--2-8-1814; W D & T S A; John Brown Fam Cem in Washington Co; Pvt mkr.

BROWN, JOSEPH (--d Giles Co); Md   (   ); Captured at Nickajack in 1788; Ramsey's Annals of Tenn; Mt Moriah Cem in Giles Co; Pvt mkr.

BROWN, JOSHUA (11-26-1792--12-30-1841 Knox Co); Md Frances Blakely 9-27-1818 (2-25-1798--3-26-1883); Pvt, Capt Nicholas Gibbs' Co, Col Sam Bunch's Regt E T Drftd Mil, 1-10-1814-Left at Camp Ross sick-3-6-1814; W D & T S A; Brown Fam Cem 1 m S Hall's Cross Rds, 7th Distr, Knox Co; Pvt mkr.

BROWN, Col RICHARD (1772--1-26-1818 Rogersville, Hawkins Co); Single; Capt of Cherokee Co at Tohopeka, 3-27-1814; T S A; d at Joseph Rogers' Tavern en route to Washington; Knoxville Register, 2-3-1818; Rogers Fam Cem, Rogersville, Hawkins Co; Unmkd.

BROWN, THOMAS (9-15-1779--10-15-1848 Roane Co); Md Jane Adams McElwee 2-16-1801 (3-22-1782--5-6-1860); 2nd Maj, 14th Cav, E T V, 5-28-1812; T S A; Bethel Pres Cem in Kingston, Roane Co; Monument. (Twin bro of Col John Brown, also bur there.)

BROWN, THOMAS (--1849 Hawkins Co); Md Sarah Sizemore 1815 (   ); Capt in Etowah Campaign 1792-3; Ramsey's Annals of Tenn; Brown Fam Cem in Hawkins Co; Unkn.

BROWN, WILLIAM (--d Roane Co); Md Carolina Gamble (   );
Pvt, Capt Wm Christian's Co, Col John Brown's 2nd Regt, 10-13-
1813--1-13-1814; W D & T S A; Post Oak Christian Ch Cem near
Rockwood, Roane Co; Pvt mkr.

BROYLES, CORNELIUS (1786-- 1861 Rhea Co); Md Polly Farley 1814
(   ); Pvt, Capt Wm McLin's Co, Col Wm Lillard's 2nd
Regt E T V, 10-12-1813--2-8-1814; Fam Cem in Rhea Co; Unkn.

BRUCE, JOHN (--1840 List aged 45 yrs Rutherford Co); Md
(   ); War of 1812; Pension List 1840 & 2400 Pensioners,
Armstrong; likely in Rutherford Co; Unkn.

BRUMBOUGH, JAMES (--d Greene Co); Md   (   );
War of 1812; data sent by Mrs LeRoy Brown, Greeneville; Old
Cem in Greeneville, Greene Co; Unkn.

BRYAN, PETER (1755-- 1810 Sevier Co); Md Betty Hubbard 1777
(   ); Capt in Col John Sevier's Etowah Campaign 1793;
Ramsey's Annals of Tenn; likely in Sevier Co; Unkn.

BRYAN, RICHARD (1792--6-30-1855 Wilson Co); Md Mary Brown 1818
(1800--3-27-1884); War of 1812; Goodspeed Wilson Co; likely in
Wilson Co; Pvt mkr.

BRYAN, WILLIAM (--1837 McMinn Co); Md Lucy Cote (--1837);
Quartermaster in War of 1812; Goodspeed E T H; likely in
McMinn Co; Unkn.

BUCHANAN, ALEXANDER (3-22-1794--4-9-1836 Davidson Co); Md
(   ); at Buchanan's Station, 1791; Acklen's Records;
Cem on Knapp Demonstration Farm of Peabody College, near
Nashville, Davidson Co; Pvt mkr.

BUCHANAN, JOHN (1772-- 1820 Williamson Co); Md Margaret Edmondson 1798 (1774--1858); Capt 21st Regt Williamson Co Mil; John
Sevier's Commission Bk; likely in Williamson Co; Unkn.

BUCHANAN, JOHN (1-12-1759--11-23-1832 Davidson Co); Md Sarah
Ridley 1791 (11-28-1774--11-22-1831); Pvt, Capt Patterson's Co,
Col Wm Metcalf's 1st Regt W T Mil, 11-12-1814--5-13-1815; W D
& T S A; Nashville, Davidson Co; Pvt mkr.

BUCHANAN, ROBERT (--d Davidson Co); Md   (   );
at Buchanan's Station, 1791; Acklen's Records; Cem on Knapp
Demonstration Farm of Peabody College near Nashville, Davidson
Co; Unkn.

BUCHANAN, SAMUEL (1765-- 1783 scalped near Buchanan's Station);
Single; killed prior to the attack on Feb 20th; Ramsey's Annals
of Tenn; Cem on Knapp Demonstration Farm of Peabody College,
near Nashville, Davidson Co; Illegible stone.

BUCK, BETHUEL (3-16-1802--3-16-1858 Carter Co); Md Elizabeth Rockhold 3-20-1821 (3-15-1805--7-12-1836); Pvt, Capt Adam Winsell's Co, Col Ewen Allison's Regt E T Drftd Mil, 1-5-1814--5-26-1814; W D & T S A; Bethuel Buck Fam Cem in Carter Co; Unmkd.

BUCK, EPHRAIM (1792--6-7-1874 Carter Co); Md Nancy Agnes Taylor 5-26-1813 (1793--11-4-1885); 1st Lieut, Capt Adam Winsell's Co, Col Ewen Allison's Regt E T Drftd Mil, 1-5-1814--5-26-1814; W D & T S A; Buck Fam Cem at Okalona, Carter Co; Govt mkr, 1938.

BUCKNER, EZRA (8-5-1797--10-28-1861 Union Co); Md Elizabeth Duncan 9-17-1818 (11-4-1801--3-12-1882); Pvt, Capt Nicholas Gibbs' Co, Col John Williams 39th Regt U S Inf, 1-10-1814--5-13-1814; W D & T S A & P D; Cem in Union Co; Pvt mkr.

BULLARD, JOSEPH (--d in Tenn); Md   (   ); Capt at Battle of Lookout Mt, 1788; Hamilton Co Hist-Armstrong; likely in Tenn; Unkn.

BULLOCK, JAMES P (1789-- 1858 Sumner Co); Md Mildred Didlake 1811 (1790--1876); under Gen Wm H Harrison, War of 1812; Goodspeed Sumner Co; Cem in Sumner Co; Unkn.

BUNCH, Col SAMUEL (12-4-1786--9-5-1849 Rutledge, Grainger Co); Md Amanda Mariah Anderson 10-22-1820 (1806--aft 1866) (2nd husband was Mark Lawry of White Co); Capt in Col John Williams Regt E T V, 12-1-1812--3-25-1813; & Col of Mtd Regt, E T V, 10-14-1813--1-14-1814, Col E T Drftd Mil, 1-10-1814--4-21-1814; later Sheriff Grainger Co, 1814; W D & T S A; Bunch Fam Cem 2 m W Rutledge, Grainger Co; Govt mkr by Tenn U S D of 1812.

BURGESS, N G (--3-19-1862 Bradley Co); Md   (   ); War of 1812; Edwards Acct Bk-Wooten; Fort Hill Cem in Cleveland, Bradley Co; Pvt mkr.

BURLESON, ISAAC (1795--1-24-1865 Rutherford Co); Md Julia B Holloway 1856 (1820-1895); Pvt, Capt Jones' Co, Col Dyer's Regt Mtd Gunmen, W T Mil, 9-28-1814--1-1-1815; W D & T S A; Burleson Fam Cem near Murfreesboro, Rutherford Co; Official 1812 mkr.

BURNS, GEORGE (--d Bradley Co); Md   (   ); Pvt, Capt Hood's Co, Col Smith's Regt; Edwards Acct Bk-Wooten & P D; likely in Bradley Co; Unkn.

BURNS, JOHN (--liv 1828 List Hardeman Co); Md (   ); served in Tenn Mil; 1828 List & 2400 Pensioners, Armstrong; likely Hardeman Co; Unkn.

BURROUGHS, PETER (BURRUS) (4-11-1796-- 1840 Franklin (Coffee) Co); Md Elizabeth P Atkinson 11-26-1816 (--d 1837); Pvt, Capt Cornelius Sales' Co, Va Mil, 8-30-1814--2-21-1815; Va S A; Cem in Franklin, later Coffee Co; Pvt mkr.

BUSHONG, GEORGE (1754-- 1815 Sullivan Co); Md
(   ); Pvt, Capt Wm King's Co, Col Ewen Allison's Regt
E T Drftd Mil, 1-6-1814--5-18-1814; Weavers Union Cem in
Sullivan Co; Official 1812 mkr, 1930. (Also Rev War)

BUTCHER, WILLIAM (--d aft 1852 Bradley Co); Md
(   ); Pvt, Capt Neal's Co; Edwards Acct Bk & P D; Cem
in Bradley Co; Unkn.

BUTLER, HENRY T (10-19-1794--2-24-1878 Giles Co); Md Musidora
McNairy 2-22-1824 (2-27-1801--2-24-1876); Pvt, --- Co, Col
Philip Pipkin's 1st Regt W T Mil, 6-20-1814--12-20-1814; W D
& T S A; Cem in Pulaski, Giles Co; Pvt mkr.

BUTLER, WILLIAM (--liv 1828 List Jackson Co); Md
(   ); served in Tenn Mil; P D & 2400 Pensioners, Armstrong; likely Jackson Co; Unkn.

BUTLER, Dr WILLIAM E (1789-- 1882 aged 95 yrs in Jackson,
Madison Co); Md Martha Thompson Hays 1813 (   ); Surgeon
on Staff, Col Thomas Hart Benton's 2nd Regt W T Inf; W D &
T S A; Cem in Jackson, Madison Co; Pvt mkr.

BYRD, JOSEPH (1-9-1785--8-5-1858 Kingston, Roane Co); Md Ann
Pride 5-6-1819 (7-20-1797--8-25-1885); Pvt, Capt Wm Neilson's
Co, Col --- ; Hist of Roane Co-Wells; Bethel Pres Cem in
Kingston, Roane Co; Pvt mkr.

CAIN, PETER (--c 1791--liv 2-8-1874 aged 83 yrs Overton Co);
Md Anna Covington 11-20-1807 (--d 1856); 3rd Srgt, Capt Andrew
Lawson's Co, Col Wm Johnson's 3rd Regt E T Drftd Mil 9-20-1814--
5-9-1815; W D & T S A & P D; likely Overton Co; Unkn.

CALBOUGH, JOHN (COLBOUGH) (--d Carter Co); Md Miss Mottern
(   ); Pvt, Capt Wm King's Co, Col Ewen Allison's Regt
E T Drftd Mil, 1-6-1814--5-18-1814; W D & T S A; Colbough Fam
Cem N W Elizabethton, Carter Co; Unkn.

CALDWELL, ADAM (1763--1819 Nashville, Davidson Co); Md
(   ); Pvt, Capt Montgomery's Co, Tenn Mil; Texas 1812
Records; Cem in Nashville, Davidson Co; Unkn.

CALDWELL, JEB (--d 2-25-1829 Knox Co); Md   (   );
Pvt, Col Triplett's Regt, Va Mil, War of 1812; Va S A & P D in
Va, transfrd to Tenn & 2400 Pensioners, Armstrong; likely Knox
Co; Unkn. (Also Rev War. Pensioned in 1785 in Va.)

CALDWELL, JOHN CAMPBELL (1-8-1791--7-17-1867 Bedford Co); Md
Jane Northcott of Ky (   ); at Tohopeka 3-27-1814 & N O
1-8-1815; Goodspeed Bedford Co; Cem in Bedford Co; Pvt mkr.

CALDWELL, PERRIN (7-12-1764--12-2-1854 Knox Co); Md Elizabeth
Worsham 9-4-1785 (1771--1865); Pvt, Capt Peter Jordan's Co, Col
Barbee's 7th Regt Ky Mil, 8-23-1812--3-17-1813; W D & Ky S A;
Cem in Knox Co; Pvt mkr.

CALDWELL, SAMUEL (1776--d Clarksville, Montgomery Co); Md
(   ); War of 1812; W D & T S A; Cem in Clarksville,
Montgomery Co; Unkn.

CALVERT, WILLIS (--6-15-1829 Nashville, Davidson Co); Md
Rebecca   (--liv 1835 aged 47 yrs in Ky); P D & 2400
Pensioners, Armstrong; likely in Nashville, Davidson Co; Unkn.

CAMPBELL, ALEXANDER (12-22-1789-- 1870 Sneedville, Hancock Co);
Md Nancy McNeil c 1808 (--d bef husband); Pvt, Capt Wm Gillenwaters' Co, Col Wm Lillard's 2nd Regt, E T V, 10-2-1813--2-6-
1814; W D & T S A; Campbell Fam Cem outskirts of Sneedville,
Hancock Co; Pvt mkr.

CAMPBELL, COLIN (1792-- 1860 Sumner Co); Md Martha Parish 1814
(1794--1855); Pvt, Capt Wallace's Co, Col --- ; Goodspeed
Sumner Co; Cem in Sumner Co; Pvt mkr.

CAMPBELL, Judge DAVID (1750--11-21-1812 Washington, Rhea Co);
Md Elizabeth Outlaw 1779 (   ); Judge, Terr S of River
Ohio 1790, Fed Judge Miss Terr, 1811; T S A & Miss S A; Wash-
ington, Rhea Co; Pvt mkr & D A R mkr. (Also Rev War)

CAMPBELL, DAVID (8--1753--8-18-1832 Wilson Co); Md Margaret
Campbell (   ); Treaty of Dumplin, 1785, Campbell's Sta-
tion, 1787 & Knox Co Mil 1796, & Representative Knox Co, 1803;
T S A; Campbell Fam Cem Wilson Co; Pvt mkr.

CAMPBELL, GEORGE WASHINGTON (2-29-1762--2-17-1848 Nashville, Davidson Co); Md Harriett Stottard (1789--1849); U S Senator 1811-14, Sec of Treas of U S 1814; T S A & Acklen's Records; Old City Cem in Nashville, Davidson Co; Pvt mkr.

CAMPBELL, ISAAC (1766-- 1832 Carter Co); Md Anna Delashmit 7-21-1827 (   ); Pvt, Capt Jesse Cole's Co, Col Sam Wear's 1st Regt, E T V, 10-18-1813--1-17-1814; W D & T S A; Isaac Campbell Fam Cem near Hampton, Carter Co; Unmkd.

CAMPBELL, JAMES (6-6-1796--5-21-1879 Knox Co); Md 1-(   ), 2-Charlotte Barbus (   ); Pvt & Capt with Jackson at Tohopeka, 3-27-1814; T S A; Campbell Fam Cem on Schnick Farm, River Dale, Knox Co; Pvt mkr.

CAMPBELL, JAMES (--d Hamilton Co); Md   (   ); listed as War of 1812; Hamilton Co Hist--Armstrong; likely in Hamilton Co; Unkn.

CAMPBELL, JOSEPH (--d Blount Co); Md   (   ); Pvt, Capt Adam Winsell's Co, Col Ewen Allison's Regt E T Drftd Mil, 1-10-1814--5-10-1814; W D & Blount Co Court Minutes 1854; likely Blount Co; Unkn.

CAMPBELL, THOMAS JEFFERSON (2-22-1793--4-13-1850 in Wash, D C); Md Sallie L Bearden 11-20-1817 (2-9-1796--11-1-1852); Asst Inspctr Gen, Maj Gen John Cocke's Regt in Creek War, 9-25-1813--3-12-1814; W D & T S A; Old Citizens Cem Chattanooga, Hamilton Co; Pvt mkr. (Sallie Bearden Campbell was buried in grave with her husband.)

CANNON, CLEMENT (--1-19-1860 Bedford Co); Md Susan Locke (   ); War of 1812; Goodspeed Bedford Co; Cem in Bedford Co; Pvt mkr.

CANNON, Gen NEWTON (5-22-1781--9-16-1841 Williamson Co); Md 1-Leah P Perkins 8-27-1813 (--d 1816), 2-Rachel Starnes Wellborn 8-26-1818 (   ); Brig Gen 2nd Regt W T Mil, 9-24-1813--12-28-1813; W D & T S A; Fam Estate "Alisonia" on Harpeth River, Williamson Co; Pvt mkr.

CANNON, THOMAS (--c 1776--10-24-1863 Overton Co); Md Martha Lea 1806-7 (1792--Pensioned 1871); Pvt, Capt James Turner's Co, at Battle of Talledega, 11-9-1814; T S A & P D; Cannon Fam Cem in Overton Co; Mkd with rock- "T Cannon".

CARDIN, LEONARD (--1857 Monroe Co); Md Tobitha Peace (--1847); War of 1812; Goodspeed Monroe Co; likely Monroe Co; Unkn.

CARR, GEORGE WASHINGTON (--c 1789--3-4-1862 Sullivan Co); Md Sarah Moulton 1817-8 (c 1796--aged 82 yrs 1878--d aft 1883); Pvt, Capt James Landen's Co, Col Sam Bayless' 4th Regt E T Drftd Mil, 11-13-1814--5-18-1815; W D & T S A & P D; Cem near Fall Branch, Washington Co or Sullivan Co; Unkn. (Sarah M Carr W #7968 liv 1883.)

CARR, MOSES (12-8-1778--7-13-1854 Coffee Co); Md Lucy Jones 7-18-1805 (7-23-1780--1846); 1st Lieut, Capt Martin's Co Inf, 7th Regt N C Mil; W D & N C S A; Carr Fam Cem in Coffee Co; Pvt mkr.

CARR, WILLIAM (1755-- 1833 Knox Co); Md Margaret (1756--1847); Capt 3rd Regt U S Inf, stationed at Old Block House in Knoxville, 1792-5; W D & Kate White clipping, Knoxville press ? date; First Pres Cem in Knoxville, Knox Co; Pvt mkr. (Also Rev War - "Died Jan, 1833 aged 78 yrs - A Rev Father".)

CARRICK, Rev SAMUEL (7-17-1760--8-17-1809 Knox Co); Md 1-Elizabeth Moore (--d 9-24-1793), 2-Annis McClellan 1794 (1-27-1774--); Minister for Gen Assembly S W Terr, 1792 & Constitutional Convention 1796; T S A; First Pres Cem in Knoxville, Knox Co; Pvt mkr.

CARRIGER, CHRISTAIN (7-28-1779--d Carter Co); Md Levicy Ward 8-3-1811 (   ); Col Carter Co Mil 1811 & State Leg 1812-1819; T S A; Carriger Fam Cem, Carter Co; Unkn.

CARRIGER, GODFREY (5-15-1769--5-6-1827 Carter Co); Md Mrs Elizabeth Lovelace Crawley 10-27-1803 (--2-27-1826); Lieut, Carter Co Mil, 1796; John Sevier Commission Bk; Carriger Fam Cem, Carter Co; Pvt mkr.

CARROLL, Gov WILLIAM (3-3-1788--3-20-1855 Nashville, Davidson Co); Md Cecilia Bradford 1811 (   ); Gen, Gen Jackson's Right Wing in Creek War & N O; W D & T S A; City Cem in Nashville, Davidson Co; Mkd by State of Tenn & Official 1812 mkr, 1957.

CARSON, JOSEPH (--d likely in Knox Co); Md Carolina C Green in Ala (   ); Col of Regt, Miss Vol in Creek War; Goodspeed Knox Co; likely Knox Co; Unkn.

CARSON, MOSES W (9-22-1783--8-21-1852 Washington Co); Md Margaret Ross 1-4-1816 (10-10-1794--2-11-1875); Pvt, Capt Jonathan Waddle's Co, Col Sam Bayless' 4th Regt E T Drftd Mil, 11-13-1814--5-18-1815; W D & T S A; Old Providence Pres Cem near Millburnton, Green Co-Washington Co line; Pvt mkr.

CARTER, JESSE (9-15-1779--10-17-1851 Bolivar, Hardeman Co); Md Lucy Stoker (   ); Pvt, Capt Kilpatrick's Co, Col Philip Pipkin's Regt W T Mil, 6-20-1814--12-1814, Battles of Chalmette & N O; W D & T S A; Bolivar, Hardeman Co; Pvt mkr.

CARTER, LANDON (1-29-1760--1-5-1800 Carter Co); Md Elizabeth McLin 2-2-1784 (1765--1842); Lieut Col Washington District Mil, 1790; Tenn Comm Bk-Gov Wm Blount; Carter Fam Cem near Elizabethton, Carter Co; Pvt mkr & monuments 1936 by D A R, U S D of 1812 & descendants. (Carter Co was named for Landon Carter, and the county seat, Elizabethton, named for his wife, Elizabeth McLin Carter.)

CARTER, WILLIAM (1791-- 1860 Trousdale Co); Md Nancy Rickman (1797--aft 1878); Pvt, Capt Martin's Co, War of 1812; Goodspeed Trousdale Co; likely Cem in Trousdale Co; Unkn.

CARTER, WILLIAM BLOUNT (10-22-1792--4-17-1848 Carter Co); Md wid-Elizabeth Lytle West (   ); Col & Forage Master, Brig Gen Nathaniel Taylor's Brigade 9-20-1814, res 10-17-1814; T S A & Congressional Dir; Carter Fam Cem near Elizabethton, Carter Co; Pvt mkr & monuments 1936 by D A R & U S D 1812 & descendants.

CARTWRIGHT, ROBERT (2-22-1722--12-24-1809 Davidson Co); Md 1-Ann Huggins (   ), 2-Mary Hunter (   ); served in Capt James Ore's Expd vs Creeks & Cherokees in 1794; Cem near Goodlettsville, Davidson Co; Mkd by D A R. (Also Rev War)

CARUTHERS, JAMES (--d Jackson, Madison Co); Md Frances McCrory bef 1824 (   ); War of 1812; Tenn Cousins-Ray; Cem in Jackson, Madison Co; Pvt mkr.

CASTLEMAN, ABRAHAM (--d Davidson Co); Md   (   ); Capt of Co of men in Mero District 1793 to go vs Indians - Called "Foolish Warrior"; also in Buchanan's Station when attacked; Ramsey's Annals of Tenn; likely Cem in Davidson Co; Unkn. (See Ramsey's Annals for details.)

CASTLEMAN, ANDREW (--d Davidson Co); Md   (   ); served as Indian Scout in early days in Mero District vs Indians during early settlements; Ramsey's Annals, likely Cem in Davidson Co; Unkn.

CASTLEMAN, BENJAMIN (--likely Davidson Co); served with Capt Rains 1787 as Indian Scout in Mero District; Ramsey's Annals-p 467; Unkn Cem in Davidson Co; Unkn.

CASTLEMAN, HANS (--likely Davidson Co); Md   (   ); served as Indian Scout in Mero District, wounded 7-1-1793 when Joseph & Jacob were killed; Ramsey's Annals; Unkn Cem; Unkn.

CASTLEMAN, JACOB, Jr (--killed 1793 Davidson Co); likely single; killed by Indians in attack on Hays Station on Stone's River, Davidson Co, 1793; Ramsey's Annals-p 605; Bur likely where killed; Unkn.

CASTLEMAN, JACOB, Sr (--1781 Davidson Co); Md   (   ); "One Jacob Castleman killed in 1781 while hunting near Stoner's Lick", Ramsey Annals of Tenn-p 455; bur likely where fell; Unkn. (This site was where John Castleman has since lived-Ramsey.)

CASTLEMAN, JOHN (-- Davidson Co); Md   (   ); Indian Scout with Capt John Rains, lived on Stoner's Lick Creek in 1781; Ramsey's Annals of Tenn; Unkn Cem in Davidson Co; Unkn.

CASTLEMAN, JOSEPH (--killed 7-1-1793 Davidson Co); Md
(   ); killed on Stoner's Lick Creek same time that Jacob
Jr was killed; Ramsey's Annals of Tenn; likely bur in vicinity;
Unkn.

CATLETT, BENJAMIN (--4-29-1833 Sevierville, Sevier Co); Md
Nancy Lovelady c 1815 (--c 1795--liv 10-28-1850); Pvt, Capt
Isaac Williams' Co, Col Sam Bunch's 2nd Regt, E T Drftd Mil,
1-10-1814--5-16-1814 & Pvt, Capt Wm Henderson's Co Mtd Spies
& Gunmen, Gen Nathaniel Taylor's Brig; W D & T S A; Old Bapt
Cem at Sevierville, Sevier Co; Pvt mkr.

CATLETT, JOHN (1784--liv 10-28-1850 & 1855 Sevierville, Sevier
Co); Md   (   ); Lieut, Capt Isaac Williams'
Co, Col Sam Bunch's 2nd Regt, E T Drftd Mil, 1-10-1814--disch
5-14-1814; W D & P D; Alder Branch Bapt Cem, Sevier Co; Unkn.

CATLETT, RICHARD (--10-25-1837 Sevier Co); Md Ailcy
(--liv 1850); Pvt, Capt Simeon Perry's Co, Col Sam Bunch's Regt
9-23-1813--1-10-1814 & Pvt, Capt Wm Henderson's Co, Spies, Brig
Gen Nathaniel Taylor's Brig 9-20-1814--5-20-1815; W D & P D;
likely at Alder Branch Bapt Cem, Sevier Co; Unkn.

CHANDLER, RICHARD P (--d Blount Co); Md   (   );
Paymaster at Tellico Blockhouse & Southwest Point 1793-1798 &
War of 1812; #138,566 on Pension List; Henley Waste Book & P D;
Mt Moriah Meth Cem in Blount Co; Unkn.

CHAPMAN, BENJAMIN (1788-- 1861 Sumner Co); Md Rebecca Ann Bull
(1802--1848); at New Orleans 1-8-1815; Goodspeed Sumner Co;
likely in Sumner Co; Unkn.

CHEATMAN, Col LEONARD P (--1863 Nashville, Davidson Co); Md
Elizabeth Robertson (--12-23-1881); War of 1812 with Gen Jackson;
T S A & Goodspeed Shelby Co; Cem in Nashville, Davidson Co; Pvt
mkr.

CHERRY, BENJAMIN (8-18-1790--5-23-1876 Alto, Franklin Co); Md
Emily E Nugent 4-27-1854 (1820--12-30-1911); Pvt, Capt Wm
Christian's Co, Col John Brown's 2nd Regt E T Mil, 10-13-1813--
1-13-1814 & 2nd Lieut, Col Wm Johnson's 3rd Regt E T Drftd Mil,
9-20-1814--5-20-1815; W D & T S A & P D; Alto, Franklin Co;
Official 1812 mkr. (Mrs Hugh L Crownover-nee Jennie M Cherry
1861--1955, was a Real Daughter of the Tenn Society, U S D of
1812, Decherd, Rt 3, Tenn.)

CHESNEY, JOHN (--d Union Co); Md   (   );
War of 1812; W D; Prospect Ch Cem, Union Co; Govt mkr.

CHESNEY, STERLING (--d Union Co); Md   (   );
War of 1812; W D; Prospect Ch Cem, Union Co; Govt mkr.

CHESTER, Col ROBERT I (7-21-1793-- 1891 Jackson, Madison Co);
Md 1-Miss Hays, neice of Rachel Jackson, 2-Mrs Jane P Donelson
(   ); Quartermaster in Col Wm Johnson's 3rd Regt E T
Drftd Mil; W D & Tenn Cousins-Ray; Jackson, Madison Co; Pvt mkr.

CHILDRESS, ROBERT (--d Tenn); Md Rachel Eastridge (   );
Pvt, Capt Reuben Tipton's Co, Col John Chiles' Battln, E T Mtd
Mil, 9-20-1814--5-1-1815; W D & T S A; likely in Tenn; Unkn.

CHILES, JOHN (--d Grainger Co); Md   (   );
Ensign, Capt Wm Walker's Co, Col John Williams' Regt U S Inf,
12-1-1812--3-25-1813, & Capt in Col John Brown's 2nd Regt Mtd
Inf, 1-10-1814, promoted to Maj 9-20-1814--5-20-1815; W D &
T S A; likely in Grainger Co; Unkn.

CHISAM, JOHN (1780-- 1855 White Co); Md Mary Harris bef 1810
(1782--); Pvt, Capt Wm Russell's Co Mtd Spies, 10-4-1813-- ;
W D & T S A; Chisam Fam Cem in White Co; Pvt mkr.

CHISAM, JAMES (-- Hardeman Co); Md   (   );
Pvt, Capt Wm Russell's Co, Mtd Spies, 10-4-1813-- ; W D & T S A
& Texas 1812 Records; Hardeman Co; Unkn.

CHRISTIAN, HENRY (--d Knox Co); Md   (   );
War of 1812; Goodspeed Knox Co; likely Knox Co; Unkn.

CHUMLEY, JACOB Jr (--d Ft Williams, Ala, 1814); Md
(   ); Pvt, Creek War; W D & T S A; at Ft Williams,
Talledega Co, Ala; Unmkd.

CHURCH, HENRY (2-17-1779--11-7-1844 Hawkins Co); Md Olive
Sergeon (Surginer) (4-25-1796--8-8-1853); Pvt, Capt John Fagan's
Co, Col John Williams' 39th Regt, U S Inf, 12-12-1812--3-25-1813;
T S A & B L Wt; Cem in Hancock Co-then Hawkins; Pvt mkr.

CLABAUGH, WILLIAM (1782--1850-60 Sevier Co); Md Lavina King c
1815 (1796--1850-60); Pvt, Capt Alexander Hill's Co, Col Wm
Carroll's Regt, 10- 1813--6- 1815; W D; Middle Creek Cem, Sevier
Co; Unmkd.

CLACK, SPENCER (3-28-1740--7-9-1832 Sevier Co); Md Mary Beevers
11-2-1766 (   ); J P Sevier Co 1794, Constitutional Convention 1796; T S A & Sevier Co Records; Forks of Pigeon Bapt
Cem, Sevierville, Sevier Co; Pvt mkr & Rev War mkr. (Also Rev
War)

CLACK, SPENCER (1783--d Giles Co); Md Lucy Williams Jones
1-9-1818 (   ); War of 1812; Kinfolks-Bond; likely in
Pulaski, Giles Co; Unkn.

CLAIBORNE, THOMAS (5-17-1780--1-7-1856 Nashville, Davidson Co);
Md   (   ); Maj, Gen Jackson's Staff in
Creek War; T S A; Old City Cem, Nashville, Davidson Co; Pvt mkr.

CLAPP, SOLOMON (6-20-1795--8-3-1881 Knox Co); Md Therba Smith
(   ); Pensioner War of 1812 after 1840 List; P D;
Clapp's Chapel Meth Cem, near Harbison's Cross Rds, Knox Co;
Pvt mkr.

CLARK, JOHN (--9-9-1852 Bradley Co); Md Elender Sisk in S C
(--liv 5-15-1855 aged 77 yrs Bradley Co); Pvt, Capt Andrew
Lawson's Co, 10-31-1812--3-31-1813; W D & T S A & P D; Bradley
Co; Unkn.

CLARK, JOHN T (--liv 2-21-1852 Grainger Co); Md
(   ); Pvt, Capt Andrew Lawson's Co, Col Wm Johnson's 3rd
Regt E T Drftd Mil, 9-20-1814--5-9-1815, also Sub for Robert
Dugan in Blount Co Co, Col Sam Bayless' 4th Regt, Drftd Mil,
served as Ferryman at Ft Strother, disch 7-1815; W D & T S A
& P D; likely Grainger Co; Unkn.

CLARK, WILLIAM (1792-- 1869 Lincoln Co); Md 1-Barbara Tolbert
(   ), 2-Harriet Shugart (--d Pensioner 1812); War of 1812;
Goodspeed Lincoln Co & P D; Cem in Lincoln Co; Unkn.

CLAY, WOODSON (10-14-1777--8-17-1824 Nashville, Davidson Co); Md
Orphia Kennedy 12-21-1818 (   ); Pvt, Capt Thomas Williamson's Co, Col Pillow's 2nd Regt W T Mil, 9-25-1813--12-22-1813;
W D & T S A; Cem in Nashville, Davidson Co; Pvt mkr.

CLAYTON, JOHN (1790--8-10-1864 Lewis Co); Md 1-Ellen Mayfield
Bridges (   ), 2-Mrs Margaret C Peery (   ); Pvt,
Capt John Looney's Co, Col --- , 9-20-1814--4-20-1815; W D & P D;
Clayton Fam Cem on Swan Creek near Hohenwald, Lewis Co; Pvt mkr.

CLICK, HENRY (--liv 1840 List aged 59 yrs Cocke Co); Md
(   ); served 4th Regt U S Inf; P D & 2400 Pensioners,
Armstrong; likely Cocke Co; Unkn.

CLIFT, WILLIAM (12-5-1794--2-11-1886 Hamilton Co); Md Nancy A
Brooks (2-22-1795--8-17-1847); listed as Col; Hamilton Co Hist-
Armstrong; Soddy Pres Cem, Hamilton Co; Pvt mkr.

CLINARD, JOHN (--d 1849 Davidson Co); Md Mary Cameron (   );
with Andrew Jackson at N O; W D; Cem in Davidson Co; Unkn.

CLOUD, WILLIAM (--killed 3-27-1814 Tohopeka, Ala); Md
(   ); Pvt, Capt Joseph Everett's Co, Col Ewen Allison's
Regt E T Drftd Mil, 1-7-1814--3-27-1814 killed; W D & T S A;
likely at Tohopeka, Ala; Unkn.

CLOYD, JAMES BARR (12-25-1779--2-22-1861 Washington Co); Md
1-Mary Patton (1780--bef 1832), 2-Katherine Click 2-15-1832
(1803--1869); Pvt, Capt Henry McCray's Co, Col Ewen Allison's
Regt E T Drftd Mil 1-5-1814--5-23-1814 & later at N O 1-8-1815;
W D & T S A & P D; likely in Fairview Meth Cem, Washington Co
or Cloyd Fam Cem, Washington Co; Pvt mkr.

CLOYD, JOHN (5-17-1793--d Washington Co); Md 1-Rachel Gester
(   ), 2-Rebecca Patton (   ), 3-Rachel Boyd (   );
wounded at Tohopeka 3-27-1814; Cloyd Fam History; likely Washington Co; Unkn.

COBB, ETHELRED (--liv 1828 List Lincoln Co); Md
(   ); served Col Dark's Regt U S Inf; Pension List
1828 Lincoln Co & 2400 Pensioners, Armstrong; likely Lincoln
Co; Unkn.

COCKE, Maj Gen JOHN (12- 1772--2-16-1854 Rutledge, Grainger Co);
Md Sarah Stratton Cocke (coz) c 1794 (1777--7-13-1853); Maj Gen,
E T Mil in Creek War & Col of Regt Riflemen at N O 1815; W D &
T S A; Cocke Fam Cem at Rutledge, Grainger Co; Pvt mkr.

COCKRELL, JOHN (12-19-1757--4-11-1837 Nashville, Davidson Co);
Md Ann Robertson (2-10-1757--10-13-1821); War of 1812; W D &
Acklen's Records; Old City Cem, Nashville, Davidson Co; Pvt mkr.
(Maj & Capt in Rev War)

COFFMAN, ANDREW (12-22-1864--9-1-1861 Hamblen Co); Md Nancy Legg
1812 (--d 1872); Pvt, Capt Zachaes Copeland's Co, Col Wm Lillard's 2nd Regt E T V, 10-8-1813--2-8-1814; W D & T S A; Bent
Creek Bapt Cem, Hamblen Co; Pvt mkr.

COLDWELL, JOHN CAMPBELL (CALDWELL) (1-23-1792--7-12-1867 Bedford
Co); Md Jane Northcutt 7-13-1819 (10-25-1799--8-30-1867); Capt
under Jackson at Tohopeka & N O; T S A; Willow Mt Cem, Shelbyville, Bedford Co; Pvt mkr.

COLE, Capt JESSE (--d Carter, now Johnson Co); Md Celia Brown
(dau Benjamin Brown); Capt, Col Sam Wear's 1st Regt, E T V, 10-
19-1813--1-17-1814; W D & T S A; Unkn Cem in Johnson Co; Unkn.

COLLINS, HENRY (1783-- 1848 5th Distr, Rhea Co); Md Rebecca
Pierce (1783--1847 Dekalb Co, Ala); Srgt, 3 mos in War of 1812,
later with Jackson; Pvt, Capt Wm Alexander's Co, Col Wm Johnson's 3rd Regt E T Drftd Mil, under Gen John Coffee; Goodspeed
E T Hist & Rhea Co Hist- T J Campbell; likely in Rhea Co; Unkn.

COLLINS, THOMAS (--c 1848 Grassy Cove, Cumberland Co); Md Peggy
         (--aft 1848); Pvt at Battle of N O; Cumberland Co Hist-
Bullard & Kreschniak; likely in Cumberland Co; Unkn.

COLLINS, WM D (--liv 10-15-1850 Meigs Co); Md   (   );
Pvt, Capt Mitchell's Co, Col Sam Wear's 1st Regt, E T V, 10-23-
1813--12-31-1813; W D & P D; likely Meigs Co; Unkn.

COLLINGSWORTH, EDMOND (--d Davidson Co); Md   (   );
Col in --- (?) --- Regt ; Collingsworth Fam Cem, 12 m from
Nashville on Charlotte Rd, Davidson Co; Pvt mkr.

CONNER, WILLIAM (1-29-1790--9-24-1860 Knox Co); Md Sarah Cox
1-9-1806 (3-26-1785--8-29-1879); 1st Srgt, Capt Daniel Yarnell's
Co, Col Sam Bunch's Regt Mtd Gunmen; W D & P D; Conner Fam Cem,
6th Distr, Knox Co; Unmkd.

COOK, ALEXANDER (11-4-1793--4-4-1864 Blount Co); Md Louiza Ball
1-22-1818 (   ); Pvt, Capt James Tedford's Co, Col Sam
Wear's 1st Regt E T V, 9-28-1813--12-31-1813; W D & T S A;
Centenary Bapt Cem, Blount Co; Pvt mkr.

COOK, ALSTON (--liv 1828 List Maury Co); Md
(   ); served in N C; 1812 Pension List transfrd from
N C to Tenn & 2400 Pensioners, Armstrong; likely Maury Co; Unkn.

COOK, JAMES (--d Blount Co); Md Margaret Gould 1-22-1802
(   ); War of 1812; P D; likely Centenary Meth Cem in
Blount Co; Unkn. (Margaret Gould Cook W #14,973 Blount Co
Pension)

COOK, JESSE (7-27-1790--c 1875 White Co); Md Mary Ann Clay 1829
(1811--); War of 1812 in Tenn; The North Carolinian-Wm Johnston, June 1957; likely in White Co; Unkn.

COOK, WILLIAM (1-5-1797--11-28-1873 Blount Co); Md
(   ); Pvt, Capt John Trimble's Co, Maj Wm Russell's
Battln, Gen John Coffee's Brig, 10-5-1814--4-5-1815; W D &
Blount Co Hist-Burns; Centenary Bapt Cem, Blount Co; Pvt mkr.

COOKE, RICHARD FIELDING (7-6-1787--10-15-1870 Putnam Co); Md
Margaret Cox 3-31-1813 (3-28-1791--12-14-1849); 2nd Lieut, Capt
Abraham Dudley's Co, Maj Wm Woodfolk's 3rd Regt W T Mil, 9-20-
1814-Srgt, 3rd Lieut 10-1-1814, 2nd Lieut 12-3-1814, disch 4-10-
1815; W D; Cooke Fam Cem near Baxter, Putnam Co; Pvt mkr.

COOKSEY, JESSE (1793-- 1866 Montgomery Co); Md Sarah Heathman
(1803--1882); War of 1812; W D; in Montgomery Co; Unkn.

COOPER, E (--liv 1840 List aged 45 yrs McMinn Co); Md
(   ); War of 1812; P D & 2400 Pensioners, Armstrong;
likely in McMinn Co; Unkn.

COOPER, MATTHEW DELAMERE (--12-20-1878 Maury Co); Md 1-Mary
Agness Frierson (1801--1834), 2-Elizabeth Jane   1835
(1819--1838), 3-Mary Ann W   (1822--1861); Pvt, Capt
McEwen's Co, Col T H Benton's Regt Vol Inf, 12-23-1812, Pvt,
Capt McEwen's Co, Col T H Nemton's Regt Vol Inf, 2-19-1813,
1st Lieut, Capt McEwen's Co, Col Wm Pillow's Regt, Vol Inf,
9-26-1813; W D & T S A; Old Zion Pres Cem, 6 m from Columbia,
Maury Co; Large Marble Flat Slab with all 3 wives beside him.

COOPER, THOMAS (--d aft 1852 Bradley Co); Md
(   ); Pvt, Capt Dodson's Co; P D & Edwards Acct Bk;
likely in Bradley Co; Unkn.

COPE, BARAKIAS (--liv 1828 List Blount Co); Md
(   ); served Tenn Mil; P D & 2400 Pensioners, Armstrong;
likely in Blount Co; Unkn.

COPELAND, WESLEY (--liv 1828 List Wayne Co); Md
(   ); served Col Wilkinson's 7th Regt Inf; P D 1828 List
& 2400 Pensioners, Armstrong; likely Wayne Co; Unkn.

COSBY, JAMES (--d 1831 Hamilton Co); Md Isabella Woods (--d
1830); Maj in Battle of Lookout Mt, 1788; Hamilton Co Hist-
Armstrong; Cosby-Pitt Cem N of Falling Water, Hamilton Co; Pvt
mkr. (Also Rev War)

COSBY, JAMES WOODS (--d Hamilton Co); Md   (   );
War of 1812; Hamilton Co Hist-Armstrong; Cosby-Pitt Cem N of
Falling Water, Hamilton Co; Pvt mkr.

COTTON, JOHN (10-10--d Nashville, Davidson Co); Md Martha
(10- 1796--6- 1840); War of 1812; Acklen's Records; Old City
Cem, Nashville, Davidson Co; Pvt mkr.

COUCH, JOSEPH (10-9-1787--3-19-1861 Bedford Co); Md Catherine
Bolton 1813 (7-10-1796--3-10-1886); served under Gen Jackson;
Goodspeed Bedford Co; Bedford Co; Pvt mkr.

COUCH, WILLIAM (--8-31-1840 Hancock Co); Md   , who
remar by 1855; Pvt, Capt Jonas Laughmiller's Co, Col Ewen Allison's Regt E T Drftd Mil, 1-12-1814--7-16-1814; W D & T S A &
P D; Cem in Hancock Co; Unkn. (Pensions file- George Livesay,
Letter from John W Livesay, 1855.)

COULTER, THOMAS (6-25-1795--5-14-1876 Hamilton Co); Md Rebecca
Parks 4-16-1815 (4-20-1793--12-29-1880); 2nd Lieut, Capt Allen
Bacon's Co, Col John Brown's 2nd Regt Mtd Gunmen, 9-3-1813--
12-3-1813, & Srgt, Capt Joseph Rich's Co, Col Sam Bayless' 4th
Regt E T Drftd Mil, 11-13-1814--3-6-1815; W D & T S A; Hutcheson
Fam Cem, Hamilton Co; Pvt mkr.

COVINGTON, JOHN (1791-- 1873 Knox Co); Md   (   );
Pvt, Capt John Lewis' Co, Col Edwin Boothe's 5th Regt E T Mil,
11-13-1814--5-15-1815; W D & T S A & Texas 1812 Records; Bearden,
Knox Co; Unkn.

COVINGTON, WILLIAM (9-14-1782--11-28-1871 Williamson Co); Md
Catherine Robertson (1782--10-16-1861); Pvt, Capt John W Byrn's
Co, Col John Coffee's Regt W T Mil, 12-10-1812--2-9-1813; W D
& T S A; Williamson Co; Pvt mkr.

COWAN, ANDREW (--d Monroe Co); Md Esther Houston 9-25-1816
(   ); Pvt, Capt Wallace's Co, Col John Williams' 39th Regt
U S Inf, 12-1-1812--3-25-1813 & Pvt, Capt Nicholas Gibbs Co, Col
T H Benton's Regt; W D & T S A; likely Monroe Co; Unkn.

COWAN, Capt JAMES B (1777-- 1831 Franklin Co); Md Nancy
Williams 1797 (1782--1812); Capt in War of 1812; Goodspeed Lincoln Co; likely in Franklin Co; Unkn.

COWAN, JOHN (--d Franklin Co); Md   (   );
Capt Co Mtd Vol, Franklin Co, Gen John Coffee's Brig in Creek
War, 9-28-1814--3-28-1815; W D & T S A & Leaves of the Family
Tree-Allen, 1-7-1834; likely Franklin Co; Unkn.

COWARD, ISAAC (1791--liv 10-30-1875 Anderson Co--d aft 1887);
Md Margaret Young (--liv 4th Distr Anderson Co--); War of 1812;
Goodspeed E T H-Anderson Co; likely Anderson Co; Unkn.

COX, CALEB BOSLEY (1-15-1796--2-11-1879 Washington Co); Md Nancy Ann Carriger 1-27-1825 (3-10-1802--6-9-1891); Pvt, Capt John Byler's Co, Col Copeland's 2nd Regt, E T Mil, 1-28-1814--5-13-1815; W D & T S A; Old Watauga Academy Cem at Hunter, Carter Co; Pvt mkr.

COX, COLEMAN (1798-- 1858 Knox Co); Md Roxanna Foster (1803--liv 1887); War of 1812 from Knox Co; Goodspeed E T Hist Knox Co; likely Knox Co; Unkn.

COX, J BARTLEY (1791--11-17-1851 Limestone Co, Ala); Md Eliza J N Freeman (who mar 2nd James A Allen); Pvt, Capt John Roper's Co, Col Wm Lillard's 2nd Regt E T V, later under Col Sam Wear's 1st Regt E T V, 10-13-1813--2-8-1814, & Corp, Capt John Underwood's Co, E T Mil at Hiwassee Garrison; W D & T S A; Fam Cem at Brown's Ferry, Limestone Co, Ala; Mkd by 15 ft marble shaft.

COX, JOSHUA (-- Unkn); Md ( ); Pvt, Capt Wm White's Co, Col John Brown's 2nd Regt, E T Mtd Gunmen, 9-13-1813--12-29-1813, apptd Srgt Maj and transfrd to Field & Staff & served to 3-11-1814, then rejoined old Co; T S A; likely bur in Ala; Unkn.

COX, WILLIAM (--d 1883 Washington Co); Md Mary Ruth Boring 1791 ( ); Pvt, Capt George McPherson's Co, Col Sam Bunch's Mtd Mil, 1-4-1814--7-14-1814; W D & T S A; Cox Fam Cem Washington Co; Pvt mkr.

CRAIGMILES, JOSEPH (4-2-1782--8-3-1854 Cleveland, Bradley Co); Md Lucinda Henderson (--8-3-1854); War of 1812; P D & Edwards Acct Bk; Ft Hill Cem in Cleveland, Bradley Co; Pvt mkr.

CRAWFORD, JAMES L (--liv 1828 List Maury Co); Md ( ); served Tenn Mil; P D & 2400 Pensioners, Armstrong; likely Maury Co; Unkn.

CRAWFORD, SAMUEL (6-2-1758--5-14-1822 Knox Co); Md Nancy Forgey 1788 (8-13-1768--3-13-1837); Early Indian Wars; Goodspeed Knox Co; Washington Pres Cem Knox Co; Pvt mkr. (Also Rev War)

CRAWFORD, THOMAS (8-4-1794--4-4-1872 Knox Co); Md Maria Harris 9-20-1825 (1802--12-19-1881); Pvt, Capt John Bayless' Co, Col Sam Wear's 1st Regt E T V, 9-23-1813--12-33-1813; W D & T S A; Washington Pres Cem Knox Co; Unmkd.

CREED, WILSON C N (1-8-1793--bef 1830 Hawkins Co); Md Lucinda Stubblefield 1-8-1818 (1802--1873); 3rd Lieut War of 1812, 3-7-1814--res 4-12-1814; Heitman; Cem near Mooresburg, Hawkins Co; Unkn.

CROCKETT, WILSON (--c 1784 Unkn); Md Jane Morrow c 1810 (1790--); War of 1812-Land Grants on Marrowbone Creek; W D & Crockett Fam Hist; likely in Tenn; Unkn.

CROSS, ABRAHAM (1792--9-19-1885 Sullivan Co); Md Peachy Gitts (Getz) (--d aft husband); Corp, Capt Rogers Co, 24th U S Inf, 8-29-1812 for 18 mos, Muster Roll at Sackett's Harbor shows him absent 12-31-1813 from Camp Meigs, later Pvt, Capt James Landen's Co, Col Sam Bayless' 4th Regt E T Drftd Mil, 11-14-1814--5-26-1815; W D & T S A; Smith-Cross Fam Cem on banks Holston River, Sullivan Co; Unmkd.

CROSS, GEORGE (--d 1814 at Ft Williams, Ala); Md ( ); War of 1812, d Ft Williams, Ala; T S A; Bur at Ft Williams, Ala; Unmkd.

CROZIER, JOHN (5-12-1769 Ireland--10-12-1828 Knoxville, Knox Co); Md Hannah Barton 1-1799 ( ); Capt, Vol Co Knox Co, 1796-98-1800 & P M Knoxville, 1804-1848; John Sevier Commission Bk & Knox Co Records; Cem in Knoxville, Knox Co; Pvt mkr.

CRUMLEY, AARON (--d Greene Co); Md Lydia Brown 8-23-1814 ( ); Pvt, Capt Jacob Hoyal's Co, Col Ewen Allison's Regt E T Drftd Mil, 1-10-1814--5-15-1814; W D & T S A; likely in Greene Co; Unkn.

CRUMLEY, JACOB Jr (--d Sullivan Co); Single; Pvt, Capt Wm King's Co, Col Ewen Allison's Regt, E T Drftd Mil, 1-6-1814--5-18-1814; W D & T S A; Crumley Fam Cem, Sullivan Co; Unmkd.

CRUMLEY, JACOB Sr (--d 4-28-1814 Ft Strother, Ala); Md Nancy (12-20-1782--1838-40); Pvt, Capt Wm King's Co, Col Ewen Allison's Regt E T Drftd Mil, 1-6-1814--4-28-1814, 3 mos 23 days at death; W D & T S A; likely at Ft Strother, Ala; Unkn.

CRUTCHER, THOMAS (2-18-1760--3-8-1844 Nashville, Davidson Co); Md ( ); Treasurer Mero Distr & Mayor Nashville 1819; T S A; Old City Cem, Nashville, Davidson Co; Pvt mkr.

CRUZE, JAMES (1797--d Knox Co); Md Lennes Childress ( ); War of 1812; Goodspeed Knox Co; likely Knox Co; Unkn.

CUMMINGS, GEORGE (1764--1830-9 Wilson Co); Md Mary McQuiston 1792 (1780--1816-20); Pvt, Capt Ezekiel Ross' Co, Maj Woodfolk's Regt W T Mil, 9-20-1814-- ; W D & T S A; likely Wilson Co; Unkn.

CUNNINGHAM, SAMUEL (--liv 1828 List Stewart Co); Md ( ); served Clark's 3rd Regt U S Inf; P D & 2400 Pensioners, Armstrong; likely Stewart Co; Unkn.

CURL, JARRETT (--d aged 100 yrs 2 mos, Hickman Co); Md (dau Mary Curl md Dr D D Flowers, Dickson, Tenn); War of 1812; Notable Men of Tenn-Allison; Cem in Hickman Co; Unkn.

CURLEE, CULLEN (1-5-1786--1-18-1858 Tipton Co); Md Eleanor McFerrin 8-25-1818 ( ); Pvt, Musician & Trumpeter, Capt George Brandon's Co, Col Newton Cannon's 2nd Regt, W T Riflemen, 9-24-1813--1-1-1814; W D & T S A; Cem in Tipton Co; Pvt mkr.

CURRIER, WILLIAM (-- in Tenn); Md Martha Frier (   ); War of 1812; W D; likely in Tenn; Unkn. (Drummer in Rev War)

CURRY, WILLIAM (1787--d Roane Co); Md   (   ); Pvt, Capt Uriah Allison's Co, Col Edmond P Gaines' 8th Regt U S Inf, 3-15-1812; W D & Roane Co Hist-Wells; Unkn Cem in Roane Co; Unkn.

CYPERT, JESSE (6-1-1781-- 1857 Wayne Co); Md Jemima Worthen 1802 (--d 1853); Pvt, Capt Alexander Hill's Co, & Capt John Cunningham's Co, Col Wm Metcalf's 1st Regt, W T Mil; W D & T S A; Waynesboro, Wayne Co; Pvt mkr.

DAIL, ABNER (--d Grainger Co); Md Jane McDonough (   );
War of 1812; Goodspeed E T H-Grainger Co;: Cem in 14th Distr,
Grainger Co; Unkn.

DAIL, WILLIAM (1-5-1795--8-17-1877 Anderson Co); Md Nancy Overton
(1-1-1792--3-30-1860); War of 1812; P D & W D & Goodspeed E T H-
Anderson Co; likely in Anderson Co; Unkn.

DALE, ADAM (--d Maury Co); Md   (   ); Capt,
Col Wm Y Higgins' 2nd Regt W T Mil; T S A & Texas 1812 Records;
Rose Hill Cem in Columbia, Maury Co; Pvt mkr & Official 1812 mkr.

DALE, THOMAS Jr (1778--d Smith Co); Md Elizabeth Hammond 1806
(1788--); Pvt, Capt Adam Dale's Co, Col Wm Y Higgins' 2nd Regt
W T Mil; W D & T S A; Liberty, Smith Co; Unkn.

DANIEL, JAMES (--liv 1840 aged 54 yrs Dickson Co); Md
(   ); served Col Williams Regt Mil; P D & 2400 Pensioners,
Armstrong; likely Cem in Dickson Co; Unkn.

DANIEL, JESSE (--liv 1828 List Lincoln Co); Md
(   ); served Regt W T Mil; P D & 2400 Pensioners, Armstrong; likely in Lincoln Co; Unkn.

DANIEL, PAUL (--d Morgan Co); Md Mary Hendricks (--d Morgan Co);
War of 1812; Goodspeed E T H; likely Morgan Co; Unkn.

DANIELS, JAMES (1796-- 1872 Dickson Co); Md   (   );
Corp, Capt Joseph Williams Co Tenn Mil; T S A & Texas 1812
Records; Dickson Co; Unkn.

DARDIS, JAMES (7-26-1766--12-25-1846 Winchester, Franklin Co);
Md Lucy Simms (   ); Lieut, Vol Cav Hawkins Co, 1797-98;
John Sevier's Commission Bk; Winchester, Franklin Co; Pvt mkr.

DARK, JAMES (--d Marshall Co); Md 1-Martha Gates in Wilson Co
(   ), 2-Sarah Fisher (   ); at New Orleans; Goodspeed
Marshall Co; likely Marshall Co; Unkn.

DAVIS, JOHN (--d 10-1814 in service); Md   (   );
served Col John Williams' 24th Regt U S Inf; P D & 2400 Pensioners, Armstrong; heirs were Anna, Mary & John Davis in Sullivan
Co; likely in Ala; Unkn.

DAVIS, ROBERT C (--liv 1828 List Wilson Co); Md
(   ); served 2nd Regt Mtd Gunmen; P D & 2400 Pensioners,
Armstrong; likely Wilson Co; Unkn.

DAVIS, PETER P (--d Blount Co); Md Viney   (Pension #8,539);
Pvt, Capt David McKamey's Co, Col Wm Johnson's 3rd Regt E T
Drftd Mil, 9-29-1814--5-18-1815; T S A & P D & Blount Co Hist,
Burns; likely Ellijoy Bapt Cem in Blount Co; Unkn.

DAVISON, BRACKETT (--liv 1828 List Maury Co); Md
(   ); served Gen John Coffee's Brig, W T Mil; P D & 2400 Pensioners, Armstrong; likely in Maury Co; Unkn.

DAVISON, THOMAS (DAWSON) (--d 1812 Ft Williams, Ala); Md
(   ); Pvt, Capt Jonathan Waddle's Co, Col Sam Bayless' 4th Regt E T Drftd Mil, 11-13-1814--d 1814 Ft Williams, Ala; W D & T S A; likely Ft Williams, Ala; Unmkd.

DAY, JOHN (1-15-1795--3-26-1853 Hancock Co); Md Frances Holleway (11-28-1797--5- 1887); Corp, Capt Berry's Co, Col Sam Bunch's Regt E T Mtd Mil; W D & T S A; Hancock Co; Pvt mkr.

DEADERICK, DAVID (10-10-1754--10-28-1823 Jonesboro, Washington Co); Md 1-Nancy Knight (--d 1787), 2-Margaretta Anderson 12-30-1794 (5-25-1775--10-21-1857); Tenn Senate 1799-1800; T S A; Old City Cem in Jonesboro, Washington Co; Pvt monument. (Also Rev War)

DEADERICK, GEORGE MICHAEL (1756--1816-7 Davidson Co); Md (2nd wife of Col Dunn, Davidson Co) (--d aft 1816); Pvt, --- Regt with Jackson at Tohopeka, 3-27-1814; W D & Deaderick Fam Hist; Deaderick Fam Cem at "Westwood", Davidson Co; Pvt mkr.

DEAN, LUKE H (--10-26-1813 en route); Md   (   ); Corp, Capt Robt Jetton's Co, Col John Allcorn's Regt W T V Cav, 9-24-1813--10-26-1813 died; W D & T S A; likely in Ala; Unkn.

DEARLING, WM LYNCH SMITH (4-17-1796--6-12-1876 Warren Co); Md Mary Terry Harrison 8-21-1817 (3-8-1799--9-6-1864); Pvt, Capt James M Hayden's Co, Va Mil, 8-30-1814--12-16-1814; Va S A; Warren Co; Pvt mkr.

DEARMOND, JOHN (--c 1769--liv 9-28-1850 aged 81 yrs McMinn Co); Md (   ); Pvt, Lieut Robt May & Lieut Davis in Garrison at Tellico Blockhouse & Southwest Point 1790s & Pvt, Capt Wm Henderson's Co, Mtd Gunmen or Spies, Gen Nath Taylor's Brig, 1814-15; P D & T S A; likely McMinn Co; Unkn.

DELOACH, SIMON (--liv 1840 aged 51 yrs Dickson Co); Md
(   ); War of 1812; P D & 2400 Pensioners, Armstrong; likely Dickson Co; Unkn.

DEMARCUS, SOLOMON (--5-10-1841 Knox Co); Md Mary James 10-19-1802 (--c 1875); Pvt, Capt Richard Marshall's Co E T Mil; W D & P D; Graham Fam Cem, Anderson Co; Official 1812 mkr, 1938.

DENHAM, WASHINGTON (1790--aft 1850 Hawkins Co); Md Elizabeth   (--liv 1850 aged 50 yrs - One Denham md 9-27-1842 Elizabeth Stile in Hawkins Co); War of 1812 Invalid List, Pensioned 1820, 54 in 1840 List; P D; likely Hawkins Co; Unkn.

DENNY, WILLIAM (--liv 1840 aged 47 yrs in Smith Co); Md
(   ); served in Tenn Mtd Inf; P D & 2400 Pensioners, Armstrong; likely Smith Co; Unkn.

DENTON, JOSIAH (--9-18-1866 3rd Distr, Sevier Co); Md Catherine Sehorn 1809 (1783--liv 3-24-1871 Sevier Co); Pvt, Capt Wm Henderson's Co, Mtd Spies, Gen Nath Taylor's Brig Vol, 6-18-1812--11-1814; W D & P D & T S A; Cem in 3rd Distr, Sevier Co; Unkn.

DIBRELL, CHARLES L (1757-- 1840 Union Co); Md ( ); Capt of Ky Troops, Gen Wm Harrison's Expd 1790; Ky S A; Union Co; Unkn.

DICKSON, WILLIAM (--liv 1840 aged 54 yrs in Marshall Co); Md ( ); War of 1812; P D & 2400 Pensioners, Armstrong; likely Marshall Co; Unkn.

DICKASON, JOHN H (1779-- 1855 Wilson Co); Md ( ); Lieut, Capt Wm Alexander's Co & Capt Wm Lauderdale's Co, W T Mil; T S A & Texas 1812 Records; Wilson Co; Unkn.

DICKINS, SAMUEL (1781--9- 1840 Tazewell Co, N C); Md ( ); Civil Service & Gen Assembly in N C; Elmwood Cem Bk, Memphis; Elmwood Cem, Memphis, Shelby Co; Govt mkr.

DIVINE, JAMES (--d McMinn Co); Md ( ); Pvt, Capt Wm Turner's Co Inf, Lieut Col John A Alston's Regt, S C Mil, 11-6-1814--3-12-1815; S C S A; McMinn Co; Unkn.

DIXON, WILLIAM (--liv 1828 List Maury Co); Md ( ); served Tenn Mil; P D & 2400 Pensioners, Armstrong; likely Maury Co; Unkn.

DOBBS, JESSE (--aft 1852 Bradley Co); Md ( ); Corp, Capt Andrew Lawson's Co, Col Wm Johnson's 3rd Regt, E T Drftd Mil, 9-20-1814--5-9-1815; W D & Edwards Acct Bk; likely Bradley Co; Unkn.

DOBBS, JOHN (1773-- 1859 Maury Co); Md ( ); Lieut, Capt John Doak's Co, 2nd Regt Tenn Mil at N O; Texas 1812 Records; Columbia, Maury Co; Unkn.

DODD, SAMUEL (1795--d Williamson Co); Md Xernia Johnson (1796--); Pvt at N O in 1815; Goodspeed Williamson Co; likely Williamson Co; Unkn.

DOHERTY, Col GEORGE (1-18-1745--d Jefferson Co); Md Priscilla Goforth 1763 ( ); Early Indian Wars on Watauga, Repr from Jefferson Co, Natchez Expd 1803 & Brig Gen in Creek War, E T Brig at Tohopeka 1814; W D & T S A; "Shady Grove" Cem, 4 m W Dandridge, Jefferson Co; Pvt mkr.

DONELLY, RICHARD (8-17-1790--8-26-1870 Johnson Co); Md Rebecca Doran 10- 1817 (9-9-1796--12-28-1876); Enl War of 1812, served 1 mo; T S A & Goodspeed E T H Johnson Co; Cem in Johnson Co; Pvt mkr. (Also in Indian Removal 1837)

DONELLY, WILLIAM (2-15-1792--2-16-1842 Johnson Co); Md Sarah McQueen 2-24-1824 (6-4-1801--12-24-1876); Pvt, Capt McClain's Co, N C Regt Vol at Wilkesboro, Wilkes Co; W D & N C S A; Robinson Fam Cem in Johnson Co; Pvt mkr.

DONELSON, Maj ALEXANDER (11- 1784--killed 1-22-1814 at Emuckfau, Ala); Single; Lieut & Paymaster, Enl 9-24-1813, Lieut & Aide-de-Camp Gen John Coffee, 10-30-1813--killed 1-22-1814; W D & T S A; likely in Ala; Unkn.

DONELSON, JOHN IV (4-23-1787--4-28-1840 Davidson Co); Md Eliza Butler 11-8-1823 (   ); Lieut 9-4-1813 in Creek War & at N O; W D & T S A; likely Donelson Fam Cem, Davidson Co; Pvt mkr.

DONELSON, LEMUEL (6-6-1789--d Davidson Co); Md Elizabeth Wythe 1819 (1802--1832); Pvt, Capt Hutchings Co, Vol Mtd Gunmen, 9-14-1814-- , Col Williamson's Regt; W D & T S A; likely in Donelson Fam Cem, Davidson Co; Unkn.

DONELSON, SAMUEL (-- Unkn --   ); Md   (   ); Assembly at Knoxville; Nothing more known.

DONELSON, WILLIAM (5-17-1795--   ); Md Rachel Donelson 6-22-1822 (   ); Pvt, Capt Moore's Co, Col Thomas Williamson's Co, Col Wm Pillow's Regt W T Mtd Gunmen, 9-25-1813--12-22-1813; W D & T S A; likely Donelson Fam Cem, Davidson Co; Unkn.

DORAN, ALEXANDER (6-2-1760-- 1814 Carter, now Johnson Co); Md Elizabeth Lowry 1780 (   ); 2nd Lieut, Capt Jesse Cole's Co, Col Sam Wear's 1st Regt, E T V, 10-18-1813--1-7-1814; W D & T S A; Shoun's Cross Rds, Johnson Co; Pvt mkr. (Also Rev War)

DOSS, AZARIAH (--d 1869 Robertson Co); Md Elizabeth Groves (   ); Pvt, War of 1812; W D & T S A; Cem in Robertson Co; Unkn.

DOSSETT, EDMOND (--d Campbell Co); Md   (   ); Pvt, War of 1812; Goodspeed E T H; Delap Cem between Jacksboro & LaFollette, Campbell Co; Pvt mkr.

DOSSETT, ROBERT (1787--5-12-1889, aged 101 yrs Campbell Co); Md Elizabeth Willoughby (--6-19-1836); War of 1812 under Gen Jackson; Goodspeed E T H; Cem in Powell's Valley, Campbell Co; Unkn.

DOSSETT, WILLIS (--killed 11-3-1813 Talledega, Ala); Md (   ); Pvt, Capt John W Byrn's Co, Col John Allcorn's Regt Mtd Mil, W T; 9-24-1813--11-3-1813 killed; W D & T S A; likely Ala; Unkn.

DOUGLAS, JOHN (--d McMinn Co); Md   (   ); Pvt, Capt Jehu Stephens' Co, Vol Mtd Gunmen E T, Brig Gen John Coffee's Brig, 10-6-1814--4-6-1815; W D & T S A; Salem Bapt Cem near Coghill, McMinn Co; Pvt mkr.

DOUGLAS, JOHN Jr (--d 12-14-1814 in service); Md
(   ); Pvt, Capt Jehu Stephen's Co Vol Mtd Gunmen E T, Brig
Gen John Coffee Brig, 10-6-1814--d 12-14-1814; W D & T S A;
likely in Ala; Unkn.

DOUGLAS, ROBERT (--c 1756--7-10-1837 McMinn Co); Md
(   ); War of 1812; P D; Salem Bapt Cem near Coghill, McMinn
Co; Pvt mkr. (Also Rev War)

DUGAN, DANIEL (--c 1793--liv 12-17-1850 aged 57 yrs Sevier Co);
Md   (   ); Pvt, Capt Andrew Lawson's Co, Col Wm
Johnson's 3rd Regt E T Drftd Mil, 9-20-1814--5-9-1815; W D &
T S A & P D; likely Sevier Co; Unkn.

DUGGAN, HUGH (--bef 1852 Bradley Co); Md (nameless wid had pension); Pvt, likely from Sevier Co; Edwards Acct Bk- Widow Duggan,
& P D; Cem in Bradley Co; Unkn.

DUGGAN, WILLIAM (--liv 1840 aged 49 yrs Monroe Co); Md
(   ); Pvt, Col John Williams' 24th Regt U S Inf; P D & 2400
Pensioners, Armstrong; likely in Monroe Co; Unkn.

DUGGAN, WILLIAM (--liv 1-30-1858 aged 94 yrs McMinn Co); Md
(   ); Srgt, Capt Andrew Lawson's Co, Col Wm Johnson's 3rd
Regt E T Drftd Mil, 9-20-1814--5-9-1815; P D & T S A; likely
McMinn Co; Unkn.

DUGGER, JOHN (10-1-1780--8-2-1869 Carter Co); Md Mary Engle 2-26-
1801 (12-22-1785--2-2-1869); Pvt & Ensign, Capt Adam Winsell's
Co, Col Ewen Allison's Regt E T Drftd Mil, 1-5-1814--5-18-1814;
W D & T S A; moved from Dugger Fam Cem Carter Co to Sugar Grove
Bapt Cem near Butler, Carter Co; Unmkd. (One of Cem covered by
Watauga Lake.)

DUGGER, JULIUS C (9-9-1760-- 1838 Carter Co); Md
(   ); Pvt, Capt Adam Winsell's Co, Col Ewen Allison's Regt
E T Drftd Mil, 1-5-1814--5-18-1814; W D & T S A; moved from Dugger
Fam Cem near Fish Springs, Carter Co, by T V A to --- Carter Co;
Pvt mkr. (One of Cem covered by Watauga Lake.)

DUGGER, JULIUS A (--d 1862 Carter Co); Md Nancy Overbay 4-17-1824
(   ); Pvt, Capt Henry Hunter's Co, Col Wm Johnson's 3rd Regt
E T Drftd Mil, 9-13-1814--5-11-1815; W D & T S A; Fam Cem on Stony
Creek, Carter Co; Unkn.

DUGGER, WILLIAM (3-4-1750--6-18-1839 Carter Co); Md
(   ); Chicamauga Expd vs Indians 1788; T S A & Ramsey's
Annals; Dugger Fam Cem at Fish Springs, Carter Co - moved by
T V A to Cem in Carter Co; Pvt mkr. (Also Rev War)

DULIN, WILLIAM (--d 1813 in service); Md   (   );
heirs were Sally, Jane & Jefferson Dulin in Smith Co; P D & 2400
Pensioners, Armstrong; likely in Ala; Unkn.

DUNCAN, JOSEPH (-- 1850 Blount Co); Md Susannah Norwood 10-14-1828 (   ); Capt, Col Sam Bunch's Regt E T Drftd Mil, 1-10-1814--4-21-1814; W D & T S A; Cem in Morganton, Blount Co; Unkn.

DUNLAP, JAMES (--liv 1828 List Monroe Co); Md (   ); Pvt, --- Co, Col Wm Johnson's 3rd Regt E T Drftd Mil; P D & 2400 Pensioners, Armstrong; likely Monroe Co; Unkn.

DUNNEGAN, JOHN (--d Polk Co); Md (   ); Pvt, Capt Daniel Ross' Co, Col John Coffee's Regt, later Col Allen's Regt Vol, 9-24-1813--12-31-1813; W D & T S A; Unkn Cem in Polk Co; Unkn.

DURHAM, Rev THOMAS (1760-- 1823 Smith Co); Md Rebecca Allen 1780 (1762--1823-?); Juryman in Smith Co; Smith Co Records; likely in Smith Co; Unkn.

DYER, BALDY (--11-20-1814 in service); Md (   ); heirs were Willie, James, William, David, Susanna, Simpson & Mary Dyer of Davidson Co; P D & 2400 Pensioners, Armstrong; likely in Ala; Unkn.

DYER, JOEL (1754--6-11-1825 Madison Co); Md 1-Sophia (   ), 2-Sallie Jones Christmas 7-16-1802 (   ); 2nd Maj, Hawkins Co Mil, 1796; John Sevier's Commission Bk; Madison Co; Pvt mkr.

DYER, ROBERT HENRY (-- 1828 Madison Co); Md (   ); On Nickajack Expd vs Chicamauga Indians, & Lieut in Cav Regt, 5th Tenn Brig, 1807, Capt 1810, Lieut Col on Natchez Expd, 1812-13, & Col 1st Regt, Mtd Gunmen, W T 1814-15; W D & T S A & Beg West Tenn- Williams; Madison Co; Pvt mkr.

DYKE, JACOB (--d Greene Co); Md (   ); Capt, Col Wm Lillard's 2nd Regt E T V, 10-14-1813--2-8-1814, mustered out Greeneville; W D & T S A; likely in Greene Co; Unkn.

EARLY, ANDREW (OERLICH, ANDREW) (10-23-1784--5-5-1864 Blount Co); Md Winifred R Frazier 7-26-1808 (5-3-1787--1-26-1861); 2nd Srgt, Capt Alexander Biggs' Co, Col Zachariah Boothe's 5th Regt Tenn Mil, 11- 1812--5- 1815; W D & T S A; New Providence Pres Cem, Maryville, Blount Co; Pvt mkr.

EARNEST, HENRY (12-13-1772--11-21-1851 Greene Co); Md Kitty Reeve (5-4-1801--11-19-1848); Col, Mtd Inf in Indian Wars; Fam Records; Ebenezer Meth Cem in Greene Co; Pvt mkr.

EASLEY, DRURY (--liv 1828 List Sumner Co); Md   (   ); served in 44th Regt U S Inf; P D & 2400 Pensioners, Armstrong; likely in Sumner Co; Unkn.

ECKLEBERGER, DAVID (--liv 1840 List aged 43 yrs Madison Co, with Isaac Malett); Md   (   ); War of 1812; P D & 2400 Pensioners, Armstrong; likely in Madison Co; Unkn.

EDENS, AUSTIN (--d Carter Co); Md Martha Murray 10-22-1796 (   ); Pvt, Capt Solomon Hendrix's Co, Col Sam Bayless' 4th Regt E T Drftd Mil, 11-18-1814--1-17-1815; W D & T S A; likely in Carter Co; Unkn.

EDMUNDSON, ANDREW JACKSON (1793--4-30-1872 Memphis, Shelby Co); Md   (   ); served as Capt in Campaigns vs Indians & the British; Record Bk of Elmwood Cem; Elmwood Cem in Memphis, Shelby Co; Official 1812 mkr.

EDWARDS, DAVID (1778--8-28-1817 near Centerville, Hickman Co); Md Eve Lazell 1798 (--bef 1814); Pvt, Capt Dooley's Co, Col Thomas McCrory's 2nd Regt W T Mil, 10-4-1813--   ; T S A; Edwards Fam Cem near Centerville, Hickman Co; Govt mkr 1933 by U S D 1812.

EFFLER, LAWRENCE (--liv Unicoi, Unicoi Co, 1883); Md (   ); War of 1812; P D; likely in Unicoi Co; Unkn.

ELLIOTT, ROBERT (--liv 1828 List Maury Co); Md (   ); served 17th Regt U S Inf; P D & 2400 Pensioners, Armstrong; likely in Maury Co; Unkn.

ELLIOTT, THOMAS (1765-- 1863 Carter Co); Md Basay Bullengar 1-23-1805 (   ); Pvt, Capt Jesse Cole's Co, Col Sam Wear's 1st Regt E T V, 10-18-1813--1-17-1814; W D & T S A; likely in Grindstaff Cem on Stony Creek, Carter Co; Unkn.

EMMERSON, THOMAS (6-23-1773--7-22-1837 Jonesboro, Washington Co); Md 1-Rachel Burwell 2-7-1795 (--d 1832), 2-Catherine Jacobs 3-27-1833 (11-9-1789--12- 1858); Judge Superior Ct 1807; John Sevier Commission Bk; Old Cem in Jonesboro, Washington Co; stone broken and illegible by tree thru it.

EMMETT, DANIEL (--liv 5-2-1851 Sevier Co); Md   (   ); Pvt, Capt Isaac Williams' Co, Col Sam Bunch's 2nd Regt E T Drftd Mil, 1-10-1814--5-16-1814, disch Roane Co; W D & P D; Emmerts Cove Cem, Sevier Co; Unkn.

EMMERT, FREDERICK (EMMETT) (12-14-1791--d Blount Co); Md Drusilla Reagan (   ); Pvt, Capt Isaac Williams' Co, Col Sam Bunch's 2nd Regt E T Drftd Mil, 1-10-1814--5-16-1814; W D & T S A; Tuchaleeche Meth Camp Ground Cem, Blount Co; Unkn.

ENSOR, THOMAS P (--d aged 89 yrs Sullivan Co); Md Hannah Jobe 5-9-1812 (5-21-1791--2-12-1856); Pvt, Capt John Hampton's Co, Col Ewen Allison's Regt E T Drftd Mil, 1-5-1814--7-26-1814; W D & T S A; Weaver's Union Ch Cem in Sullivan Co; Pvt mkr.

ERVIN, PATRICK (ERWIN) (--4-30-1835 aged 56 yrs Washington Co); Md Malinda Taylor (--1861); Pvt, Capt Henry McCray's Co, Col Ewen Allison's Regt E T Drftd Mil, Enl 1-5-1814, transfrd 4-27-1814 to Capt Francis Register's Co, Col Sam Bunch's Regt Mtd Mil, 8-1-1814, also in Capt George McPherson's Co, Col Sam Bunch's Regt Mtd Mil; W D & T S A; Fairview Meth Ch Cem 2 m S Jonesboro, Washington Co; Govt mkr 1924 by U S D 1812.

ESTES, JOEL (1-22-1780--9-16-1833 near Waverly, Humphreys Co); Md 1-Sarah L Bates 10-13-1801 (1781--c 1825), 2-Mary Lee Wilson 6-30-1831 (   ); Capt of Co Vol Riflemen in 43rd Regt Va Mil, attchd to 4th Regt Va Mil in War of 1812; Muster Roll dated Norfolk, Va, 9-16-1813--10-15-1813; W D & Va S A; Estes Fam Cem near Waverly, Humphreys Co; Govt mkr 1937 by descndt.

EVANS, RICHARD (--7-11-1854 Sevier Co); Md Catherine Emmert 3-4-1812 (--3-23-1888); Pvt, Capt Isaac Williams' Co, Col Sam Bunch's 2nd Regt E T Drftd Mil, 1-10-1814--5-10-1814; W D & P D; Cem in Emmerts Cove, Sevier Co; Unkn.

EVERETT, JOSEPH (1-3-1773--2- 1850 Sullivan Co); Md 1-Agness Gaines 12-17-1797 (3-31-1780--), 2-Phoebe Childress 1817 (1788 --aft 1850); Capt in Col Ewen Allison's Regt E T Drftd Mil, 1-17-1814--5-18-1814; W D & T S A; Groseclose Fam Cem in Sullivan Co; Pvt mkr.

FAIN, JOHN (--liv 1840 List aged 51 yrs Jefferson Co); Md
(   ); served Col Ball's Regt; P D & 2400 Pensioners, Armstrong; likely in Jefferson Co; Unkn.

FAIN, THOMAS (12-11-1785--2-2-1862 Sullivan Co); Md Sarah Crawford 3-26-1812 (   ); Pvt, Capt John Hampton's Co, Col Ewen Allison's Regt, E T Drftd Mil, 1-5-1814--7-26-1814; W D & T S A; Crawford Fam Cem 5 m W Blountville at Holston Institute, Sullivan Co; Pvt mkr.

FANCHER, ISAAC (--liv 1828 List Overton Co); Md   (   );
served 7th Regt U S Inf; P D & 2400 Pensioners, Armstrong; likely Overton Co; Unkn.

FARMER, SAMUEL (1784--3-20-1866 Robertson Co); Md Sarah Childress 1808 (1790--1876); Pvt, Capt John Crane's Co & Capt James Cross' Co, Col John Williamson's Mtd Gunmen, Regt W T Mil, 9-1814--3- 1815; T S A; Cem in Robertson Co; Pvt mkr.

FIELD, GEORGE (--liv 1828 List Giles Co); Md   (   );
served in Tenn Mil; P D & 2400 Pensioners, Armstrong; likely in Giles Co; Unkn.

FIKES, ELISHA (--liv 1828 List Robertson Co); Md
(   ); served in 2nd Regt Tenn Mil; P D & 2400 Pensioners, Armstrong; likely in Robertson Co; Unkn.

FINDLEY, WILLIAM (--d Bradley Co); Md   (   );
Pvt, Capt John Trimble's Co, Col John Brown's 2nd Regt E T V; W D & Edwards Acct Bk; likely in Bradley Co; Unkn.

FINE, JOHN (1-2-1782--1-26-1857 Cocke Co); Md Nancy Lee 1800 (11-10-1782--2-18-1859); War of 1812; Hist of Cocke Co -Odell; Cem on Old Rutherford Farm on Sinking Creek, Cocke Co; Unkn.

FISHER,   (--1-8-1815 at N O); Single; killed at Battle of N O 1-8-1815; Rev War Pension statement of father John Fisher & stepmother Lucinda Tramel, Warren Co Tenn; at N O; Unkn.

FIVE, KILLER (--d Polk Co, near Benton); Md   (   );
Pvt, Cherokee Regt in Creek War; W D & T S A; Cem 1½ m from Benton, Polk Co, where his mother, Nancy Ward, is bur beside him on hill above hiway; Govt mkr. ("Nancy Ward d 1-22-1828".)

FLEMING, JOHN DICKEY (3-2-1792--8-12-1882 Maury Co); Md Margaret M Williams (2-8-1801--11-30-1842); Pvt, Capt Johnson's Co, Col N T Perkins' Regt W T Inf, 12-20-1813-- ; W D; Zion Pres Cem near Columbia, Maury Co; Pvt mkr.

FLENNIKEN, JAMES WALLACE (1776--8-19-1840 Knox Co); Md Mary S   (7-10-1775--9-21-1859); War of 1812, called Major; W D & D'Armond Gen- D'Armond; Fam Cem on farm, 4 m S Knoxville, Knox Co; Pvt mkr.

FLETCHER, WILLIAM (--killed 11-9-1813 Ala); Md
(   ); Pvt, Capt John J Winston's Co, Col John Allcorn's Regt
Mtd Riflemen, W T Mil, 10-9-1813--11-9-1813 killed; W D & T S A;
likely in Ala; Unkn.

FLOWERS, WILLIAM (--d Washington Co); Md   (   );
Pvt, Capt David G Vance's Co, Col Sam Bunch's Regt Mtd Inf, 10-
1813-- 2- 1814; W D; Unkn Cem in Washington Co; Unkn.

FOLSOM, MALCOLM NEVILLE (1793--2-21-1878 Elizabethton, Carter
Co); Md Nannie Hughes (1797--4-16-1877); aged 20 yrs, served in
2nd War with Gr Britain, disch at Norfolk, Va; Fam Hist; Green
Hill Cem at Elizabethton, Carter Co; Pvt mkr.

FORD, JOHN C D (alias John D Ford) (--d in service 1-6-1813);
Md   (   ); heirs were Isaac, Hannah, Cromwell &
Thomas Ford in Sullivan Co; served in 2nd Regt, Artillery; P D
& 2400 Pensioners, Armstrong; likely where died; Unkn.

FORESTER, ISAAC (1790--d in Lincoln Co); Md Matilda Hodges 1817
(   ); served under Gen John Coffee; Goodspeed Lincoln Co;
likely in Moore Co (then Lincoln); Unkn.

FORMAN, JOHN (--liv 1828 List Jefferson Co); Md
(   ); served in Tenn Mil; P D & 2400 Pensioners, Armstrong;
likely Jefferson Co; Unkn.

FORRESTER, WILLIAM (--d Bradley Co); Md   (   );
Pvt, Capt James Gillespie's Co, Col Sam Wear's 1st Regt E T V,
9-23-1813--12-31-1813; W D & Edwards Acct Bk; likely in Bradley
Co; Unkn.

FORT, ROBERT D (5-23-1795--4-9-1886 Memphis, Shelby Co); Md
Elizabeth Ann Joyner 12-4-1821 (9-29-1805--3-17-1886); Pvt, W T
Mil; W D & P D; Elmwood Cem in Memphis, Shelby Co; Govt mkr.

FOSTER, ANTHONY (1795--4-8-1825 Nashville, Davidson Co); Md
Eleanor   (1778--1825); Commissioner of West Tenn for Land
Claims, 6-12-1808; T S A; Old City Cem in Nashville, Davidson
Co; Pvt mkr.

FOSTER, EPHRAIM (9-12-1794--9-6-1854 Nashville, Davidson Co); Md
Jane M   1828 (1792--11-12-1847); U S Senator & Pvt Sec to
Gen Jackson during Creek War; Vol State- Moore; Old City Cem in
Nashville, Davidson Co; Pvt mkr.

FOSTER, RICHARD (--d in service 12-19-1813 in Ala); Md
(   ); heirs were Alcey, Thomas & Mary Foster in Rutherford
Co; served in 24th Regt U S Inf; P D & 2400 Pensioners, Armstrong; likely in Ala; Unkn.

FOSTER, ROBERT COLEMAN (7-18-1769--9-27-1844 Nashville, Davidson
Co); Md Anne S Hubbard 1790 (4-27-1770--11-27-1850); Speaker of
House & Candidate for Gov of Tenn in 1815; T S A; Old City Cem
in Nashville, Davidson Co; Pvt mkr.

FOX, ADAM (--d 1867 Sevier Co); Md Mary Schrader 1815 (--liv 1909); Pvt, Capt Simeon Perry's Co, Col Sam Bunch's Regt E T V, 9-23-1813--12-23-1813; W D & P D; likely in Fox Fam Cem at Old Dutch Settlement, Sevier Co; Unkn.

FRANCISCO, JOHN (--c 1761--Inv Est 4-2-1849 Meigs Co); Md Elizabeth (?) Hagood (--bef 1823); Lieut, Capt Ezekiel's Co, Mtd Cav, Maj Gen Charles Scott's Regt Ky Cav, 7-15-1793--11-14-1793; Ky S A; Francisco Fam Cem Bradley Co, near Meigs Co line; Unmkd.

FRASER, Dr JAMES (1787--1833 Lebanon, Wilson Co); Md Hannah Brown ( ); Surgeon's Mate, Col Robt H Dyer's Regt, Mtd Gunmen W T V, 9-28-1814--4-27-1815; W D & T S A; Lebanon, Wilson Co; Pvt mkr.

FRAZIER, ABNER (--d Greene Co); Md ( ); War of 1812; Goodspeed E T H; likely in Greene Co; Unkn.

FRAZIER, HENRY (--aged 57 yrs in 1840 List & 60 yrs in Henry Church File, 1855, Hawkins Co); Md ( ); Pvt, Capt John Fagan's Co, 39th Regt, U S Inf; W D & 2400 Pensioners, Armstrong; likely Hancock Co; Unkn.

FREEMAN, JOHN (--d Greene Co); Md Mary ( ); War of 1812; Baptist Preachers- Burnett; likely in Greene Co; Unkn.

FREEMAN, MOSES (--d 1-10-1814 in service); Md ( ); Pvt, Capt Jacob Dyke's Co, Col Wm Lillard's 2nd Regt E T V; 10-13-1813--1-10-1814 died; W D & T S A & Hartsell Diary; died at Ft Strother, Ala on Coosa River; Unkn.

FREEMAN, ZADOCK (--c 1785--d Washington Co); Md Hannah Grayham 9-23-1815 ( ); Pvt, 39th Regt U S Inf, Col John Williams 11-23-- ; W D & P D (pensioned in 1838); Cem near Mauk Fam Cem at Mt Carmel Meth Ch, Washington Co; Unkn.

FREY, PETER (7-26-1792--3-10-1856 Robertson Co); Md Evelina Hutchinson 1-11-1818 (8-11-1797--10-8-1854); Pvt, Capt Richard Krunk's Co, Col John Cocke's 2nd Regt, W T Mil, 11-13-1814--5-13-1815; T S A; Cem in Robertson Co; Pvt mkr.

FROST, STEPHEN (--c 1787--8-6-1865 Union Co); Md 1-Mary Hill ( ), 2-Nancy Kitts 2-1-1836 (1802--1880); Pvt, Capt Joseph Rich's Co, Pvt, Capt Joseph B Bacon's Co, Col Sam Bayless' 4th Regt E T Drftd Mil, 11-7-1814--5-21-1815; W D & T S A; Dyer Fam Cem in Union Co near Luttrell; Pvt mkr.

FUGATE, TOWNSEND (1780-- 1878 Rutherford Co); Md Jane Campbell (1784--1837); War of 1812; Goodspeed Rutherford Co; likely in Rutherford Co; Unkn.

FULLER, Lieut JAMES (--liv 1840 List aged 49 yrs Jefferson Co); Md ( ); served 20th Regt U S Inf; P D & 2400 Pensioners, Armstrong; likely in Jefferson Co; Unkn.

FULMER, JOHN (10-17-1795--11-12-1883 Washington Co); Md 1-Elizabeth White 2-24-1817 (--9-10-1882), 2-Rebecca   (named in his Will of 1883); Pvt, Capt Jacob Hartsell's Co, Col Wm Lillard's 2nd Regt, E T V, 10-12-1813--2-8-1814; W D & T S A & Hartsell Diary; Galloway Fam Cem near mouth of Boones Creek in Washington Co; Pvt mkr with 1812 service on it.

GAINES, JAMES (1742-- 1830 Sullivan Co); Md Elizabeth Strother 1761 (9-22-1738--8-3-1845); Presidential Elector; T S A; Groseclose Cem at Morrison City, Sullivan Co; Pvt mkr. (Capt of N C troops in Rev War.)

GAINES, JAMES TAYLOR (1775-- 1821 Gaines Bend near Church Hill, Hawkins Co); Md 1-Jane McMinn Campbell (dau Gov Joseph McMinn) 11-20-1808 (8-27-1787--1-27-1815), 2-Frances Gale Rogers 5-16-1816 (1-21-1795--2-7-1883) [dau Joseph Rogers, she md 2-Dr Hugh Walker (1802--1866)]; Asst Quartermaster, 7th Mil Distr, Ft Deposit, Ala, 1815; W D & T S A; likely in Groseclose Cem at Morrison City, Sullivan Co; likely unmkd. (Son of James Gaines & bro of Edmond P Gaines.)

GAMBLE, JAMES (4- 1793--1- 1873 Chattanooga, Hamilton Co); Md 1-Anne Dickey (1800--1847 Roane Co), 2-Susan Beelers 9-7-1847 (1-25-1825--8-28-1895); Pvt, Capt James Gillespie's Co, Col Sam Wear's 1st Regt E T V, 9-13-1813--12-31-1813; W D & T S A & P D; National Cem in Chattanooga, Hamilton Co; Official 1812 mkr.

GAMBLE, MOSES (8-2-1794--9-5-1870 Blount Co); Md Jane McCallie 11-28-1822 (8-17-1801--10-3-1887); Pvt, Capt Jehu Stephens' Co, Col Sam Wear's Regt Mtd Gunmen, 10-6-1814--4-6-1815; W D & T S A; Walker's Chapel Meth Cem near Walland, Blount Co; Pvt mkr.

GANN, NATHAN (--7-18-1839 Washington Co); Md Sarah   (   ); Capt, Mil Co for Washington Co 1797-98; John Sevier's Commission Bk; Gann Fam Cem near Brownsboro, Washington Co; Govt mkr. (Marked by Govt mkr for Rev War, Lieut in Capt Milliken's Co.)

GARDNER, CULLEN BRYANT (--d 1874 near Gallatin, Sumner Co); Md Sarah Lauderdale Franklin 1-8-1817 (   ); Quartermaster Srgt, Gen John Coffee in Jackson's Command; W D & T S A; Gardner Fam Cem 4 m S E Gallatin, Sumner Co; Official 1812 mkr.

GARNER, WILLIAM (8-11-1781--c 1860 Blount Co); Md Williamson (   ); Corp, Capt Jehu Stephens' Co, Col John Chiles' Regt, Gen John Coffee's Brig, 10-6-1814--4-6-1815; W D & T S A; Crye Fam Cem near Lanier High School, Blount Co; Govt mkr.

GARRETT, GEORGE W (1790-- 1867 Marshall Co); Md Miss Davis (1818--1876); War of 1812; Goodspeed Marshall Co; Marshall Co; Unkn.

GARRETT, JAMES (1775-- 1852 Maury Co); Md   (   ); Pvt, Capt Doak's Co, Col N T Perkins' 1st Regt W T Mtd Vol, 12-20-1813--2-8-1814; W D & T S A; Columbia Cem, Maury Co; Pvt mkr.

GASS, ANDREW (--d aged 65 yrs Jefferson Co); Md Mary C Collins (--liv 1840 aged 60 yrs Jefferson Co); Goodspeed E T H Jefferson Co; 4th Srgt, Capt Reuben Tipton's Co, Maj John Chiles' Batln, 9-20-1814--5-1-1815; likely Jefferson Co; Unkn.

GEORGE, JOHN (--5-25-1814 Greene Co); Md   (   ); Pvt, Lieut Joseph Graham's Co, Col Ewen Allison's Regt E T Drftd Mil, 1-6-1814--5-23-1814; Greene Co Inventory Bk, 1810-1843, by Wm George, Admr; likely Greene Co; Unkn.

GIBBS, GEORGE W (1785-- 1870 Davidson Co); Md   (   ); Capt, 2nd Regt Tenn Mil; T S A; d Nashville, Davidson Co; Unkn.

GIBBS, Capt NICHOLAS (--killed 3-27-1814 Tohopeka, Ala); Md Rachel Doyle (   ); Capt, Col Sam Bunch's Mtd Regt, Col John Williams' 39th Regt U S Inf, 1-10-1814--3-27-1814 killed; W D & T S A; likely in Ala;   likely unmkd.

GIBSON, Col JOHN H (--d Madison Co); Md   (   ); Lieut, 28th Regt Tenn Mil, 2-21-1811, 2nd Maj Cav Regt, Gen John Coffee, under Jackson on Natchez Expd 1812-13, Lieut Col, Brig Gen John Coffee, Creek War & at N O; W D & T S A & Beg West Tenn-Williams; Madison Co; Pvt mkr.

GIBSON, Capt   (--Unkn--); Md   (   ); Capt in Battle Lookout Mt, 1788; Armstrong's Hamilton Co; likely Hamilton Co; Unkn.

GIDDENS, JAMES (1784--10-14-1818 Williamson Co); Md Priscilla R Buford (7-2-1789--11-29-1856); Capt, Col Cheatham's 2nd Regt W T Mil, 1-20-1814--5-10-1814; W D & T S A; Williamson Co; Pvt mkr.

GILLELAND, WILLIAM (1788--5-11-1867 Washington Co); Md (   ); 1st Lieut, Capt Joseph Bacon's Co, Col Sam Bayless' 4th Regt E T Drftd Mil, 11-13-1814--5-21-1815; W D & T S A; Old Salem Pres Cem, Washington College, Washington Co; Pvt mkr.

GILLES, JAMES (--d likely Bradley Co); Md   (   ); Capt of Co E T V in War of 1812; Edwards Acct Bk; likely Bradley Co; Unkn.

GILLESPIE, ALLEN (7-29-1769--8-29-1842 Greene Co); Md Sarah
(--aft 1842); Pvt, Vol Co Cav, Washington Co; P D & Laws of Tenn-
p 1803; New Providence Pres Cem near Millbrook, Greene Co-Washington Co line; Pvt mkr.

GILLESPIE, GEORGE (--bef 2- 1794 Washington Co); Md Martha
(   ); Sheriff Washington Co, 1780s; Washington Co Records;
Gillespie Fam Cem or Old Salem Pres Cem, Washington College, Wash-
ington Co; Unkn.

GILLESPIE, JACOB (1773-- 1864 Sumner Co); Md Nellie   (   );
War of 1812; Sumner Co Records; likely Sumner Co; Unkn.

GILLESPIE, JAMES (--d Blount Co); Md 1-Peggy Houston (   );
2-Jane Gallaher (   ), 3-Patsy W Wallace 8-12-1823 (   );
Capt, Col Sam Wear's 1st Regt E T V, 9-23-1813--12-31-1813; W D
& T S A; Gillespie Fam Cem near Louisville, Blount Co; Unkn.

GILLESPIE, JAMES T (--killed 3-27-1814 Tohopeka, Ala); Md
Clarkie Gillespie (--1870 Franklin Co); Pvt, in Tenn Regt at
Tohopeka; Goodspeed Franklin Co; likely in Ala; Unkn.

GILMORE, JOSEPH (--2-23-1825 Davidson Co); Md   (   );
War of 1812 -   1828 List, transfrd from S C to Davidson Co
Pension List; P D & 2400 Pensioners, Armstrong; likely Davidson
Co; Unkn.

GIST, JOHN (GUESS) (7-13-1791--11-13-1852 White Co); Md Eliza-
beth Robinson (7-15-1797--8-13-1850); Pvt, Capt James Cole's Co,
W T Mil, Creek War; W D & B L Wt #34978; Mt Gilead Cem near
Sparta, White Co; Pvt mkr.

GIST, JOSHUA (1-12-1789--2-2-1831 Maury Co); Md Mary Cherry
(1796--aft 1855); Pvt, Capt Evans' Co, 1st Regt W T V Mil; 1-10-
1812--4-20-1813; W D & T S A; Maury Co; Pvt mkr.

GIST, NEILL (--c 1778--aft 1830 Anderson Co); Md   (   );
Pvt, Capt James Tunnell's Co, Col Wm Johnson's 3rd Regt E T Drftd
Mil; W D & T S A & Gist Genealogy- Dorsey; likely in Anderson Co;
Unkn.

GLASS, WILLIAM (--d Maury Co); Md Nancy or Agness McCollough
4-12-1811 (   ); 5th Srgt, Capt Jehu Stephens' Co, Mtd Gunmen, Col Sam Wear's Regt, 10-6-1814--4-6-1815; W D & T S A;
likely Maury Co; Unkn.

GODFREY, ZACHARIAH (--liv 1828 List Roane Co); Md   (   );
served 9th U S Inf; P D & 2400 Pensioners, Armstrong; likely
Roane Co; Unkn.

GOFORTH, JOHN (--d 9-8-1813 in service); Md   (   );
heirs were Nancy, Preston, Cornelius & John Goforth in Jefferson
Co; served 7th U S Regt Inf; P D & 2400 Pensioners, Armstrong;
likely where died; Unkn.

GOODMAN, ANDREW (1783--9-24-1864 near Buffalo, Washington Co);
Md Catherine Saunders 5-15-1812 Sullivan Co (--liv 1883 Carr-
ville, Washington Co); Pvt, Capt James Landen's Co, Col Sam Bay-
less' 4th Regt E T Drftd Mil, 11-13-1814--5-18-1815 for 6 mos;
W D & T S A & P D; Cem near Buffalo Ridge, Washington Co; Unkn.
(Pension #52,839 & Wid #6721)

GOODNER, JAMES (1792-- 1883 Nashville, Davidson Co); Md
(   ); Corp, Capt Anthony Metcalf's Co, Col Thomas McCrory's
2nd Regt W T Mil, 10-4-1813--1814; T S A; Cem in Nashville,
Davidson Co; Pvt mkr.

GOULD, JOHN (--d Blount Co); Md Jane Ritchie 11-10-1826 (   );
Pvt, Capt John Trimble's Co, Mtd Inf, Col John Coffee's Regt,
10-5-1814--4-5-1815; W D & T S A & Blount Co Hist- Burns; Centenary Meth Cem in Blount Co; Unkn.

GORDON, Capt JOHN (7-15-1763-- 1819 Maury Co); Md Dolly Cross
7-15-1794 (7-15-1779--12-5-1859); Capt, Co Spies under Gen Andrew
Jackson in Creek War, 9-24-1813--5-10-1814; W D & T S A; Rose
Hill Cem, Columbia, Maury Co; Pvt mkr.

GOURLEY, EDWARD (--d Blount Co); Md Jane Robinson 7-17-1827
(   ); Pvt, Capt Samuel Thompson's Co, Col Edwin Boothe's
5th Regt Drftd Mil, 11-13-1814--5-15-1815; W D & T S A; Unkn Cem
near Louisville, Blount Co; Unkn.

GOURLEY, WILLIAM (1779--7-1-1860 Carter Co); Md Elizabeth
Shultz 1796 (3-15-1780--2-25-1847); Pvt, Capt Jesse Cole's Co,
Col Sam Wear's 1st Regt E T V, 10-18-1813--1-17-1814; W D &
T S A; Edens Fam Cem in Carter Co; Unmkd.

GRACE, DAVID (1773--aft 1845 Blount Co); Md   (   );
Pvt, Capt Wm Walker's Co, Col John Williams' 39th Regt U S Inf,
12-22-1813--12-22-1814; W D & P D & T S A; Unkn Cem on Nine
Mile Creek in Blount Co; Unkn.

GRANT, WILLIAM Sr (2-25-1792--9-16-1863 Bradley Co); Md Miss
Henderson (   ); Pvt, Capt Ish's Co; Edwards Acct Bk; Ft
Hill Cem, Cleveland, Bradley Co; Pvt mkr.

GRAY, JOSHUA (--d Greene Co); Md   (   ); War
of 1812; W D; Pleasant Hill Meth Cem at Afton, Greene Co; Govt
mkr. "Clark's Co - 4th Va Mil - War of 1812".

GRAYHAM, JAMES (--10- 1814 Ft Montgomery, Ala); Md Nancy Collins
c 1800 (--liv 10-26-1816 Washington Co); Pvt, Capt John Phegan's
Co, Col John Williams' 39th Regt U S Inf; W D & Washington Co
Court Minutes 10-26-1816; likely Ft Montgomery, Ala; Unkn.

GREEN, DAVIS (--d 9- 1814 Ft Williams, Ala); Md
(   ); 2nd Corp, Capt Newlin's Co, Col Philip Pipkin's Regt
W T Mil, 6-20-1814-- ; W D & T S A; likely at Ft Williams, Ala;
Unmkd.

GREEN, SAMUEL (--d in Tenn); Md   (   ); War of 1812; Armstrong's Hamilton Co Hist; likely in Tenn; Unkn.

GREEN, SAMUEL (1789--10-15-1855 Hamilton, then James Co); Md Martha Ferguson (1791--1858 Ooltewah); War of 1812; Goodspeed E T H; James Co; Unkn. (Could this be same as one above?)

GREENE, RICHARD (1755-- 1823 in Tenn); Md Sarah Virginia 1785 (1760--1826); Pvt, Capt Henry Higgs' Co, 61st Va Mil, 2-28-1814--6-11-1814; Va S A; likely in Tenn; Unkn. (Also Rev War)

GREENWAY, WILLIAM (3-5-1796--4-5-1880 Washington Co); Md Margaret McCracken 8-22-1834 (7-4-1802--7-13-1844); Pvt, Capt Joseph Bacon's Co, Col Sam Bayless' 4th Regt E T Drftd Mil, 11-13-1814--2-15-1815; W D & T S A; Old Salem Pres Cem at Washington College, Washington Co; Official 1812 mkr.

GREER, JOHN (2-17-1764--6-3-1844 Sullivan Co); Md Nancy Owen (   ); Pvt, Capt James Gray's Co, Gen Wm Cocke's Regt U S Inf, 11-13-1814--5-13-1815; W D & P D; Crumley Fam Cem in Sullivan Co; Unmkd. (Also Rev War Pensioner)

GREER, WILLIAM (--1-1-1858 Carter Co); Md Mary Crumley 11-11-1812 (2-27-1792--2-8-1877); Pvt, served 233 days Capt Henry Hunter's Co, Col Wm Johnson's 3rd Regt E T Drftd Mil, 9-13-1814--5-11-1815; W D & T S A & P D; Old Greer Fam Cem on Dry Creek, Carter Co; Pvt mkr.

GREEG, ABRAHAM (9-19-1790--9-21-1876 Sullivan Co); Md Janette Davidson (1796--1-22-1851); Ensign, Capt Benjamin King's Co, Col Wm Lillard's 2nd Regt E T V, 10-12-1813--2-8-1814; also under Lieut Wm Snodgrass at Ft Armstrong; W D & T S A; New Bethel Pres Cem, Sullivan Co; Pvt mkr. (Also in Capt Abraham McClellan's Co, Cherokee Removal 1837.)

GREGORY, Capt GEORGE (--liv 1840 List aged 61 yrs Jefferson Co); Md   (   ); served in Col George Doherty's Tenn Mil; P D & 2400 Pensioners, Armstrong; likely Jefferson Co; Unkn.

GREGORY, TARPLEY (--d Smith Co); Md   (   ); War of 1812;   ; likely in Smith Co; Unkn.

GRESHAM, GEORGE (2-12-1795--5-7-1878 Washington Co); Md Mary Boone Hoss (2-11-1797--10-31-1871); Pvt, Capt David G Vance's Co, Col Sam Bunch's Regt E T V, 10-16-1813--1-22-1814; W D & T S A; Gresham Fam Cem on Buffalo Ridge, Washington Co; Pvt mkr.

GRIFFETH, LEE (came to Rhea Co bef 1807 --d bef 1875 Rhea Co); Md Jane Shelton 1801 (--d 4-26-1875 aged 92 yrs); at N O, 1-8-1815; Rhea Co Hist- Campbell; likely in Rhea Co; Unkn.

GRIMET, JOHN (--liv 3-20-1855 Monroe Co); Md   (   ); Pvt, Capt Andrew Lawson's Co, Col Wm Johnson's 3rd Regt E T Drftd Mil; T S A & B L Wt; likely in Monroe Co; Unkn.

GRIMMETT, JACOB (--c 1786--liv 1871 aged 85 yrs Wilson Co); Md Martha Hudson 12-24-1807 (--liv 1871); Pvt, Capt Andrew Lawson's Co, Col Wm Johnson's 3rd Regt E T Drftd Mil; W D & T S A & P D; likely Green Vale Cem, Wilson Co; Unkn.

GRUNDY, FELIX (9-11-1777--12-19-1840 Nashville, Davidson Co); Md ( ); Congressman 1811-14; U S A; Mt Olivet Cem, Nashville, Davidson Co; Pvt mkr.

GUICE, SOLOMON (--d Perry Co); Md ( ); Pvt, War of 1812; Data from R J Bandy, V A, Mountain Home, Tenn; Unkn Cem near Denson's landing, Perry Co; Unkn.

GUTHRIE, HENRY (--d Nolensville, Williamson Co); Md ( ); War of 1812; W D; Nolensville Cem, Williamson Co; Pvt mkr.

GWIN, JAMES (--killed 11-9-1813 Talledega, Ala); Md ( ); Pvt, Capt John W Byrn's Co, Col John Allcorn's Regt W T Mil, 9-24-1813--11-9-1813 killed; W D & Tenn Soldiers in War of 1812-Vol 1-Allen; likely in Ala; Unkn.

HADLEY, JOHN LIVINGSTONE (3-27-1788--12-26-1870 Davidson Co);
Md Amelia Hadley 1816 (9-3-1793--2-11-1875); Surgeon in Navy in
War of 1812; Hist Davidson Co- Clayton, p-462; Hadley Fam Cem at
Old Hickory, Davidson Co; Pvt mkr.

HAILEY, HENRY (--d 1854 Williamson Co); Md Joanna   1828
(   ); War of 1812; Goodspeed Williamson Co; Cem near
Nolensville, Williamson Co; Unkn. (Also Rev War)

HAINES, GEORGE (HAYNES) (1736-- 1834 Carter Co, now Unicoi);
Md Margaret McInturff c 1758 (   ); Pvt, Capt Solomon
Hendrix' Co, Col Sam Bayless' 4th Regt E T Drftd Mil, 11-13-1814
--5-26-1815; W D & T S A; Haynes-Swingle Fam Cem in Unicoi Co
(Carter); Pvt mkr.

HALE, GEORGE (--d Washington Co); Md   (   );
Pvt, Gen John Coffee's Regt, Enl Hickman Co, 9-28-1814--4-15-1815;
W D & P D; Unkn Cem in Washington Co; Unkn.

HALE, JOHN BILLINGSLEY (1-3-1793-- 1860 Blount Co); Md Jane
McClung 6-17-1817 (11-16-1797--5-15-1868); Pvt, Capt James Gil-
lespie's Co, Col Sam Wear's 1st Regt E T V, 9-23-1813--12-31-1813;
W D & T S A & Hist Blount Co- Burns; Baker's Creek Pres Cem near
Brick Mill, Blount Co; Pvt mkr.

HALE, JOSEPH (2-9-1789--1-6-1883 Greene Co); Md Rebecca Landrum
(--aged 66 yrs in 1873 Greene Co); Capt in Col Sam Bayless' 4th
Regt E T Drftd Mil, 11-13-1814--5-26-1815; T S A & Goodspeed
E T H Greene Co; likely Cem in Greene Co; Unkn.

HALE, LEWIS (7-5-1794--9-18-1880 Washington Co); Md 1-Elizabeth
Bragg (4-8-1798--11-15-1863), 2-Elizabeth McCrary Whitlock 1865
(--d 1895); Pvt, Capt James Landen's Co, Col Sam Bayless' 4th
Regt E T Drftd Mil, 11-13-1814--5-18-1815; W D & T S A; Fall
Branch Bapt Cem, Washington Co; Pvt mkr.

HALE, PHILIP SMITH (11-8-1793--6-2-1867 Stanley Valley, Hawkins
Co); Md Elizabeth Bachman (11-8-1799--7-13-1891); Storekeeper -
G & P S Hale at Boatyard, War of 1812; Autobiography of bro
George Hale; Hale Fam Cem, Stanley Valley, Hawkins Co near Va
line; Pvt mkr.

HALE, RICHARD (--d Washington Co); Md Mary Cox (   );
served 3 tours in War of 1812; W D & Goodspeed E T H; likely a
Fam Cem in Washington Co; Unkn.

HALE, THOMAS (--d 12-1-1813 in service); Md   (   );
Pvt, Capt Frederick Stump's Co, Col John Allcorn's Regt Cav
W T V, 9-24-1813--12-1-1813 died; W D & T S A & Soldiers of
War of 1812 Vol 1- Allen; likely in Ala; Unkn.

HALL, BENJAMIN (11- 1785-- 1862 Knox Co); Md Lucy Hansard c 1814
(--d 1855); Pvt, Capt John Sharp's Co, Col Edwin Boothe's 5th
Regt E T Drftd Mil; W D & T S A; Hall Fam Cem N of Fountain City
Knox Co, Hall's Cross Rds; Official 1812 mkr 1938.

HALL, EDMOND (12-16-1798--7-10-1878 Knox Co); Md Hester Renfro 8-17-1820 (1795--10-27-1871); Pvt, Capt Nicholas Gibbs' Co, Col Sam Bunch's Regt E T Drftd Mil, 1-1-1814-- ; W D & T S A; Hall Fam Cem, 7th Distr Knox Co, Beaver Creek Valley; Official 1812 mkr 1938.

HALL, JAMES (--d 1888 Washington Co); Md Sallie Biddle (   ); War of 1812; Fam Records; Hall Fam Cem on Watauga-Holston River, Washington Co; Unkn. (Cem flooded by water of Patrick Henry Dam - T V A.)

HALL, OBEDIAH (5-31-1787--11-2-1851 Knox Co); Md Sarah Bayless 4-30-1818 (2-25-1799--8-9-1870); Srgt, Capt Nicholas Gibbs' Co, Col Sam Bunch's Regt E T Drftd Mil, 1-1-1814-- ; W D & T S A; Hall Fam Cem on Racoon Valley Rd, 6th Distr Knox Co; Pvt mkr.

HALL, THOMAS (3-1-1758--9-25-1833 Knox Co); Md Nancy Hayes 9-25-1783 (11-23-1760--1836); Ensign, War of 1812; W D & P D; Hall Fam Cem, Hall's Cross Rds, Knox Co; Pvt mkr. (Also Rev War)

HALL, Brig Gen WILLIAM (2-11-1775--10-7-1856 Sumner Co); Md Mary B Alexander (   ); Brig Gen W T Mil under Gen Andrew Jackson; T S A; Hall Fam Cem at Castillian Springs, Sumner Co; Pvt mkr & monument. (Estate called "Green Gardens")

HALL, ZACHARIAH (1790--12-24-1861 Knox Co); Md 1-Mary Nelson 8-8-1817 (   ), 2-Martha M Bradley 10-21-1847 (4-11-1819--10-24-1899); Pvt, Capt Nicholas Gibbs' Co, Col Sam Bunch's Regt E T Drftd Mil, 1-1-1814; W D & T S A; Hall Fam Cem on Demarcus Farm, 5th Distr Knox Co; Official 1812 mkr 1938.

HAMBLEN, THOMAS (11-20-1788--3-29-1867 Choptack, Hawkins Co); Md 1-Elizabeth McCarty 10-10-1807 (10-3-1790--9-7-1847), 2-Emeline Farris 1-25-1849 (6-27-1806--5-11-1882); Pvt, Capt Wm Gillenwater's Co, Col Wm Lillard's 2nd Regt E T V, 10-2-1813--2-8-1814; W D & P D & B L Wt; Hamblen Fam Cem on E V Payne Farm, Choptack, Hawkins Co; Pvt mkr.

HAMBLEN, WILLIAM H (10-29-1794--11-17-1869 Davidson Co); Md Verrina H Folkes c 1822 (6-15-1802--11-13-1882); Maj, W T Mil; T S A; Hamblen Fam Cem near Hall's Lane on Dry Creek, Dickerson & Gallatin Pikes, Davidson Co; Pvt mkr.

HAMILTON, JAMES (--d 9-21-1814 Ft Williams, Ala); Md (   ); Pvt, Capt Newlin's Co Inf, Col Philip Pipkin's Regt W T Mil, 6-20-1814--9-21-1814 died; W D & T S A; likely at Ft Williams, Talladega Co Ala; Unmkd.

HAMILTON, Capt WILLIAM (--d 1-24-1814 at Battle of Enotochopco, Ala); Md   (   ); Capt, Col Wm Lillard's 2nd Regt E T V, 10-12-1813--1-24-1814 killed; W D & T S A & J Hartsell's "MEMORA"; likely near battleground, Ala; Unkn.

HAMLETT, JAMES (--d Robertson Co); Md Jane Cullen Atkinson bef 1844 (   ); Pvt, Capt Richard Benson's Co, Col --- 2nd Regt W T Mil, 1-28-1814--5-23-1814; T S A; likely in Robertson Co; Unkn. (Real Daughter, Margaret Ann Hamlett, b 5-4-1844 liv 1936 in Tenn Real Daughters)

HAMMONTREE, JAMES (--d Loudon Co); Md Nancy Divine 12-28-1826 (   ); Pvt, Capt Joseph Duncan's Co, Col Sam Bunch's Regt Drftd Mil, 1-10-1814--7-21-1814, transfrd to Capt Berry's Co 4-27-1814, transfrd to Capt Buchanan's Co 5-10-1814; Craig's Chapel Cem near Greenback, Loudon Co; Govt mkr.

HANDLEY, Capt SAMUEL (7- 1748--8-4-1840 Winchester, Franklin Co); Md 1-Susanna Cowan (1761--c 1794), 2-Mary Adams bef 1795 (   ); early Indian Wars, Tellico Blockhouse 1793, Representative Washington Co, 1796 Constitutional Convention; T S A; Winchester, Franklin Co; Monument. (also Rev War - Pt Pleasant, Kings Mt, Boyd's Creek, et al)

HARALSON, Capt HERNDON (10-12-1757-- 1847 Haywood Co); Md Mary Murphey 10-4-1791 (   ); Clerk of Caswell Co N C, & N C Assembly 1793-1800, Sup Ct Judge 1800-1816; N C S A & Caswell Co Records; Cem in Haywood Co; Pvt mkr.

HARBISON, AARON (1-11-1793--3-14-1860 Knox Co); Md 1- (   ), 2-Dixie Tindell (--Pensioned 1879 Knox Co); War of 1812; P D & W D; Clapps Chapel Meth Cem near Harbison's Cross Rds, Knox Co; Pvt mkr.

HARBISON, WILLIAM PLEDGE (3-17-1797--4-15-1868 Knox Co); Md Mary Graves 2-10-1819 (--Pensioned March 1879 Knox Co); War of 1812; P D & W D; Clapps Chapel Meth Cem near Harbison's Cross Rds, Knox Co; Pvt mkr.

HARDGRAVE, SKELTON (5-7-1792-- 1828 Davidson Co); Md Susanna Lofton 1-6-1812 (1794--c 1830); Lieut, Capt Joseph Williamson's Co, Col Lowry's Regt, 9-20-1813, also in 1814 2nd Regt U S Inf; T S A; Providence Cem near Nashville, Davidson Co; Unmkd. (Govt mkr appld for 1939)

HARDEMAN, THOMAS JONES (--d likely in Texas); Md Mary Polk 1814 (--d at Bolivar 1830); Capt in War of 1812, taken prisoner bef N O; W D & T S A & Beg of West Tenn- Williams; went to Texas after 1830; Unkn.

HARDEN, WILLIAM (--d 3-23-1814 at Ft Williams, Ala); Md (   ); Pvt, Capt Johnson's Co Inf, Col Cheatham's Regt, 1-28-1814-- ; W D & T S A; at Ft Williams, Talladega Co, Ala; Unmkd.

HARDIN, ASA (--killed 11-9-1813 Talledega, Ala); Md (   ); Pvt, Capt John Baskerville's Co Vol Cav, Col John Allcorn's Regt W T Mil, 9-24-1813--11-9-1813 killed; W D & T S A; likely Ala; Unkn.

HARDIN, Col JOSEPH (4-18-1734--4-7-1801 Knox Co); Md Jane Gibson 1762 (1742--3-25-1817); member S W Terr Assembly & Gen Assembly 14 yrs; T S A; Hickory Creek Bapt Cem, Knox Co; Pvt mkr. (Also Rev War - Maj 2nd N C Minute Men Salisbury Distr monument)

HARDIN, JOHN (--d likely Hamilton Co); Md ( ); Capt, Battle of Lookout Mt 1788; Armstrong's Hamilton Co; likely Hamilton Co; Unkn.

HARPER, WILEY (--liv 1828 List Dickson Co); Md ( ); served 44th U S Regt; P D & 2400 Pensioners, Armstrong; likely Dickson Co; Unkn.

HARRIS, BENJAMIN CRAMPTON (--d likely Carter Co); Md ( ); Pvt, Capt David G Vance's Co, Col Sam Bunch's Regt E T V, 10-16-1813--1-22-1814; W D & T S A; likely in Elizabethton Carter Co; Unkn. (He owned a Hatter's Shop in Elizabethton, Carter Co.)

HARRIS, JAMES (--d 1863 Bedford Co); Md Nancy Thompson (--d 1870); Capt under Gen Andrew Jackson; Goodspeed Bedford Co & T S A; likely Bedford Co; Unkn.

HARTMAN, HENRY (6-22-1784--3-31-1838 Washington Co); Md Polly Brown 1806 (12-28-1784--1860); War of 1812; Fam Records; Hartman Fam Cem, 14th Distr Washington Co; Pvt mkr.

HARTSELL, Capt JACOB (1786--5-2-1843 Washington Co); Md Nancy Million 10-3-1805 (1787--Will-12-4-1868 Washington Co); Capt, Col Wm Lillard's 2nd Regt E T V, 10-12-1813--2-8-1814; W D & T S A & J Hartsell-Memora-E T H S Publications 1939-40; Cherokee Bapt Cem, Washington Co; Govt mkr 1956.

HASSELL, JENNETT (1789-- 1868 Sumner Co); Md Jane Pervine (1780 --1866); Pvt, under Andrew Jackson in Creek War; Goodspeed Sumner Co; likely Sumner Co; Unkn.

HAUN, JOHN (9-27-1790--7-12-1858 Carter Co); Md Jane Hyder 1811 (8-8-1792--3-27-1880); Pvt, Capt Adam Winsell's Co, Col Ewen Allison's Regt E T Drftd Mil, 1-5-1814--5-26-1814; W D & T S A; Haun Fam Cem on Dry Creek, Carter Co; Pvt mkr.

HAWORTH, RICHARD (3-5-1794--2-3-1875 Jefferson Co); Md Mary Ann Lyle (6-6-1800--12-13-1883); War of 1812; Goodspeed E T H Jefferson Co; West View Cem, Jefferson Co; Pvt mkr.

HAYES, HUGH (--liv 1828 List Wilson Co); Md ( ); served Col Williamson's Regt W T Mil; P D & 2400 Pensioners, Armstrong; likely in Wilson Co; Unkn.

HAYS, STOKELY D (--d Davidson Co); Md Lydia Butler ( ); Lieut & Q M Gen in Creek War; W D & T S A; likely in Davidson Co; Pvt mkr.

HAYES, ROBIN (--liv 1840 List aged 46 yrs in Smith Co); Md
(   ); War of 1812; P D & 2400 Pensioners, Armstrong;
likely in Smith Co; Unkn.

HAYES, W   (1793--11-5-1866 Lincoln Co); Md Cynthia
(--d 12-19-1865); War of 1812 under Jackson; Goodspeed Lincoln
Co; likely in Lincoln Co; Unkn.

HEADERICK, HENDERSON (--d aft 1852 Bradley Co); Md
(   ); Pvt, Capt Simpson's Co; Edwards Acct Bk; likely in
Bradley Co; Unkn.

HEATH, JOHN (--d 9-21-1814 in service in Ala); Md
(   ); heirs were Edith, Nancy & Polly Heath in Cocke Co;
P D & 2400 Pensioners, Armstrong; likely in Ala; Unkn.

HELLWIG, GEORGE (--d 3-28-1814 at Ft Williams, Ala); Md
(   ); Pvt, Capt John Chiles' Co, Col John Brown's 2nd Regt
E T Mtd Mil, 1-10-1814--d 3-28-1814; W D & T S A; at Ft Williams,
Talledega, Ala; Unmkd.

HENDERSON, DAVID (--liv 1840 List aged 49 yrs in Lincoln Co);
Md   (   ); served W T Mil; P D & 2400 Pensioners,
Armstrong; likely Lincoln Co; Unkn.

HENDERSON, Col JAMES (--killed 1814-15 in skirmish near N O);
Md   (   ); War of 1812; Rutherford Co Hist-   ;
likely near N O; Unkn.

HENDERSON, JOHN Sr (10-16-1796--6-16-1864 Bradley Co); Md
(   ); Srgt, Capt Christopher Cook's Co E T Mil, 9-29-1814
--5-3-1815; W D & T S A; Ft Hill Cem in Cleveland, Bradley Co;
Pvt mkr.

HENDERSON, WILLIAM (--liv 1828 List Anderson Co); Md
(   ); served 29th U S Inf; P D & 2400 Pensioners, Armstrong;
likely Anderson Co; Unkn.

HENDERSON, WILLIAM (2-1-1778--6-3-1860 in Tenn); Md Elizabeth
Baldridge 3-7-1804 (3-5-1777--5-29-1867); Pvt, Capt George
Saver's Co, Col Lowry's Regt W T Mil, 9-20-1814--11-20-1814;
W D & T S A; likely in Tenn; Pvt mkr.

HENDERSON, WILLIAM (--d 1-15-1877 Hamilton Co); Md
(   ); War of 1812; W D; Grave #12938, National Cem, Chattanooga, Hamilton Co; Govt mkr.

HENDERSON, WILLIAM (--d bef 1851 Jefferson Co); Md Elizabeth
Cowan 2-22-1821 (1797--liv 1851 Jefferson Co); Ensign, Capt
Gregory's Co, Brig Gen George Doherty's Brig; W D & P D; likely
in Jefferson Co; Unkn.

HENEGAR, Capt HENRY (11-15-1785--2-10-1839 Greene Co); Md Charlotte Henderson 5-21-1807 (10-18-1788--6-18-1853); Capt, Col
John Williams' 39th Regt; W D & Goodspeed E T H Greene Co; Unkn.

HENDRIX, SOLOMON (4-28-1790--2-8-1864 Carter Co); Md 1-Susanna Hart 3- 1812 (3-6-1793--2-7-1855), 2-Margaret Duncan (   ); Capt, Col Sam Bayless' 4th Regt E T Drftd Mil, 11-13-1814--5-18-1815; W D & T S A; Hendrix Fam Cem on Sinking Creek, Carter Co; Govt mkr.

HENLEY, ARTHUR HAZELRIGG (3-17-1783-- 1848 Monroe Co); Md Ann Evalina Moore 4- 1814 (9-29-1798--2-27-1860); War of 1812; Fam Data; Henley Fam Cem at Chota, Monroe Co on Little River; Pvt mkr.

HENLEY, ISAAC (1-5-1785--12-4-1846 Washington Co); Md Elizabeth Bayless 10-28-1819 (7-20-1789--11-18-1869); Srgt, Capt John Hampton's Co, Col Ewen Allison's Regt E T Drftd Mil, 1-5-1814--7-26-1815; W D & T S A; Cherokee Bapt Cem in Washington Co; Pvt mkr.

HENLEY, Lieut JOHN (--c 1760--5-27-1821 Washington Co); Md Catherine   c 1784 (1765--4-23-1855); Lieut Cav Regt Washington Co & War of 1812; T S A; Henley Fam Cem in Washington Co; Pvt mkr.

HENRY, HUGH (1786--d Blount Co); Md Nancy Whittle Henry 10-18-1825 (6-24-1803--5-6-1868); 3rd Srgt, Capt Jehu Stephens' Co, Col Sam Wear's Regt E T Mtd Gunmen, 10-6-1814--4-6-1815; W D & T S A; Henry Fam Cem at Mouth of Ellijoy, Blount Co; Unmkd.

HENRY, JAMES (1791--7-11-1833 Blount Co); Md Narcissa Howard (5-11-1800--8-21-1868); 2nd Lieut, Capt Jehu Stephens' Co, Col Sam Wear's Mtd Gunmen, 10-6-1814--4-6-1815; W D & T S A; Baker's Creek Pres Cem, Blount Co; Pvt mkr.

HENRY, JAMES (11-20-1782--8-5-1847 Blount Co); Md 1-Jane Garner (11-17-1783--12-4-1820), 2-Nancy Keeny 1-7-1827 (   ); Pvt, Capt James Gillespie's Co, Col Sam Wear's 1st Regt E T V, 9-23-1813--12-31-1813; W D; Henry Fam Cem, Mouth of Ellijoy, Blount Co; Unmkd.

HENRY, JOHN - Fifer (--d Blount Co); Md   (   ); Fifer, Capt James Allison's Co, Col Ewen Allison's Regt E T Drftd Mil, 1-10-1814-- ; W D; Unkn Cem likely on Ellijoy, Blount Co; Unkn.

HENRY, JOHN (--d Blount Co); Md Sarah Smith 10-22-1831 (   ); 3rd Corp, Capt Jehu Stephens' Co, Col Sam Wear's Regt Mtd Gunmen, 10-6-1814--4-6-1815, ordered to Tenn 3-5-1815; W D; Henry Fam Cem Blount Co; Unkn.

HENRY, SAMUEL (--d Blount Co); Md Elizabeth Garner 3-28-1798 (   ); Pvt, Capt Jehu Stephens' Co, Col Sam Wear's Regt Mtd Gunmen, 10-6-1814--4-6-1815; W D; likely Henry Fam Cem on Ellijoy, Blount Co; Unkn.

HENRY, WILLIAM (--d Monroe Co); Md 1-Polly Gamble 10-10-1800 (   ), 2-Mary Upton (   ); Pvt, Capt Jehu Stephens' Co, Col Sam Wear's Regt Mtd Gunmen, 10-6-1814--4-6-1815; W D; likely Sweetwater, Monroe Co; Unkn.

HENSON, JOHN (1792-- 1876 Knox Co); Md Mary Cottrell (1800--8-14-1855); War of 1812; Goodspeed E T H; likely in Knox Co; Unkn.

HESTER, WILLIAM (--liv 1828 List Roane Co); Md ( ); served Tenn Mil; P D & 2400 Pensioners, Armstrong; likely Roane Co; Unkn.

HICKS, ELIJAH (--d Bledsoe Co); Md ( ); War of 1812; Hamilton Co Hist, Armstrong; likely Bledsoe Co; Unkn.

HICKMAN, GEORGE (--d Washington Co); Md ( ); Pvt, enl for 5 yrs Capt Hamilton's Co, 1st Regt U S Inf; W D & P D & Nelson papers, McClung Room, Knoxville; Cherry Grove Cem, Washington Co; Unkn.

HILL, ALLEN (12-27-1769-- 1857 Madison Co); Md ( ); Capt under Gen Jackson War of 1812; W D & Fam Bible & Jacob Hill's Diary; Hill Fam Cem near Jackson, Madison Co; Pvt mkr.

HILL, DANIEL (1750-- 1848 McNairy Co); Md ( ); Pvt, Capt Wm Moore's Co, Col Thomas Hart Benton's Regt Tenn Mil; T S A & Texas 1812 Records; likely McNairy Co; Unkn.

HILL, JACOB (8-28-1796-- 1878 Madison Co); Md Jane Lemons of N C ( ); War of 1812; W D & Fam Bible & Jacob Hill's Diary; Hill Fam Cem near Jackson, Madison Co; Pvt mkr.

HINES, ISAAC (9-15-1795-- 1872 Knox Co); Md Mary L Don Carlos (1800-1863); Pvt, Capt Reuben Tipton's Co Mtd Gunmen, Maj John Chiles' Regt, 9-20-1814--5-2-1815; W D & T S A & Goodspeed Knox Co; Knox Co; Unkn.

HINES, ROBERT (--d likely Knox Co); Md (One Rhoda Hines listed as Pensioner in Knox Co); War of 1812; French-Broad-Holston Hist-Rothrock; likely in Knox Co; Unkn.

HINDS, SIMEON (4-11-1769--12-13-1840 Overton Co); Md Elizabeth Stone 1796 (6-18-1773--1845); wounded by Indians while Capt Tenn Mil, 1807-15; T S A; Union Ch Cem in Overton Co; Pvt mkr.

HIXON, EPHRAIM (10-14-1797--12-25-1855 Hamilton Co); Md Margaret (6-17-1799--10-9-1888); War of 1812; Hamilton Co Hist, Armstrong; Hixon Cem, Hamilton Co; Pvt mkr.

HODGES, HOWELL (--Inv 1863 Washington Co); Md Sarah Ann Crouch 11-23-1837 ( ); Pvt, Capt Jacob Hoyal's Co, transfrd 5-2-1814 from Capt McPherson's Co, Col Ewen Allison's Regt E T Drftd Mil, 1-10-1814--5-15-1814, & Pvt, Capt Jacob Hoyal's Co, Col Sam Bayless' 4th Regt E T Drftd Mil, 11-13-1814--5-18-1815; W D & T S A; Unkn Cem in Washington Co; Unkn.

HODGES, MICAJAH (9-1-1795--6-30-1881 Washington Co); Md Elizabeth Gray 1-29-1818 (2-4-1799--12-2-1852); Pvt, Capt James Landen's Co, Col Sam Bayless' 4th Regt E T Drftd Mil, 11-13-1814--5-18-1815; W D & T S A; Hodges Fam Cem near Gray Station, Washington Co; Pvt mkr. (Bro of Howell Hodges)

HOGG, Dr SAMUEL (4-18-1783--5-28-1842 Davidson Co); Md Polly Talbott 4-1-1806 (1-22-1786--12-13-1860); Surgeon, 1st Regt Vol Inf 11-21-1812--4-22-1813, Hospital Surgeon Staff with Andrew Jackson in Creek War 2-22-1814--5-25-1814, Hospital Surgeon, Gen Wm Carroll's Staff 11-13-1814--5-13-1815; W D & T S A & Hist of Sweetwater Valley- Lenoir; Old City Cem in Nashville, Davidson Co; Pvt mkr.

HOLLOWAY, EDMOND (--disch 4-10-1814 at Ft Williams, Ala); Md (   ); Pvt, Capt Edward Buchanan's Co, Col Sam Bunch's Regt E T Drftd Mil, 1-10-1814--5-20-1814; W D & T S A; likely at Ft Williams, Talledega Co, Ala; Unmkd. (Holloway is in List of those who died there.)

HOLMES, ABIJAH (--d 10-30-1813 Ala); Md   (   ); Pvt, Capt Frederick Stump's Co, Col John Allcorn's Regt Cav E T V, 9-24-1813--10-30-1813 died; W D & T S A; likely in Ala; Unkn.

HOPE, JAMES (1777-- 1840 Roane Co); Md Barshaba Walker 1798 (--aft 1842); Lieut, Capt Wm White's Co, 2nd Regt E T Mtd Gunmen; W D & T S A; Hickory Creek Bapt Cem, Knox Co; Official 1812 mkr 1938.

HOPE, JOHN (-- Unkn --); Md   (   ); Pvt, 24th U S Inf, Prisoner & pay due him by Admr Samuel Hope; Inv Bk 1810-1843 in Greene Co; Unkn place; Unkn.

HORNE, WILLIAM (1791--10-5-1883 aged 94 yrs Bradley Co); Md (   ); Pvt, Capt James Lillard's Co, Col Wm Lillard's 2nd Regt E T V, 10-17-1813--2-8-1814; W D & T S A & Bradley Co- J M Wooten, & P D; Lebanon Bapt Cem 6 m E Cleveland, Bradley Co; Pvt mkr.

HORNSBY, JAMES (10-25-1792--10-22-1863 Roane Co); Md Eleanor McCidy (1800--liv 1887 Roane Co); War of 1812; Roane Co Hist- Wells & Goodspeed E T H Roane Co; likely in Roane Co; Unkn.

HORTON, HOWELL (--1828 List Hamilton Co, --d 5-24-1832 Hamilton Co); Md   (   ); served Col Eaton's Regt N C Mil; P D & 2400 Pensioners, Armstrong & N C S A; likely Hamilton Co; Unkn.

HORTON, ISAAC (1790-- 1856 Hawkins Co); Md Rhoda Richardson in Va (1795--1850); Pvt, Capt Washington Smith's Co, 59th Regt Va Mil, 3-20-1813--4-17-1814; Va S A; likely in Hawkins Co; Unkn. (One ISAAC HORTON served in Tenn - Pvt, Capt McPherson's Co, transfrd 5-2-1814 to Capt Jacob Hoyal's Co, Col Ewen Allison's Regt E T Drftd Mil, disch 5-15-1815, T S A.)

HORTON, JOSEPH W (8-15-1792--10-31-1846 Nashville, Davidson Co); Md Sophia W Davis (7-11-1799--3-23-1874); Pvt, Capt David Deaderick's Co Artillery under Gen Andrew Jackson, 10-1-1813--3-31-1814; W D & T S A; Old City Cem, Nashville, Davidson Co; Pvt mkr.

HORTON, WILLIAM (1758-- 1798 Jefferson Co); Md   (   );
Civil Service Jefferson Co; Jefferson Ct Records; in Jefferson
Co; Unkn.

HOSS, ISAAC (1787--2-24-1828 Washington Co); Md Hannah Bayless
4-20-1808 (9- 1774--6-30-1859); Pvt, 24th U S Inf, enl by Lieut
Stewart 5-13-1813 for 5 yrs, Prisoner of War at Quebec & recvd
in exchange at Cumberland Head 4-28-1814, Pvt, Capt Hampton's Co
& Capt James Stewart's Co, 2-16-1814--8-3-1815; W D; Cherokee
Bapt Cem in Washington Co; Pvt mkr.

HOURNEY, Lieut ALFRED (--liv 1828 List in Tenn); Md
(   ); served 44th Regt U S Inf; P D & 2400 Pensioners, Armstrong; Unkn Co; Unkn.

HOUSE, JACOB (--liv 1828 List Davidson Co); Md   (   );
served 44th Regt U S Inf; P D & 2400 Pensioners, Armstrong;
likely Davidson Co; Unkn.

HOUSE, SAMUEL (--d Knox Co); Md   (   ); Pvt, Capt
Jesse Cole's Co, Col Sam Wear's 1st Regt E T V, 10-18-1813--1-17-1814; W D & T S A; likely Knox Co; Unkn.

HOUSE, WILLIAM (--killed in Service); Md   (   );
Pvt, Capt John Wallace's Co, Col Wm Hall's 1st Regt W T Mil,
12-10-1812--4-22-1813; W D & T S A; likely where killed; Unkn.

HOUSTON, Maj JAMES (11-12-1757--11-22-1840 Blount Co); Md 1-
Esther Houston 11-3-1780 (--bef 1791), 2-Polly Gillespie 10-10-
1791 (4-26-1770--6-23-1830); Maj, early Indian raids at Houston's
Station, Constitutional Convention 1796; T S A & Ramsey's Annal
of Tenn; New Providence Pres Cem, Maryville, Blount Co; Govt mkr.
(Also Rev War Govt mkr - "Ensign Va Troops - Edmondson's Co".)

HOUSTON, ROBERT (1760--d Knox Co); Md 1-   (   ),
2-Martha Black (   ); Sheriff Knox Co; Knox Co Records; in
Knox Co; Unkn.

HOUSTON, ROBERT (1790-- 1840 Blount Co); Md Margaret Cunningham
1811 (1792--1843); Pvt & Srgt, Capt Samuel Cowan's Co, Maj James
P H Porter's Regt, 9-23-1813--12-23-1813; W D & T S A; New Providence Pres Cem, Maryville, Blount Co; Unmkd.

HUBBARD, DAVID (--liv 1828 List in Tenn); Md   (   );
served Tenn Mil; P D & 2400 Pensioners, Armstrong; Unkn Co; Unkn.

HUBBS, W N (7-26-1773--8-22-1879 Union Co); Md Phebe   (--liv
1883 Union Co); War of 1812; W D & P D; Dyer Fam Cem near Luttrell, Union Co; Govt mkr. (Wid Pension #28,739 Union Co)

HUDDLESTON, JOHN (--liv 1828 List in Tenn); Md   (papers
destryd in War Off); P D in Tenn & 2400 Pensioners, Armstrong;
Unkn Co; Unkn.

HUDGEONS, WILLIAM (--liv 1828 List Davidson Co, --d Loudon Co); Md Rebecca McClure 6-20-1826 (   ); Pvt, Capt Joseph Duncan's Co, Col Sam Bunch's Regt E T Drftd Mil, 1-10-1814--7-21-1814; W D & T S A & P D; Hudgeons Fam Cem near Meadow, Loudon Co; Govt mkr by 1812 Chapter.

HUFFACRE, GEORGE (8-7-1757--d Knox Co); Md   (   ); Corp in Henry's Fort 1792 in Blount Co; Ramsey's Annals of Tenn; Seven Islands Meth Cem in Knox Co; Pvt mkr.

HUFFMASTER, Capt JOSEPH (4-4-1782--4-3-1878 Hawkins Co); Md Elizabeth Weitsell 12-8-1808 (8-27-1787--2-18-1872); Capt in Creek War under Gen Jackson; W D & T S A & P D; Old Pres Cem in Rogersville, Hawkins Co; Pvt mkr.

HUGER, FRANCIS KINLOCK (--d Knox Co); Md   (   ); Col in S C in War of 1812; Goodspeed Knox Co & S C S A; likely in Knox Co; Unkn. (Also Capt in Rev War)

HUGHES, JOHN (8-3-1776--12-26-1860 Williamson Co); Md Sallie Martin 2-7-1798 (1779--9-10-1842); Pvt, Patrick Co Va Mil, Col Sam Staples' Regt 1814; Va S A; Hughes Fam Cem at "Meadowbrook" Williamson Co; Pvt mkr.

HUGHES, JOHN (--liv 1883 Sumner Co); Md   (   ); War of 1812; Pension #14,410 Sumner Co; P D; likely Gallatin, Sumner Co; Unkn.

HUGHES, WILLIAM (--liv 1828 List Weakley Co); Md   (   ); served Tenn Vol; P D & 2400 Pensioners, Armstrong; likely Weakley Co; Unkn.

HUGGINS, JONATHAN (--9-30-1870 Manchester, Coffee Co); Md Elizabeth W Smith (   ); War of 1812; Goodspeed Coffee Co; likely Coffee Co; Pvt mkr.

HUMPHREYS, RICHARD (8-4-1793--8-16-1879 Washington Co); Md 1-Rebecca Miller 8-13-1822 (5-20-1802--3-7-1838), 2-Matilda Hartman 8-29-1839 (3-15-1809--7-1-1890); Corp, Capt Stephen Lacey's Co, 4th Regt Va Mil, 4-1-1813--7-7-1813; Va S A; Mt Zion Meth Cem at Leesburg, Washington Co; Govt mkr by 1812 Chapter.

HUMPHREYS, U L (--d 6-24-1813 in service); Md Sally B Humphreys (listed as heir by P D); Pvt, 10th Regt U S Inf; P D & 2400 Pensioners, Armstrong; likely where died; Unkn.

HUNT, DAVID (10-9-1778--8-8-1841 Franklin Co); Md Elizabeth Larkin (   ); War of 1812; T S A & Tombstone record; Larkin Fam Cem near Winchester, Franklin Co; Pvt mkr. (Tombstone says "Maj in War of 1812 with Gen Andrew Jackson".)

HUNT, SAMUEL (--c 1779--7-2-1852 Washington Co); Md Sarah Crouch 12-26-1797 (1779--8-29-1852); Maj of Washington Co Mil & Sheriff Washington Co 1814--1827; Washington Co Records; Hunt Fam Cem 1 m S Johnson City, Washington Co; Pvt mkr.

HUNTER, JACOB (1764-- 1827 Washington Co); Md Ann Clark (1766--1836); Pvt, --- Co, 1st Regt E T V, 1-31-1814; T S A; Unkn Cem in Washington Co; Unkn.

HUNTER, JOHN (5-1-1792--4-25-1850 Washington Co); Md Mary Brown 2-25-1817 (11-5-1796--5-2-1867); Pvt, Capt David G Vance's Co, Col Sam Bunch's Regt Mtd Inf, 10-16-1813--1-22-1814; W D & T S A; New Salem Bapt Cem, Washington Co; Pvt mkr.

HUNTER, JOHN (--2-17-1857 Greene Co); Md Lettie Self 7-29-1822 (1802--Pensioned 1876 Greene Co); Pvt, Capt Kirk & Capt Christopher Cook's Co, Col Wm Johnson's 3rd Regt E T Drftd Mil, 9-20-1814--5-3-1815; W D & T S A & P D; in Greene Co; Unkn. (Wid Pension #19,419)

HUNTSMAN, ADAM (--d Madison Co); Md Sarah (--d 1823 Madison Co); War of 1812, lost a leg in Creek War; W D & T S A & Madison Co Hist- Williams; likely Old Salem Cem on Cotton Grove Rd, Madison Co; Unkn. (Sarah Huntsman is bur in Salem Cem, d 1823.)

HURST, KEMP W (--d 2-9-1815 in Service); Md ( ); heirs were Sally & Smith W Hurst in Maury Co; Pvt, 35th Regt U S Inf; P D & 2400 Pensioners, Armstrong; likely where died; Unkn.

HUTCHESON, CHARLES (--d likely Bledsoe Co); Md Rebecca Sigler ( ); J P in Bledsoe Co 11-20-1811; T S A; Hutcheson Fam Cem 8 m N Pikeville on Crossville Rd, Bledsoe Co; Unkn.

HUTCHENSON, REUBEN (--d 4-17-1814 at Ft Williams, Ala); Md ( ); Pvt, Capt Bridges Co, Col Sam Bunch's Regt E T Mtd Mil, 1-10-1814--4-17-1814; T S A; at Ft Williams, Ala; Unmkd.

HUTSELL, JOHN (7-13-1780-- 1854 McMinn Co); Md Christian Hounshell 4-12-1803 (1-14-1782--1859); Fifer in War of 1812; Goodspeed E T H McMinn Co p-1041; likely in McMinn Co; Unmkd.

HYDER, MICHAEL I (--1790 Washington Co, now Carter); Md Elizabeth Woods 1764 (--1-3-1841 aged 96 yrs); Pvt, vs Chicamauga Indians 1784; N C S A; Hyder Fam Cem on Powder Branch, Carter Co; Pvt mkr. (Also Rev War)

HYDER, MICHAEL II (10-24-1767--10-6-1861 Carter Co); Md 1-Martha Lockhart 3-9-1797 (8-1-1775--8-8-1812), 2-Sarah Bowman Zimmerman (widow) 11-18-1813 (--5-6-1865); Pvt, Capt Charles Whitson's Co Carter Co Cav 1804; John Sevier Comm Bk & private records; Hyder Fam Cem on Powder Branch, Carter Co; Pvt mkr. (S J Hyder, Milligan College, Tenn has record of apptmt.)

INMAN, SHADRACH (2-16-1793--8-1-1852 Jefferson Co); Md Sarah K Henderson 1-28-1819 (5-2-1798--3-14-1841); Srgt, Capt Thos McCuiston's Co, Col Wm Lillard's 2nd Regt E T V, 10-8-1813--2-8-1814; W D & T S A; Dandridge Pres Cem, Jefferson Co; Pvt mkr. (Family tradition is that he was also at Battle of N O.)

ISBELL, THOMAS (--d in Tenn); Md ( ); Pvt, 5th Regt E T Mil; T S A; Unkn Cem in Tenn; Unkn.

ISH, ALEXANDER (1790--10-17-1862 Blount Co); Md Susan Henderson 6-1-1854 ( ); Pvt, Capt James Gillespie's Co, Col Sam Wear's 1st Regt E T V, 9-23-1813--12-31-1813; W D & T S A; Ish-Henderson Fam Cem near Friendsville, Blount Co; Pvt mkr.

ISH, JOHN (--killed 7-21-1794 by Indians, Blount Co); Md Elizabeth (1759--7-22-1821); Early Indian Wars - killed at Ish's Ft near Friendsville, Blount Co; Cem at Ish's Ft, Blount Co; Pvt mkr.

JACK, JEREMIAH (--d 1825 Knox Co); Md ( ); Early Indian Wars, Hist of Lebanon-in-the-Fork- Ramsey; Lebanon-in-the-Fork Cem, Knox Co; Pvt mkr.

JACKSON, ANDREW (3-15-1767--6-8-1845 Davidson Co); Md Rachel Donelson 8-1-1791 at Natchez, Miss & 2nd 1-7-1794 Davidson Co (1767--12-22-1828 Davidson Co); Maj Gen Tenn Troops War of 1812; W D & T S A; Hermitage Cem in Davidson Co; Govt mkr & monument & 1st Official 1812 mkr in Tenn.

JACKSON, ROBERT (--d 6-12-1815 in service); Md ( ); heirs were Louisana, William, George Washington, John & Robert Jackson in Cocke Co; served in 1st Regt Riflemen; P D & 2400 Pensioners, Armstrong; likely where died; Unkn.

JAMES, JESSE (--d Blount Co); Md Polly Rooker 3-19-1819 ( ); Pvt, Capt James Gillespie's Co, Col Sam Wear's 1st Regt E T V, 9-23-1813--12-31-1813; W D & T S A; Cem near Louisville, Blount Co; Unkn.

JAMES, Judge THOMAS (--9-10-1870 Memphis, Shelby Co); Md ( ); Battle of N O; Elmwood Cem Records, Memphis; Elmwood Cem in Memphis, Shelby Co; Govt mkr.

JAMES, THOMAS (1790--1866 Mulberry, Lincoln Co); Md Martha Dukes 1825 (--1874); Pvt, under Gen John Coffee, Goodspeed Lincoln Co; James Fam Cem near Mulberry, Lincoln Co; Pvt mkr.

JAMES, WILLIAM (--liv 1840 List aged 45 yrs Dickson Co); Md ( ); Pvt, in Tenn Vol; P D & 2400 Pensioners, Armstrong; likely Dickson Co; Unkn.

JENKINS, ALEXANDER (--d 5-9-1814 in service); Md
(   ); Pvt, Capt Joseph Duncan's Co, Col Sam Bunch's Regt, attd to Col Ewen Allison's Regt, 1-10-1814--5-9-1814 died; W D & T S A & Blount Co Hist- Burns; likely where died; Unkn.

JENKINS, JOHN (--liv 10-23-1874 Hamilton Co); Md
(   ); War of 1812; P D; likely Hamilton Co; Unkn.

JOBE, ABRAHAM (--c 1778--d aft 1850 Washington Co); Md Sarah Fain (c 1796--aft 1850 census); Cornet in Washington Co Cav, 12-6-1800; John Sevier's Commission Bk; likely in unkn Cem in Johnson City, Washington Co; Unmkd.

JOBE, DANIEL (1760-- 1874 in Tenn); Md   (   ); Pvt, Capt Edmund Terrell's Co, Ky Mtd Mil, 1794 & Pvt, Capt John Jones' Co, 8th Regt Ky Mil, War of 1812; Ky S A & Texas 1812 Records; Unkn Cem in Tenn; Unkn.

JOBE, JOHN (--d in Tenn); Md   (   ); Pvt, W T Mil; T S A & Texas 1812 Records; Unkn Cem in Tenn; Unkn.

JOHNS, JOSEPH B (1-23-1776--11-8-1839 Rutherford Co); Md Elizabeth Vaughan 1801 (9-9-1778--5-26-1844); Pvt, Capt Nathan Davis' Co in Regt under Gen Andrew Jackson, 12-18-1813, also Pvt, Capt Newton's Co, Col Wm Hall's Regt W T Mil, 12-10-1812; W D & T S A; Johns Fam Cem near Murfreesboro, Rutherford Co; Pvt mkr.

JOHNSON, ABNER (--liv 1828 List Maury Co); Md   (   ); served 39th Regt U S Inf; P D & 2400 Pensioners, Armstrong; likely in Maury Co; Unkn.

JOHNSON, Hon CAVE (1-11-1793--11-23-1866 Clarksville, Robertson Co); Md Mrs Elizabeth Dortch Brunson (   ); Brig Q M under Brig Gen Thomas Johnson, Creek War 1813-14; W D & T S A; Clarksville Cem, Robertson Co; Pvt mkr. (In 1845 served as P M Gen of U S.)

JOHNSON, DANIEL (2-14-1789--d in Jackson Co); Md 1-(   ), 2-Polly Gray Young 1823 (--1826); Pvt, Capt James Bennet's Co, Col Robt S Steele's 4th Regt W T Mil, 2-28-1814--5-27-1814; W D & T S A; in Jackson Co; Unkn.

JOHNSON, GEORGE (3-12-1775--1-18-1852 Union Co); Md Nancy Buckner (4-1-1791--11-20-1876); at Battle of Tohopeka 3-27-1814; Goodspeed E T H Union Co; Fam Cem in Union Co; Unkn.

JOHNSON, JOHN H (4-2-1793--7-23-1889 Polk Co); Md
(   ); Lieut in War of 1812; Cem Record; Benton Cem in Polk Co; Pvt mkr.

JOHNSON, ROBERT (1777-- 1856 Lawrence Co); Md Mary McLaren (--d 1857); 1st Lieut, Capt Andrew McCarty's Co, Col Richard C Napier's 1st Regt W T Mil; W D & P D; Cem in Lawrence Co; Pvt mkr.

JOHNSON, THOMAS J (--d 11-6-1814 at Ft Williams, Ala); Md
(   ); 1st Lieut, Capt Nowlin's Co, Col Philip Pipkin's Regt
Inf, 6-20-1814--11-6-1814 died; W D & T S A; at Ft Williams, Ala;
Unmkd.

JOHNSON, Col WILLIAM (1766--d Rhea Co); Md Sarah Forbush (1769--
    ); Col of 3rd Regt E T Drftd Mil, 9-20-1814--5-9-1815; W D
& T S A; Johnson Fam Cem in Rhea Co; Unkn.

JOHNSTON, ROBERT (--d Fentress Co); Md   (   );
War of 1812; Pensioned in Fentress Co, P D & 2400 Pensioners,
Armstrong; likely Fentress Co; Unkn.

JOHNSTON, ROBERT (1781-- 1867 in Tenn); Md Barbara Ormond 1-27-
1820 Blount Co (   ); War of 1812; Record from Mrs J D
Dawson, Dallas, Tex; Unkn Cem in Tenn; Unkn.

JONES, DAVID (--d Cocke Co); Md   (   ); War of
1812; Goodspeed E T H Cocke Co; likely in Cocke Co; Unkn.

JONES, JEREMIAH H (--d Hamilton Co); Md   (   );
Pvt, Creek War; Hamilton Co Hist- Armstrong; likely in Hamilton
Co; Unkn.

JONES, JAMES (1797-- 1849 Blount Co); Md   1812 (   );
Pvt, Capt James Gillespie's Co, Col Sam Wear's 1st Regt E T V,
9-23-1813--12-31-1813; W D & T S A; Unkn Cem in Blount Co; Unkn.

JONES, JOHN (--likely Knox Co); Md Rebecca Gallaher 4-16-1811
Knox Co (   ); War of 1812; French Broad-Holston Hist- Rothrock; likely in Knox Co; Unkn.

JONES, JOHN (8-30-1789--5-25-1869 Hawkins Co); Md Annis Manes
1808 (3-14-1791--11-2-1874); Pvt, Capt Jonas Laughmiller's Co,
Col Ewen Allison's Regt E T Drftd Mil, 1-10-1814--4-27-1814, left
sick at Ft Williams, Ala; W D & T S A & P D; in Hawkins Co; Pvt
mkr.

JONES, NATHANIEL (--d 10-29-1814 "late a soldier U S Service,
1st prisoner in Canada, formerly of Greene Co"); Md
(   ); War of 1812; Inv Bk 1810--1843 Greene Co, Phineas
Jones, Admr 7-31-1817; likely in Canada; Unkn. (Data found in
Greene Co Records)

JONES, SAMUEL (1755-- 1831 Maury Co); Md Elizabeth Goodloe 1790
(8-17-1772--1854); Capt, Maury Co Mil; John Sevier's Commission
Bk; Maury Co; Pvt mkr. (Also Rev War)

JONES, Lieut THORNTON (6-26-1780--8-15-1852 Bolivar, Hardeman
Co); Md Nancy Thompson (   ); 2nd Lieut, Capt Crunk's Co,
Col John Cocke's 2nd Regt W T Mil, 1814-15, at N O; W D & T S A;
Bolivar Cem, Hardeman Co; Pvt mkr.

JONES, WESTWOOD A (--liv 1840 List aged 64 yrs Haywood Co); Md
         (   ); War of 1812, pensioned Haywood Co; P D
& 2400 Pensioners, Armstrong; likely Haywood Co; Unkn. (He was
living in Haywood Co with James Waddill.)

JONES, WILLIS (1784-- 1834 Maury Co); Md Elizabeth Gee (1792--4- 1834); Corp, Capt Mebane's Co, Col Philip Pipkin's 1st Regt W T Mil, 6-20-1814--left at Mobile 12-21-1814; W D & T S A; Columbia Cem, Maury Co; Pvt mkr.

KEEBLER, JAMES (12-26-1789--11-15-1859 Washington Co); Md 1-Polly   (--c 1824), 2-Sarah Hawes 8-9-1827 (c 1799--6-18-1888); Pvt, Capt Jonathan Waddle's Co, Col Sam Bayless' 4th Regt E T Drftd Mil, 11-13-1814--5-18-1815; W D & T S A; Keebler Fam Cem, Keebler's Cross Rds, Washington Co; Pvt mkr.

KEENEY, JAMES (--d 2-20-1814 in service); Md   (   ); heirs were Sally, Ishom, Margaret, Alfred, Betsy & Matilda Keeney in Jefferson Co); P D & 2400 Pensioners, Armstrong; likely where died; Unkn.

KEITHE, ZACHARIAH (--d 1855 Bradley Co); Md   (   ); War of 1812; W D; Liberty Cem near Cleveland, Bradley Co; Govt mkr by 1812 Chapter.

KELLUM, EDWARD (1787-- 1863 Memphis, Shelby Co); Md (   ); Pvt, 1st Regt W T Mil; T S A & Texas 1812 Records; Memphis Cem, Shelby Co; Unkn.

KELLY, ALLEN (--liv 1840 aged 55 yrs Jefferson Co); Md (   ); served 24th Regt U S Inf; P D & 2400 Pensioners, Armstrong; likely Jefferson Co; Unkn.

KELLY, JOHN (--d Marion Co); Md   (   ); War of 1812;   ; likely in Marion Co; Unkn. (Son of Alexander Kelly of Knox, Blount & Marion Co.)

KELTON, ROBERT (1776-- 1826 Rutherford Co); Md   (   ); Pvt, Capt Jetton's Co, Col John Coffee's Regt W T Mil; T S A & Texas 1812 Records; Rutherford Co; Unkn.

KENNEDY, ANDREW (8-12-1751--5-5-1834 Blount Co); Md Rachel Penny 11-17-1795 (1761--10-23-1845); furnished powder for War of 1812, N O; Kennedy Fam Records; Baker's Creek Pres Cem in Blount Co; Pvt mkr & Rev War mkr. (Also Rev War. Said to have furnished 10,000 lbs powder for Battle N O.)

KENNEDY, Rev JAMES (12-2-1786--8-30-1826 Knox Co); Md Mary (4-10-1777--10-11-1853); War of 1812; T S A; Lebanon-in-the-Fork Pres Cem, Knox Co; Pvt mkr.

KENNEDY, JAMES Jr (4-24-1794--8-13-1838 Knoxville, Knox Co); Md Jane Holt Cox 6-25-1828 (5-13-1812--1-16-1896); Pvt, Capt Francis Berry's Co, Col Sam Bunch's Regt Mtd Gunmen, 1-10-1814--for 6 mos; W D & T S A; Knox Co; Pvt mkr.

KENNER, HOWSON (2-4-1787--12-7-1820 Hawkins Co); Md Susannah Hamblen Kyle 1809 (12-3-1785--9-19-1848); Pvt, with Jackson at N O; data from sister, Elizabeth Kenner Savage; Rodham Kenner Cem N side Holston River near John Sevier Steam Plant, Hawkins Co; Pvt mkr.

KERBY, FRANCIS (1794--6-8-1880 Smith Co); Md Barbara Brown (1807--1855); Pvt, Capt Blakemore's Co, 1st Regt W T Mil, 6-20-1814--2-2-1815; W D & T S A & P D; Cedar Bluff Cem in Smith Co; Pvt mkr.

KERR, JESSE Jr (--d Loudon Co); Md Polly Anne Henry 4-3-1834 Blount Co (   ); Pvt, Capt Jehu Stephens' Co, Col Sam Wear's Regt E T Mtd Gunmen, 10-6-1814--4-6-1815; W D & T S A; Baker's Creek Pres Cem in Blount Co - or Pine Grove Pres Cem in Loudon Co; Unmkd.

KEYES, JEREMIAH (--liv 1840 List aged 43 yrs Washington Co); Md Mary Forguson 7-6-1826 (   ); served in E T Mil; P D & 2400 Pensioners, Armstrong; likely in Washington Co; Unkn.

KIBBLER, JOHN (KEBBLER) (5-30-1788-- 1882 Bradley Co); Md Anna (1-7-1788--2-16-1863); Pvt, War of 1812; P D & J M Wooten Records, Bradley Co; Ramsey Fam Cem near Cleveland, Bradley Co; Pvt mkr.

KILDAY, HENRY (--d 12-19-1813 in service); Md   (   ); heirs were Sally, Polly, Barbara, John & Prudence Kilday in Greene Co; served in 24th Regt U S Inf; P D & 2400 Pensioners, Armstrong; likely where died; Unkn.

KILGORE, CHARLES (--liv 1828 List Greene Co); Md (   ); served Col Campbell's Regt; P D & 2400 Pensioners, Armstrong; likely in Greene Co; Unkn.

KIMBROUGH, Rev DUKE (11-19-1762--9-21-1849 Jefferson Co); Md Eunice Carlock 1795 (10-24-1770--3-18-1856); Pastor Dandridge Bapt Church 50 yrs; Burnett's Bapt Preachers; Jefferson Co; Pvt mkr.

KIMBROUGH, ISAAC (4-26-1788--aft 1849 Polk Co); Md Mary Randolph (   ); War of 1812; Burnett's Bapt Preachers; likely in Polk Co; Unkn.

KINCHELOE, JAMES (3-29-1795--bef 4-2-1874 Washington Co); Md 1-Caldwell (   ), 2-Louiza Rush (--liv 1883 Pensioner in Washington Co); Pvt, Capt George McPherson's Co, Col Sam Bunch's Regt, attd to Col Ewen Allison's Regt, 1-4-1814--7-14-1814; W D & T S A & P D; Kincheloe Fam Cem near Fall Branch, Washington Co; Unkn. (His Will probated 4-2-1874 in Washington Co.)

KING, Col JAMES MOORE (11-18-1792 N C --4-5-1877 near Murfreesboro, Rutherford Co); Md Martha Batey 11-19-1821 (5-11-1805--8-18-1887); served with Andrew Jackson at N O; T S A; Rural Rest Cem at Kingwood, 6 m W Murfreesboro off Hiway 96, Rutherford Co; Govt mkr 1956 by 1812 Chapter.

KING, JOHN S (--d Knox Co); Md   (   ); Pvt, Capt James Landen's Co, Col Sam Bayless' 4th Regt E T Drftd Mil, 11- 1814--5-18-1815; W D & P D; likely in Knox Co; Unkn.

KING, THOMAS (7-10-1772--1840 Williamson Co); Md Eliza Bass (?) 1809 (1780--1849); various Civil Service in Williamson Co; Williamson Co Records, Williamson Co; Pvt mkr.

KING, WILLIAM (11-27-1796-- 1868 Rhea Co); Md 1-Martha Crouch 8-2-1819 (5-7-1797--5-1-1841), 2-Mary E Schoolfield (   ); Capt, Col Ewen Allison's Regt E T Drftd Mil, 1-6-1814--5-18-1814; W D; Unkn Cem in Rhea Co; Unkn.

KING, WILLIAM (5-25-1798--4-28-1866 Sullivan Co); Md Sarah Hall (1801--1853); Capt, Col Ewen Allison's Regt E T Drftd Mil, 1-6-1814--5-18-1814; W D & T S A; New Bethel Pres Cem, Sullivan Co; Pvt mkr. (It would seem that this is sam war service as the one above - we know the Sullivan Co Wm King has this service.)

KIRKPATRICK, JOSEPH (6-15-1786--3-12-1852 Wilson Co); Md Charity Hodge 12-26-1820 (--d 1872-4 Wilson Co); Capt, 2nd Regt W T V under Gen Jackson; W D & T S A; New Hope Cem near Lebanon, Wilson Co; Pvt mkr.

KIRKPATRICK, MARTIN (1790-1800--5-10-1838 Union Co); Md Anna Bayless 1-25-1814 (c 1793--aft 1860); Pvt & Ensign, Capt John Bayless' Co, Col Sam Wear's 1st Regt E T V, & Pvt, Capt Charles Conway's Co, Maj John Chiles' Regt E T Mtd Vol; W D & P D; Bayless Fam Cem in Union Co; Unmkd.

KIRKPATRICK, ROBERT (1792--8-30-1852 Knox Co); Md Rachel Bayless 12-30-1813 (--d aft 1860); Pvt, Capt John Bayless' Co Mtd Inf, Col Sam Wear's 1st Regt E T V, 9-23-1813--12-22-1813; W D & T S A; Milan Bapt Cem in Knox Co; Unmkd.

KIRKPATRICK, ROBERT S (b Va - came Tenn 1792 --d Anderson Co); Md Sarah R King (   ); War of 1812; Goodspeed E T H Anderson Co; likely in Anderson Co; Unkn.

KIRKPATRICK, WILKINS (8-14-1775-- 1842 near Bays Mt at Bent Creek, Hawkins Co); Md Sarah Hoskins (--d 1838); War of 1812; Goodspeed E T H; near Bent Creek, Hawkins Co; Unkn.

KITTRELL, GEORGE (--1867 Maury Co); Md Elizabeth H Rutherford (--1865); War of 1812; Goodspeed Maury Co; likely in Maury Co; Unkn.

KLEPPER, PETER (1792--12-31-1876 Hawkins Co); Md 1-Mary Myers c 1815 (   ), 2-Mary Pilant 1-1-1839 (1-18-1814--3-19-1907); War of 1812; Tombstone says "A Jackson Soldier"; Klepper Fam Cem at foot of Devil's Nose, Hawkins Co; Pvt mkr. (This couple had 19 children.)

KNIGHT, JAMES (--liv 1828 List Williamson Co); Md (   ); served in Capt Dale's Co Tenn Mil; P D & 2400 Pensioners, Armstrong; likely in Williamson Co; Unkn.

KNIGHT, WADE H (1798--d Humphreys Co); Md Elizabeth Knight (coz) 1818 (1798--); Pvt, Capt Peter Searcy's Co, Col Philip Pipkin's 1st Regt W T Mil, enl at Fayetteville 6-20-1814, disch Mobile 3-20-1815; T S A; Knight Fam Cem on Turkey Creek, Humphreys Co; Pvt mkr.

KYLE, ROBERT "of Clinch" (c 1760--7-17-1814 Hawkins Co); Md Sarah Runnells 1788 (1774--6-29-1842); as old man he enl Pvt, Capt Jonas Laughmiller's Co, Col Ewen Allison's Regt E T Drftd Mil, transfrd to Capt Jones Griffin's Co 1814, and died as result of exposure; T S A; Kyle Fam Cem, Puncheon Camp (now Kyle) Valley, Dr John Pearson's Farm near Eidson, Hawkins Co; Unmkd.

LACKEY, JAMES (1786-- 1875 Roane Co); Md Jane Matlock (--liv 1887 Roane Co); Pvt, Capt Neilson's Co in Roane Co, 9-13-1813-- 1-1-1814; Goodspeed E T H Roane Co & Roane Co Hist- Wells; Unkn Cem in Loudon Co; Unkn.

LACY, JAMES (11-3-1771-- 1847 Carter Co); Md ( ); Pvt, Capt Adam Winsell's Co, Col Ewen Allison's Regt E T Drftd Mil, & Pvt, Capt Francis Register's Co, Col Sam Bunch's Regt Drftd Mil, 1-5-1814--5-3-1814; W D; Lacy Fam Cem at Hopson, Carter Co; Pvt mkr.

LACY, PHILEMON (--d 12-17-1884 aged 90 yrs Carter Co); Md ( ); Pvt, Capt Adam Winsell's Co, Col Ewen Allison's Regt E T Drftd Mil, 1-10-1814--5-18-1814; W D & T S A; Cem in Carter Co; Unkn.

LAMB, ALEXANDER (--d Bledsoe Co); Md Elizabeth Carmack ( ); J P 1807--1815 Bledsoe Co; John Sevier Commission Bk; Lamb Fam Cem on West Valley Rd, Bledsoe Co; Unkn.

LAMBERT, AARON (--d 3-25-1814 in service); Md ( ); 1st Lieut, Capt Joseph Duncan's Co, Col Sam Bunch's Regt, attd Col Ewen Allison's Regt Drftd Mil, 1-10-1814--3-25-1814 died; W D & Blount Co Hist- Burns; likely where died; Unkn.

LANCASTER, SAMUEL (2-19-1790--2-17-1882 Hickman Co); Md ( ); Pvt, Capt James Haggard's Co Mtd Gunmen & in Capt Gray's Co, Col John Cocke's Regt, enl 5-29-1812, also enl 1-28-1814; W D; Beaver Dam Creek, Hickman Co; Pvt mkr.

LANGLEY, THOMAS (--d 11-30-1814 in service); Md ( ); heirs were William, John & Thomas Langley in Washington Co; served in 7th Regt U S Inf; P D & 2400 Pensioners, Armstrong; likely where died; Unkn.

LANE, ISAAC (2-14-1760--11-9-1851 McMinn Co); Md Sarah Russell 1782 (1760--6-1857); Capt, Grainger Co Mil 1796--1801 & J P in Claiborne Co; T S A; Lane Fam Cem at Niota, McMinn Co; Pvt mkr.

LANE, THOMAS (--d Greene Co); Md ( ); Soldier War of 1812; Acklen's Bible Records; Old Cem in Greeneville, Greene Co; Unmkd.

LARUE, FRANCIS (--likely in Knox Co); Md Nancy Ann Young 10-19-1820 ( ); War of 1812; French-Broad-Holston Hist- Rothrock; likely in Knox Co; Unkn.

LARUE, WILLIAM (--d 2-5-1816 Knox Co); Md Sarah Tindell (d 1883); Pvt, Capt Barton's Co, E T Mil, & Sub for Jacob Larue of Anderson Co, 9-30-1813--7-1-1814; W D & T S A; Larue Fam Cem on McMillan farm near Smithwood, Knox Co; Unmkd. (Sarah Larue was Pensioner of War of 1812 in Knox Co.)

LAUDERDALE, Lieut Col JAMES (--killed 12-23-1814 in Night Battle of N O); Md   (   ); Lieut, Gen John Coffee's Brig W T Mil; W D & T S A; Lauderdale Fam Cem near Templow, Trousdale Co; Pvt mkr.

LAWRENCE, JOHN (--d Jefferson Co); Md Amy McCollough (   ); War of 1812, at Tohopeka, 3-27-1814; Goodspeed E T H Jefferson Co; likely in Hamblen Co (then Jefferson); Unkn.

LEA, MAJOR (1771-- 1822 Grainger Co); Md Lavinia Jernigan 1793 (   ); Pvt, Capt Moses Collins' Co, 13th Regt Miss Terr Mil; Miss S A & Texas 1812 Records; Cem at Poplar Hill, Grainger Co; Unkn.

LEE, JAMES (--d in service 1815); Md   (   ); War of 1812; Carter Co Inv Bk 2-13-1815, Admr James Helton claims $75 due James Lee for U S service; likely where died; Unkn.

LEE, JAMES (1786-- 1866 Hawkins Co); Md Hannah Hale (1789--aft 1850 Hawkins Co); War of 1812; Goodspeed E T H p-1230; likely Cem on Dodson's Creek, S Holston River, Hawkins Co; Unkn. (Hawkins Co 1850 Census says born 1791.)

LEDMON, WILLIAM (--liv 1840 List aged 67 yrs Washington Co); Md Md   (   ); served 1st Regt Riflemen; P D & 2400 Pensioners, Armstrong; likely in Washington Co; Unkn.

LEGG, SAMUEL (10-6-1782--9-13-1866 Bradley Co); Md Jane Hafley 11-17-1802 (12-21-1788--2-1860); Pvt, Capt Jehu Stephens' Co, Col Sam Wear's Regt Drftd Mil, 10-6-1814--4-6-1815; W D & T S A; Bradley Co; Pvt mkr.

LEGG, WESLEY (1797-- 1859 Knox Co); Md Christiana Price (1801--1873); War of 1812; Goodspeed E T H Knox Co; Knox Co; Unkn.

LEONARD, GEORGE (--liv 1883 Bristol, Sullivan Co); Md (   ); War of 1812 Pension #10,960; P D & W D; likely in Bristol, Sullivan Co; Unkn.

LEONARD, Capt WILLIAM (--d Marshall Co); Md   (   ); War of 1812 in N C; N C S A; Chapel Hill Cem in Marshall Co; Unkn.

LEWALLEN, SHADE (--d Scott Co); Single; at Battle of N O; Scott Co Hist- Sanderson; Old Huntsville Cem at the Pres Academy, Scott Co; Pvt mkr.

LEWIS, HENRY (1780-- 1866 Hamilton Co); Md   (   ); War of 1812; W D; Lewis Fam Cem near Ooltewah, Hamilton Co; Mkd by U S D 1812.

LEWIS, JAMES (1756-- 1849 Franklin Co); Md Lucy Thomas 1779 (   ); Adjutant, Franklin Co Vol in War of 1812; T S A & Goodspeed Franklin Co; Franklin Co; Unkn. (Also Rev War)

LEWIS, JESSE (--liv 1883 List Union Co); Md   (   ); War of 1812; W D & P D #16,840 Racoon Valley, Union Co; likely in Union Co; Unkn.

LEWIS, MERIWETHER (10-18-1774--10-11-1809); Single; Sec, Pres Jefferson & Commander Oregon Expd, 1803--1806, Gov Terr La, 1807; U S A; Meriwether Lewis Natl Park at Hohenweld, Lewis Co; Monument erected by State Tenn 1848.

LEWIS Maj WILLIAM B (1784--11-12-1866 Nashville, Davidson Co); Md Margaret Lewis (dau W T Lewis) (   ); Q M on Natchez Expd 1812; W D & T S A; Mt Olivet Cem in Nashville, Davidson Co; Unmkd. (Maj Lewis was great supporter of Andrew Jackson in his famous "Kitchen Cabinet".)

LIGGETT, HENRY (1-11-1795--8-29-1861 Roane Co); Md Elizabeth Center 8-14-1817 (1794--11-27-1871); Srgt, Capt Alexander Biggs' Co, Col Edwin Boothe's 5th Regt Drftd Mil, 11-13-1814--1815; W D & T S A; Bethel Pres Cem at Kingston, Roane Co; Pvt mkr.

LILLARD, ABRAHAM (4-15-1791--12-17-1873 Polk Co); Md Jane Harrison 3-14-1816 (6-25-1796--8-15-1875); Pvt, Capt Branch Jones' Co, Col Sam Bayless' 4th Regt Drftd Mil, Gen Coulter's Brig, disch 6-13-1815; W D & T S A & Leaves From the Family Tree- Allen; Ocoee Bapt Cem, Lillard lot, Polk Co; Pvt mkr. (Nearby is the grave of "Bob, a faithful servant of A Lillard, D Oct, 1867 aged 81 yrs".)

LILLARD, JAMES III (3-17-1794--d likely Rhea Co); Md Polly Sandusky 2-1817 (   ); Capt, Col Wm Lillard's 2nd Regt E T V, 10-13-1813--2-8-1814; W D & T S A; likely in Rhea Co; Unkn.

LILLARD, Col WILLIAM (1744-- 1832 Polk Co); Md Rachel McCay Leith (wid) (--d 1842); Repr Jefferson Co 1797, & Cocke Co for 18 yrs & Col, 2nd Regt E T V War of 1812, 10-13-1813--2-8-1814; W D & T S A & Cocke Co Hist- Odell; Lillard Fam Cem near Benton, Polk Co; Pvt mkr. (Also Rev War)

LINDSEY, CHARLES (--bef 8-2-1856 Sevier Co); Md Ruth Shahan c 1812-3 (--bef 8-2-1856); heirs were Mary b 1825, Charles b 1827, Cassandra b 1831, David b c 1835, William b 1837; Pvt, as Mtd Gunner, Capt Wm Henderson's Co Mtd Gunmen, Gen Nath Taylor's Brig, 9-20-1814--5-3-1815; P D & T S A; likely in Sevier Co; Unkn.

LINGO, WILLIAM (--liv 1840 List aged 44 yrs Hardin Co); Md (   ); served N C Mil; P D & N C S A & 2400 Pensioners, Armstrong; likely in 1st Distr, Hardin Co; Unkn.

LIPPS, JONATHAN (10-24-1777--12-31-1877 aged 101-2-7 days Carter Co); Md 1-   (   ), 2-Nancy Lewis 2-12-1845 Carter Co (9-7-1801--8-27-1893); Pvt, Capt Adam Winsell's Co, Col Ewen Allison's Regt E T Drftd Mil, 1-10-1814--5-18-1814; W D & T S A; Buckles Fam Cem near Hunter, Carter Co; Pvt mkr. (Jonathan Lipps was a Bapt preacher.)

LITTERALL, HUTSON (LUTTRELL) (c 1784--5-18-1858 near Embree-
ville, Washington Co); Md Sarah   8-10-1800 in Greene Co
(1791--liv 1883 Jonesboro, Washington Co); Pvt, Capt Daniel
Huffman's Co Mtd Rifles, Col McDowell's Regt Va Vol Mil, enl in
Fincastle Co, Va for 6 mos; P D & Va S A; Unkn Cem in Jonesboro,
Embreeville area, Washington Co; Unkn. (Soldier Pension #168,658;
Sarah Litterall is listed liv in Washington Co 1883 by P D.)

LOCKE, GEORGE (--liv 4-29-1851 aged 53 yrs Meigs Co); Md
(   ); Pvt, Capt William Henderson's Co Mtd Gunmen or Spies,
Gen Nath Taylor's Brig, mustered at Ross' Landing 9-20-1814--
5-2-1815; P D & T S A; likely in Meigs Co; Unkn.

LOGAN, HENRY (1777-- 1845 Blount Co); Md Rachel Henry (1786--
1837); Pvt, Capt Jehu Stephens' Co, Col Sam Wear's Regt Drftd
Mil, 10-6-1814--4-6-1815; W D & T S A; Baker's Creek Pres Cem,
Blount Co; Pvt mkr.

LONAS, JACOB (LONES) (1792-- 1847 Knox Co); Md Jane Hickey
(   ); Lieut War of 1812; Goodspeed E T H Knox Co; Lonas
Fam Cem in Knox Co; Unkn.

LONG, JOHN B (--d likely Knox Co); Md   (   );
War of 1812; French Broad-Holston Hist- Rothrock; likely in Knox
Co; Unkn. (One John Long md Betsy Parker 12-7-1820 Knox Co.)

LONG, NICHOLAS (--likely Jefferson Co); Md   (   );
War of 1812; Pensioned in Jefferson Co; P D & 2400 Pensioners,
Armstrong; likely in Jefferson Co; Unkn.

LONGENOTTI, CHARLES (--burned to death 4-21-1854 Nashville,
Davidson Co); Md   (   ); Interpreter for Gen Jack-
son at N O; T S A & Acklen's Records; Old City Cem in Nashville,
Davidson Co; Pvt mkr.

LOONEY, ISAAC (--liv 1883 Gallatin, Sumner Co); Md
(   ); War of 1812 Pension #17,250; W D & P D; likely in
Sumner Co; Unkn.

LOONEY, MOSES (--1870 Roane Co); Md Patty York 2-27-1817 (   );
Musician, Capt James Preston's Co, 10-5-1813--1-5-1814, also in
Capt White's Co, 3 mos payroll; Roane Co Hist- Wells; likely in
Roane Co; Unkn. (There is another Moses Looney (c 1748--7-12-
1824 Knox Co) who is bur in Lonas-Looney Cem below Knoxville,
which has been confused with War of 1812 one.)

LOUDERMILK, SOLOMON (--d likely Monroe Co); Md   (   );
Pvt, Capt Joseph Duncan's Co, Col Sam Bunch's Regt, transfrd
from Capt McNair's Co, 4-27-1814--7-26-1814; W D; Unkn Cem,
likely Monroe Co; Unkn.

LOVING, WALTER (--10-10-1837 Sumner Co); Md Dolly Stone 4-23-
1806 (--5-20-1838); Pvt & Corp, Capt Henry Hamilton's Co, Col
--- 3rd Regt Tenn Mil, enl for 6 mos, disch 4- 1815; P D;
Sumner Co; Unkn.

LOWERY, ALEXANDER (1-30-1767--8-20-1846 Sparta, White Co); Md Amie Gist 5-25-1790 Greene Co (c 1767--bef 1846); Col, 2nd Regt Tenn Drftd Mil, enl 9-20-1814--res 11-20-1814; T S A; Old Cem in Sparta, White Co; Pvt mkr.

LOWERY, GEORGE (--in Tenn); Md ( ); Maj under Col Gideon Morgan's Regt of Cherokees; Hamilton Co Hist- Armstrong; Unkn Cem in Tenn; Unkn.

LOWERY, JOHN (--in Tenn); Md ( ); served under Col Gideon Morgan's Regt of Cherokees; Hamilton Co Hist- Armstrong; Unkn Cem in Tenn; Unkn.

LOY, PETER (3-24-1794--3-18-1862 Union Co); Md Philopena Sharp 7- 1818 (c 1800--); Pvt, Capt Robert Doak's Co, enl 9-23-1813-- 1-1-1814; W D & T S A; likely in Union Co; Unkn.

LOYD, JOHN (1762--8-8-1829 Roane Co); Md Rachel Vandeveer 1787 (1768--1833); Srgt, Capt Wm B Neilson's Co, Col John Brown's Regt, 9-30-1813--1-31-1814; Roane Co Hist- Wells & T S A; Fam Cem in Garden in Kingston, Roane Co; Pvt mkr. (Also Rev War in Penn)

LUSK, JOHN (11-4-1734--d Warren Co); Md ( ); Pvt, Capt Jonathan Taylor's Co, Col Butler's Regt Tenn Mil; P D; Fam Cem 4 m E McMinnville, Warren Co; Unkn.

LUSK, JOSEPH II (5-27-1790--2-3-1873 Bradley Co); Md Rebecca Igou 10-28-1812 Bledsoe Co (1-19-1798--11-1-1858); Pvt, Capt John Hawkins' Co, 1-10-1814--5-13-1814; P D & Edwards Account Bk; Lusk Fam Cem at Walterville, near Cleveland, Bradley Co; Pvt mkr.

LUTTRELL, LEWIS (8-28-1786--2-5-1855 Knox Co); Md Martha Gibbs 2-11-1819 (8-22-1800--9-12-1871); Pvt, Capt John Chiles' Co, Col John Brown's Regt E T V; W D & T S A; Luttrell Fam Cem on Washington Pike, Knox Co; Pvt mkr.

LUTTRELL, MARTIN (--liv 7-17-1851 B L Wt Hamilton Co); Md ( ); Pvt, Capt Bacon's Co; P D #10,220 & B L Wt, Edwards Account Bk, Leaves From Family Tree- Allen, 5-13-1934; likely in Hamilton Co; Unkn.

LYON, JACOB (--d Sullivan Co); Md Mary Ann Snodgrass (--7-9-1831 aged 56 yrs); War of 1812 in Va; Va S A & Fam Records; Snodgrass Fam Cem in Sullivan Co; Unmkd.

MAJORS, THOMAS (--3-11-1831 aged 54 yrs Sullivan Co); Md
(   ); Pvt, Capt Wm King's Co, Col Ewen Allison's Regt E T
Drftd Mil, 1-6-1814--5-18-1814; W D & T S A; Weaver's Union Cem
in Sullivan Co; Pvt mkr - coffin-shaped iron plaque made at
Kings Iron Works, Sullivan Co.

MALCOLM, WILLIAM (--d 6-12-1840 Sevier Co); Md Nancy Shadden
9-25-1800 (--liv 4-11-1855); Fusinger in Capt Andrew Lawson's Co,
Col Wm Johnson's 3rd Regt E T Drftd Mil, 9-17-1814--6 mos-4-
1815; P D & T S A; likely in Sevier Co; Unkn.

MALLORY, BENJAMIN (10-10-1789-- 1851 Robertson Co); Md
(   ); War of 1812; W D; Adams Station in Robertson Co; Unkn.

MALLORY, PHILIP (--1854 Davidson Co); Md Martha Nance (--d 1849);
War of 1812; Goodspeed Williamson Co; likely in Davidson Co; Unkn.

MALLORY, TIMOTHY (--liv 1828 List unkn Co); Md (   );
served in 5th Regt Ky Mil; P D & Ky S A & 2400 Pensioners, Armstrong; Unkn Co; Unkn.

MALONEY, ROBERT (8-25-1784 Ireland --6-16-1848 Greene Co); Md
Catherine Cooper (3-22-1788--11-15-1862); Capt, Col Wm Lillard's
2nd Regt E T V, 10-14-1813--2-8-1814, mustered out at Greeneville;
W D & T S A; Mt Pleasant Cumberland Pres Cem at Cross Anchor,
Greene Co; Unmkd.

MANSON, WILLIAM (--Pension Knoxville Agcy); Md Mary   (--d
aft husband); War of 1812; P D & 2400 Pensioners, Armstrong;
likely in Knox Co; Unkn.

MARLER, STEPHEN (--liv 1883 McMinnville, Warren Co); Md
(   ); War of 1812; P D; likely in McMinnville, Warren Co;
Unkn. (Pension #18,145)

MARLIN, HENRY W (--d Nashville, Davidson Co); Md
(   ); Creek War 1813-14; Acklen's Records; Old City Cem in
Nashville, Davidson Co; Pvt mkr. (Member of the "Nashville Blues")

MARR, Lieut GEORGE WASHINGTON (5-25-1779--9-5-1856 Obion Co);
Md   (   ); Atty Gen for West Tenn 1807-09, wounded
in Creek War; W D & Dir of Congress; Troy Cem in Obion Co; Pvt mkr.

MARS, DARBY (--liv 1828 List Knox Co); Md   (   );
served Triplets Regt; P D & 2400 Pensioners, Armstrong; likely
in Knox Co; Unkn.

MARTIN, RICHARD (--liv 1828 List Davidson Co); Md
(   ); served Tenn Vol; P D & 2400 Pensioners, Armstrong;
likely in Davidson Co; Unkn.

MARTIN, WILLIAM (--d Rutherford Co); Md Isabella   (--Pen-
sioned); War of 1812; P D & 2400 Pensioners, Armstrong; likely
Rutherford Co; Unkn.

MARTIN, Lieut Col WILLIAM (8-1781-- 1843 Williamson Co); Single; Lieut Col, 2nd Regt W T V, Staff of Gen Andrew Jackson at N O; W D & T S A; Martin Fam Cem at "Meadowbrook", Williamson Co; Govt mkr. (When Gen LaFayette visited the U S in 1825, Gen Wm Martin was in command of 9th Brig of Tenn Mil.)

MASON, DANIEL (--d 1840 Roane Co); Md 1-Mary Gillard, nee Brashear (--d 1819), 2-Patsy Hicks (--aft 1840); War of 1812; Goodspeed E T H & Wells List of 1812 Soldiers; likely in Roane Co; Unkn.

MASON, JOHN (--d Claiborne Co); Md Rhoda ( ); Pvt, Capt Henry Hunter's Co, Col Wm Johnson's 3rd Regt E T Drftd Mil, enl Tazewell 11-19-1814 to fill out Regt odr Sept 1812 & failed by 11 men to fill out number so attd to Capt Brock's Co, Knoxville; W D & P D; likely Claiborne Co; Unkn.

MATHANY, SAMUEL (--d Greene Co); Md ( ); Pvt, Capt Francis Register's Co, Col Sam Bunch's Regt E T Mil; W D & Letter of J R Smith, Jeraldstown, Greene Co, 1935; likely in Greene Co; Unkn. (Says he was disch same time as George Robertson from Capt Register's Co)

MATHES, EBENEZER LEITHE (5-11-1789--1-5-1868 Washington Co); Md Nancy Ann Nelson (2-25-1786--2-27-1867); Srgt, Capt Henry McCray's Co, Col Ewen Allison's Regt E T Drftd Mil, 1-5-1814--5-23-1814; W D & T S A; Old Salem Pres Cem at Washington College, Washington Co; Pvt mkr. (He and N A have double mkr - they had no children.)

MATHIS, JESSE (9-15-1794--7-2-1875 Henry Co); Md 1-Martha Beaty 11-29-1821 ( ), 2-Mary Murphy 6-25-1868 (3-22-1833--9-30-1910); Gunner in Detachment-Sea-Fencibles U S Vol, Capt Thomas M Newell, 2-15-1815--5-14-1815; W D; Palestine Ch Cem near Paris, Henry Co; Govt mkr 1950 by 1812 Chapter. (Mrs Martha M Owen, Real Daughter Tenn Society, d 1-20-1953.)

MATLOCK, HENRY (--liv 1840 List aged 54 yrs McMinn Co); Md ( ); served Col Williamson's Regt Mil; P D & 2400 Pensioners, Armstrong; likely McMinn Co; Unkn.

MATTHEWS, DAVID (7-18-1788--12- 1829 in Ala); Md Margaret Castner 9-22-1809 (4-9-1794--4-9-1871 Blount Co); Pvt, Capt Alexander Biggs' Co, Col Edwin Boothe's 5th Regt E T Drftd Mil, 11-13-1814 --5-18-1815; W D & T S A; Soldier bur in Ala & wife in Blount Co; Unkn.

MAUK, HENRY (--d Washington Co); Md ( ); Pvt, Capt George Keyes' Co, Col Wm Lillard's 2nd Regt E T V, 10-12-1813--des 11-6-1813; W D & T S A; Unkn Fam Cem in Washington Co; Unkn.

MAUK, JOHN (--d Washington Co); Md ( ); Corp, Capt James Landen's Co, Col Sam Bayless' 4th Regt E T Drftd Mil, 11-13-1814--5-18-1815; W D & T S A; Unkn Cem in Washington Co; Unkn.

MAUK, SAMUEL (--d bet 1875-1880 aged 95 yrs Washington Co); Md Polly (Sarah) Broyles (   ); War of 1812; W D & P D; Mauk Fam Cem near Mt Carmel Meth Ch 1 m below Bailey's Bridge in Washington Co; Unmkd.

MAXWELL, MOSES (--d Bradley Co aged 102 yrs); Md   (   ); War of 1812 in N C; P D & N C S A; Bean Dam Cem near White Oak Mt, Bradley Co; Unkn. (He settled near White Oak Mt and was Pensioner liv in Bradley Co - Edwards Account Bk.)

MAY, JOHN (--d Washington Co); Md   (   ); Lieut & Capt, Col James Wilburn's Regt N C Mil, enl 1814 for duration War; N C S A & Nelson Papers in McClung Room, Knoxville; Unkn Cem in Washington Co; Unkn.

MAYBERRY, HENRY (1755--3- 1832 Hickman Co); Md Magdalene Corn (--d 1830); Ensign, Hickman Co Mil; T S A; Hickman Co; Unkn.

MAYES, JAMES (--d 1858 Hamblen Co); Md   (   ); "James Mayes came from Shelby, N C 1830, served War of 1812, d 1858"; Tombstone Data; Kidwell's Ridge Bapt Cem, Hamblen Co; Govt mkr.

MEEK, ADAM (1746--7-8-1828 Jefferson Co); Md Martha Wallace (--11-24-1831); War of 1812; W D; Strawberry Plains Cem, Jefferson Co; Pvt mkr. (Also Rev War)

MEEK, JOSEPH (6-1-1788--10-4-1851 Knox Co); Md Rebecca Sawyers 3-24-1814 (5-7-1792--8-9-1870); Pvt, Capt John Bayless' Co, Col Sam Wear's 1st Regt E T V, 9-23-1813--12-22-1813; W D & T S A; Washington Pres Cem on Washington Pike, Knox Co; Pvt mkr.

MEIGS, RETURN JONATHAN (12-17-1734--1-28-1823 Rhea Co); Md 1-Joanna Winborn 2-14-1764 (   ), 2-Grace Starr-Rising Fawn 12-22-1774 (--d 10-10-1807); Agent to Cherokee Indians, 1801, at Hiwassee Garrison 1807--1817; W D & T S A; Hiwassee Garrison Cem, Rhea Co; Unmkd. (Also Rev War)

MEIGS, TIMOTHY (--d 1816 Hiwassee Garrison, Rhea Co); Md Jane Ross (   ); War of 1812; T S A; Hiwassee Garrison Cem, Rhea Co; Unmkd. (Son of R J Meigs)

MERRILL, Dr AYES PHILLIP (4-17-1798--11-3-1873 Shelby Co); Md Sarah Jane Moore (8-8-1808--1-11-1849); Physician in War of 1812; Record Bk Elmwood Cem in Memphis, Shelby Co; Elmwood Cem in Memphis, Shelby Co; Govt mkr.

MILBURN, JONATHAN (1775--8- 1811 Greene Co); Md Nancy Ann 10-10-1796 (1779--1855); Pvt, Capt John Caldwell's Battln Ky Mtd Vol, also Pvt, Capt Jeremiah Briscoe's Co, Maj Gen Charles Scott's Brig, 7-8-1794--10-26-1794; W D & Ky S A; Meth Cem at Milburnton, Greene Co; Unmkd.

MILLARD, ABIA (3-7-1789--1-17-1846 Sullivan Co); Md Mary Weaver (c 1791--3-23-1884 aged 92-5-3 days); Pvt, Capt George Keyes' Co, Col Wm Lillard's 2nd Regt E T V, 10-12-1813--2-8-1814; W D & T S A; Weaver's Union Cem, Sullivan Co; Pvt mkr.

MILLARD, SAMUEL (7-3-1786--2-10-1862 Sullivan Co); Md Alice Morrell (1-26-1790--1-10-1865); Pvt, Capt George Keyes' Co, Col Wm Lillard's 2nd Regt E T V, 10-12-1813--2-8-1814, served 3 mos & 28 days - pay $31.22; W D & T S A; Weaver's Union Ch Cem, Sullivan Co; Pvt mkr. (Brother of Abia Millard)

MILLER, GEORGE WASHINGTON (1791-- 1869 Carter Co); Md Susan Masengill 1824 (1806--1906 aged 100 yrs); Pvt, Lieut Dodge, Capt Henry Poston's Co Mtd Mil, Missouri Terr, 8-12-1814--10-12-1814; W D & Masengill's Gen; likely in Carter Co; Unkn.

MILLER, JACOB (6-30-1779--11-18-1858 Washington Co); Md 1-Elizabeth Range 7-21-1798 (1-31-1777--8-25-1843), 2-Mrs Hannah Bowman Broyles 1845 (   ); Pvt, Capt George Keyes' Co, Col Wm Lillard's 2nd Regt E T V, 10-12-1813--2-8-1814; W D & T S A; Mt Bethel Christian Ch Cem, near Washington-Greene Co line; Pvt mkr.

MILLER, JAMES (--killed 11-9-1813 Battle of Talledega, Ala); Md (   ); Pvt, Capt Robt Jetton's Co, Col John Allcorn's Regt W T Cav, 9-24-1813--11-9-1813 killed; W D & T S A; likely in Ala; Unkn.

MILLER, MARK (--liv 1828 List Giles Co); Md   (   ); served Tenn Mil; P D & 2400 Pensioners, Armstrong; likely Giles Co; Unkn.

MILLER, PETER (6-22-1792--4-27-1863 Washington Co); Md Mary Hunt 8-27-1817 (10-10-1798--5-19-1852); 1st Lieut, Capt Andrew Lawson's Co, Col Wm Johnson's 3rd Regt E T Drftd Mil, 9-20-1814--5-3-1815; W D & T S A; Hunt Fam Cem S Johnson City, Washington Co; Pvt mkr.

MILLER, PLEASANT MOORMAN (1773--4-26-1849 Gibson Co); Md Mary Louiza Blount 1801 (--2-14-1847); Pvt, Capt Wm Walker's Co, Col John Williams' Regt E T V, 1-21-1812--3-25-1813; W D & T S A; Miller Fam Cem at Trenton, Gibson Co; Pvt mkr.

MILLER, SAMUEL (--d Chattanooga, Hamilton Co); Md (   ); Pvt, Col John Williams' 39th Regt U S Inf; Pensioned 7-9-1814; W D & P D; National Cem in Chattanooga, Hamilton Co; Govt mkr. (Also Rev War - Tombstone says "Soldier of the Revolution".)

MILLIKEN, ELIHU (12-6-1785--12-21-1864 Grainger Co); Md 1-Nancy Hurst 9-29-1807 (   ), 2-Cynthia Lee 2-20-1838 (   ); Capt, Col Wm Johnson's 3rd Regt E T Drftd Mil, 9-20-1814--5-3-1815; W D & T S A; Milliken Fam Cem near Lea Springs, Grainger Co; Pvt mkr. (He was a Bapt minister.)

MILLS, GIDEON (--liv 1828 List Davidson Co, d 5-29-1829 Davidson Co); Md   (   ); served 1st Regt Riflemen; P D & 2400 Pensioners, Armstrong; likely Davidson Co; Unkn.

MITCHELL, GREENBERRY (9-28-1786--2-20-1860 Grainger Co); Md Susanna Vineyard (11-10-1787--2-5-1875); War of 1812; Goodspeed E T H & W D; Mitchell Fam Cem, Grainger Co; Pvt mkr.

MITCHELL, JOHN (--9-6-1841 Marion City, Marion Co); Md Sarah Andrews 12-30-1813 Sevier Co (1790--liv 1851 Marion Co); Pvt, Capt Wm Mitchell's Co, Col Sam Wear's 1st Regt E T V, 9-23-1813--12-31-1813; W D & P D; Marion Co; Unkn.

MITCHELL, JOHN (--d Knox Co); Md Martha Lyon (   ); War of 1812; Goodspeed Knox Co; likely Knox Co; Unkn.

MITCHELL, RICHARD (--d Hawkins Co); Md   (   ); Sec to Gov Wm Blount & Clerk Hawkins Co, 1790-1815; Blount's Journal & Hawkins Co Records; Mitchell Fam Cem, Hawkins Co; Unkn.

MITCHELL, SAMUEL B (1795--8-7-1854 Marion Co); Md Margaret T Stewart 8-14-1823 Marion Co (--liv 1855 Marion Co); Pvt, Capt Wm Mitchell's Co, Col Sam Wear's 1st Regt E T V, 9-23-1813--12-31-1813; W D & P D; Marion Co; likely Pvt mkr.

MITCHELL, WILLIAM (7-15-1775--11-12-1823 Sevier Co); Md Eve Knester 10-26-1797 (3-9-1776--liv 1851 Bradley Co); Capt, Col Sam Wear's 1st Regt E T V, 9-27-1813--4-4-1814; W D & P D & T S A; likely in Sevier Co; Unkn.

MODENA, HENRY (1792--1-15-1847 Franklin Co); Md Lucy A E Duncan 9-3-1835 (7-30-1817--1-15-1879); Pvt, Capt John Rothwell's Co, 7th Regt, 4th Brig Va Troops, disch 2-22-1815 at Capt Carter's; Va S A; Franklin Co; Pvt mkr.

MOIRS, WILLIAM (--d 4-8-1814 at Ft Williams, Ala); Md (   ); Pvt, Capt Jacob Hoyal's Co, Col Ewen Allison's E T Mil, enl 1-10-1814; W D & T S A; at Ft Williams, Ala; Unmkd.

MONTGOMERY, ALEXANDER (--d Roane Co); Md   (   ); War of 1812; W D & Roane Co Hist- Wells; Winton's Chapel near Rockwood, Roane Co; Pvt mkr. (Also Rev War in Va)

MONTGOMERY, JAMES (1-21-1797--2-10-1880 Monroe Co); Md Dorcas Miller Russell 12-30-1817 (2-26-1794--1-20-1870); Pvt, Capt Wm Walker's Co, Col John Williams Regt U S Inf 1-12-1812--7-8-1814; W D & T S A; Glen Rock Creek Cecedar Pres Cem, Monroe Co, near Sweetwater; Pvt mkr.

MONTGOMERY, JOHN (1784--8-9-1860 Roane Co); Md Mary Winton (10-16-1780--11-21-1831); War of 1812; T S A; Winton Chapel Cem near Rockwood, Roane Co; Pvt mkr.

MONTGOMERY, JOSIAH (--d Roane Co); Md Mary Lewis (   ); War of 1812 from Roane Co; Goodspeed Knox Co & Wells List of 1812 Soldiers; likely in Roane Co; Unkn.

MONTGOMERY, LEMUAL P (--3-27-1814 Battle of Tohopeka); Single; Maj under Col John Williams' 39th Regt U S Inf; W D & T S A; Indian Mound in Campbell Co near Jacksboro; Pvt mkr.

MONTGOMERY, SAMUEL (1785--5-23-1843 Blount Co); Md Elizabeth
Gillespie 1808 (1789--7-11-1859); Pvt, Capt James Gillespie's Co,
Col Sam Wear's 1st Regt E T V, 9-23-1813--12-31-1813; W D & T S A;
Montgomery Fam Cem near Baker's Creek in Blount Co; Govt mkr.

MOODY, GEORGE (1762-- 1820 Grainger Co); Md 1-Mary Hughes 1787
(   ), 2-Rachel Mitchell 1797-8 (   ); Clerk Grainger
Co 1812-1820; Grainger Co Records; Pres Cem at Rutledge, Grainger
Co; Unmkd - exact site unkn. (Also Rev War)

MOORE, DANIEL (1789--d likely Lincoln Co); Md Elizabeth
1816 (1796--1876); War of 1812; Goodspeed Lincoln Co; likely in
Lincoln Co; Unkn.

MOORE, ELIJAH (?- 1792-- 1834 Jefferson Co); Md Mary McClanahan
(1794--1859 aged 65 yrs); War of 1812 & Capt, Tenn Mil; Goodspeed
E T H Jefferson Co; likely Jefferson Co; Unkn.

MOORE, EPHRAIM (7-1-1793--8-5-1875 Hamblen Co); Md Nancy Lane
(   ); War of 1812; Burnett's Bapt Preachers, p-377; Moore
Fam Cem near Russellville, Hamblen Co; Pvt mkr.

MOORE, JAMES (--killed 11-2-1813 Tallushatchee, Ala); Md
(   ); Pvt, Capt Alex McKeen's Co, Col John Allcorn's Regt
W T Cav, 9-24-1813--11-2-1813 killed; W D & T S A; likely in Ala;
Unkn.

MOORE, JOHN (1780-- 1837 Maury Co); Md Nancy Ann Rogers 1806
(1790--8-26-1846); Pvt, Capt E Robinson's Co, 3rd Regt U S Inf,
11-13-1812--5-13-1815; W D; Maury Co; Pvt mkr.

MOORE, MITCHELL R (--liv 1883 Gallatin, Sumner Co); Md
(   ); War of 1812; P D & W D; likely in Sumner Co; Unkn.
(Pension #9,186)

MOORE, ROBERT (--killed 11-9-1813 Talledega, Ala); Md
(   ); 1st Lieut, Capt Thomas Bradley's Co, Vol Cav, Col John
Allcorn's Regt W T Mil, 9-24-1813--11-9-1813 killed; W D & T S A
& Tenn Soldiers of War of 1812, Vol 1- Allen; likely in Ala; Unkn.

MOORE, WILLIAM (1789-- 1853 in Tenn); Md   (   );
Pvt, N C Mil; N C S A & Texas 1812 Records; Unkn in Tenn; Unkn.

MOORE, WILLIAM (9-28-1786--c 1875 Lincoln Co); Md 1-Elizabeth Law-
son (   ), 2-Nancy Holman (   ); Capt, 2nd Regt, under
Gen William Pillow W T V, 9-26-1813--12-10-1813; W D & T S A;
Moore Fam Cem near Mulberry, Lincoln Co; Pvt mkr. (Virginia
Moore Willhite was a Real Daughter, member of Tenn Society.)

MORELAND, WILLIAM Sr (--d 1854 Carter Co); Md   (   );
Pvt, Capt Henry Hunter's Co, Col Wm Johnson's 3rd Regt E T Drftd
Mil; W D & T S A; Moreland Fam Cem in Carter Co; Pvt mkr.

MORGAN, GIDEON Jr (8-6-1778--9-18-1851 McMinn Co); Md Margaret Sevier 10-27-1813 (10-8-1799--3-25-1862); Organized the Regt of Cherokees of which he was Col, 1814; W D & T S A; Pres Cem at Calhoun, McMinn Co; Pvt mkr. (Mrs American Cherokee Morgan Rogers was Real Daughter Tenn U S D of 1812.)

MORGAN, GIDEON Sr (--d 1840 Roane Co); Md Patience Cogswell ( ); served in 26th Regt War of 1812; 1812 Pensioner in Monroe Co; W D & P D; Kingston Cem, Roane Co; Pvt mkr.

MORGAN, ROBERT (--liv 1883 Pensioner in Arcadia, Sullivan Co); Md ( ); War of 1812; P D; likely in Sullivan Co; Unkn.

MORGAN, RUFUS (2-19-1781--8-26-1826 Roane Co); Md Elizabeth Trigg 1809 at Abingdon, Va (--11-19-1859); Capt, Co in Creek War; Knox Co Hist; Kingston Cem, Roane Co; Pvt mkr.

MORRIS, JOSEPH (1790-- 1842 Knox Co); Md Rachel Waters in N C (--d 1865); War of 1812; Goodspeed Knox Co; likely Knox Co; Unkn.

MORRISON, EDWARD (11-22-1789--10-7-1865 Wayne Co); Md 1- ( ), 2-Elizabeth Toombs Butler (wid) (--Pensioner #15,832); Fifer, Capt George Winton's Co, Col --- , 11-17-1814--5-12-1815 disch at Washington, Rhea Co; Collier Fam Cem, S Waynesboro, Wayne Co; Pvt mkr.

MORRISSAT, JOSEPH (c 1786--aft 1847 Hawkins Co); Single 1840 List; Pvt, Capt John A Rogers Co, 24th U S Inf, 9-5-1812--8-20-1815; Canadian Campaign, wounded by bayonet 12-19-1813 at Ft Niagara; W D & T S A & P D & 2400 Pensioners, Armstrong; likely Morrissat's Chapel Cem, Hawkins Co; Unmkd. (Pensioned in 1816, #1291 & B L Wt)

MORROW, JOHN (--liv 1828 List Franklin Co); Md ( ); served in Tenn Mil; P D & 2400 Pensioners, Armstrong; likely Franklin Co; Unkn.

MORTON, THOMAS (--liv 1840 List aged 45 yrs Gibson Co); Md ( ); War of 1812; pensioned in Gibson Co; P D & 2400 Pensioners, Armstrong; likely Gibson Co; Unkn.

MOSBY, JOHN (1791-- 1837 Rutherford Co); Md ( ); Corp, Capt Byrd Nance's Co, 2nd Div W T Mil; T S A & Texas 1812 Records; likely Rutherford Co; Unkn.

MOSS, BENJAMIN T (1792-- 1849 Sumner Co); Md Elizabeth C Duke (1794--); War of 1812 in Va; Goodspeed Sumner Co & Va S A; Sumner Co; Unkn.

MOULTON, Lieut (--killed 3-27-1814 Tohopeka); Md ( ); Lieut, Col John Williams' 39th Regt U S Inf; W D & T S A; likely in Ala; Unkn.

MOWERY, SAMUEL (--d Bradley Co); Md   (   ); Pvt, Capt John Chiles' Co, Mtd Gunmen, Col John Brown's 2nd Regt E T Mtd Inf, 1-10-1814--5-25-1814; W D & Edwards Acct Bk; Bean Fam Cem in western part Bradley Co; Unkn.

MULLINS, ANTHONY (--liv 1828 List Lincoln Co); Md ( ); served in Washington's Cav; P D & 2400 Pensioners, Armstrong; likely in Lincoln Co; Unkn.

MURPHY, ROBERT (1757--5-15-18 Knox Co); Md Martha McNeal 1785 (1768--1847); War of 1812; French Broad-Holston Hist- Rothrock & Fam records; Old Murphy Fam Cem on Washington Pike, Knox Co; Pvt mkr. (Also Rev War)

MYERS, JOHN (--d Campbell Co); Md   (   ); War of 1812 Grainger Co; Goodspeed E T H Grainger Co; likely in Campbell Co; Unkn.

MYNATT, RICHARD (5-4-1772-- 1850 Union Co); Md Elizabeth Tobler c 1810 ( ); Srgt, Capt Daniel Price's Co, Col Sam Wear's 1st Regt E T V; W D & T S A; Mynatt Fam Cem near Luttrell, Union Co; Unmkd.

MYNATT, MARTIN (12-25-1794--12-23-1873 Knox Co); Md Isabella Roberts 5-20-1815 ( ); War of 1812; French Broad-Holston Hist- Rothrock; likely in Knox Co; likely Pvt mkr. (The service given for M L Mynatt is Srgt Co I, 1st Tenn Inf - This does not sound like service in 1812. He could be bur in Union Co.)

MYNATT, SILAS (--d Knox Co); Md   (   ); Pvt, Capt Daniel Price's Co, Col Sam Wear's 1st Regt E T V; W D & T S A; Mynatt Fam Cem in Union Co; Unkn.

MYNATT, THOMAS (--d likely Knox Co); Md   (   ); War of 1812; W D & French Broad-Holston Hist- Rothrock; Mynatt Fam Cem in Knox Co; Govt mkr.

MYNATT, WILLIAM C (1788--9-14-1837 Union Co); Md Harriett A Brown 6-27-1816 ( ); Aide-de-campe to Gen John Cocke in War of 1812, 9-25-1813--1-14-1814; Goodspeed Knox Co; Mynatt Fam Cem in Union Co; Unkn.

McADDON, THOMAS (1793-- 1825 Nashville, Davidson Co); Md ( ); Pvt, Capt Wm Lauderdale's Co, 1st Regt W T Mil; T S A & Texas 1812 Records; Nashville, Davidson Co; Unkn.

McADOO, JOHN (--d aft 1828 Anderson Co, near Clinton); Md Mary Ann Gibbs ( ); War of 1812; French Broad-Holston Hist- Rothrock; likely in Knoxville, Knox Co; Unkn.

McALPIN, ROBERT (--d in Tenn); Md ( ); Capt, Col Wm Lillard's 2nd Regt E T V, 10-14-1813--2-8-1814, mustered out Greeneville; T S A & Leaves from the Family Tree- Allen, 10-28-1938; likely in Greene Co; Unkn. (Robert McAlpin was Minister of Pres Church - lived in McMinn & Greene Co.)

McANNALLY, CHARLES (--d Knox Co); Md Elizabeth Moore ( ); Trustee Knox Co, 1806-12 & Sheriff Knox Co, 1812-21; Knox Co Records; likely in Knox Co; Unkn.

McCALEB, ANDREW (12-25-1788--7-9-1860 Rhea Co); Md Ann Boyd ( ); War of 1812, Battle of Tohopeka; W D & Goodspeed E T H; McCaleb Fam Cem in Rhea Co; Pvt mkr.

McCALEB, ARCHIBALD (--d 1813 en route to War of 1812); Md ( ); War of 1812; Goodspeed E T H & Rhea Co Hist- Campbell; Cem at Head of Turkey Creek, Knox Co; Unkn.

McCALLIE, THOMAS (--1859 Hamilton Co); Md Mary Hooke ( ); War of 1812 & Col Rhea Co Mil; T S A; Chattanooga, Hamilton Co; Pvt mkr.

McCANDLESS, ROBERT A (--aft 3-23-1852 Bradley Co); Md ( ); 1st Srgt, Capt James Berry's Co, Maj Thomas Clark's Battln E T Mil; W D & P D & Edwards Acct Bk & B L Wt; likely on Candy's Creek, Bradley Co; Unkn. (His B L Wt dated 3-23-1852 on Candy's Creek, Bradley Co.)

McCARDELL, JACOB (--killed in battle 1812-14); Md Rebecca Ball 8-18-1814 Washington Co (--aft 1816); War of 1812, killed; W D & Washington Co Ct Minutes 7-18-1816 says "Jacob McCardell was killed in late War", Inv dated 1815 Washington Co; likely where killed; Unkn.

McCLANAHAN, MATTHEW (--1835 Rutherford Co); Md Bradley ( ); War of 1812; Goodspeed Rutherford Co Hist; likely in Rutherford Co; Unkn. (Served as Col in Seminole War)

McCLANAHAN, SAMUEL (--aft 1835, aged over 100 yrs, Rutherford Co); Md ( ); Maj under Gen Jackson, War of 1812; Goodspeed Rutherford Co Hist; likely in Rutherford Co; Unkn. (Also Maj in Rev War)

McCLUNG, CHARLES (5-13-1761--8-19-1835 Knoxville, Knox Co); Md Margaret White 10-28-1790 (4-8-1771--8-27-1827); 1st Clk Knox Co 1792 & U S Comm Cherokee Boundary Line; Knox Co Records & U S A; Old Gray Cem in Knoxville, Knox Co; Pvt mkr.

McCLUNG, PATRICK (5-5-1793--8-10-1869 Blount Co); Md 1-Margaret Cowan 5-30-1821 (6-19-1802--9-3-1838), 2-Hannah Graham Swan 7-18-1839 (7-12-1803--3-14-1898); Pvt, Capt James Gillespie's Co, Col Sam Wear's 1st Regt E T V, 9-23-1813--12-31-1813; W D & T S A; Baker's Creek Pres Cem in Blount Co; Pvt mkr.

McCLOUD, JAMES (--d likely in Knox Co); Md - one James McCloud md Polly McCloud, 9-30-1817 Knox Co (   ); War of 1812; French Broad-Holston Hist- Rothrock; likely Knox Co; Unkn.

McCONNELL, ARCHIBALD (1-28-1795--3-15-1847 Marshall Co); Md Eliza Houston 4-19-1819 (8-31-1799--1-14-1884); Pvt, Capt Bird L Hurt's Co, Col Wm Metcalf's 1st Regt W T Mil, 11-13-1814--5-13-1815; W D & T S A; Lewisburg, Marshall Co; Pvt mkr.

McCONNELL, JOHN (12-7-1779--7-21-1858 Blount Co); Md Anna Stewart 12-25-1815 (1-21-1793--12-14-1853); Pvt, Capt John Trimble's Co, Maj Wm Russell's Battln, Gen John Coffee's Brig, 10-5-1814--3-5-1815; W D & T S A; Big Springs Pres Cem in Blount Co; Pvt mkr.

McCRACKEN, SAMUEL (--d aft 1852 Bradley Co); Md   (   ); Pvt, Capt Allen S Bacon's Co, Col John Brown's Regt E T V; W D & Edwards Acct Bk & B L Wt; Henegar Cem at Charleston, Bradley Co; Pvt mkr.

McCRORY, Col THOMAS (--6- 1818 Sullivan Co); Md   (   ); Col, 2nd Regt W T Mil, 10-4-1813--1-4-1814 wounded; W D & T S A; Weaver's Union Cem in Sullivan Co; Rev War mkr & Iron Plaque. (Also Rev War - The coffin-shaped iron plaque was made at Kings Iron Works in Sullivan Co.)

McCUISTON, JAMES (1758-- 1826 Bedford Co); Md   (   ); Pvt, Capt Robert McCuiston's Co, 5th Regt N C Mil, 1814-15; N C S A & Texas 1812 Records; Bedford Co; Unkn.

McDONALD, ANDREW Jr (1788-- 1879 Hamilton Co); Md Sarah Kelly 1816 (   ); Pvt, Capt Uriah Allison's Co, & Capt Miles Vernon's Co & Capt James Anderson's Co, 24th Regt U S Inf at Ft Meigs, Ala; T S A & Roane Co Hist- Wells; McDonald Fam Cem near Ooltewah, Hamilton Co; Govt mkr. (Likely same as McDonnough below)

McDONALD, HENRY B (1794-- 1873 Smith Co); Md   (   ); Pvt, Capt James Tubbs' Co, 2nd Regt W T Mil; T S A; Carthage, Smith Co; Unkn.

McDONNOUGH, ANDREW Jr (5-25-1788--1-2-1879 James Co (now Hamilton); Md Sarah Kelly 10-13-1816 Bledsoe Co (12-11-1785--11-17-1883); Pvt, Capt James Anderson's Co, Col John Williams' 24th Regt U S Inf, also in Capt Robt O Butler's Co & Capt Wm O'Dair's; disch June 1813, 18 mos; again, in Capt Miles Vernon's Co Tenn Mil, enl 11-13-1814--5-13-1815; W D & P D; McDonnough Fam Cem near Ooltewah, Hamilton Co; Govt mkr dedicated 1939 by U S D 1812.

McELDUFF, Lieut DANIEL (--liv 1828 List Franklin Co); Md (   ); served U S Army, trans from Ga; P D & 2400 Pensioners, Armstrong; likely Franklin Co; Unkn.

McELWEE, WILLIAM (6-28-1798-- 1855 Roane Co); Md Lucinda Eblen 3-29-1829 (3-6-1811--12-3-1904); Pvt, Capt Allen Bacon's Co Mtd Inf, Col John Brown's Regt E T V, 9-3-1813--; W D & T S A; McElwee Fam Cem near Rockwood, Roane Co; Pvt mkr.

McEWEN, DAVID (7-17-1756-- 1821 Williamson Co); Md Margaret Erwin 12-21-1780 (7-8-1761--1822); Lieut, 21st Regt Tenn Mil, 1813; John Sevier's Comm Bk; Williamson Co; Pvt mkr.

McEWEN, J L (1794--4-15-1879 Williamson Co); Md Tabitha Barfield 1821 (--d 12-28-1853); War of 1812; Goodspeed Williamson Co; likely Williamson Co; Unkn.

McEWEN, Maj JAMES (4-28-1782--8-26-1821 Williamson Co); Md Elizabeth Goff (1-29-1785--1-4-1818); Capt, Col Thomas Hart Benton's 2nd Regt W T Mil, & Maj, Col Wm Pillow's 2nd Regt W T V; T S A; Williamson Co; Pvt mkr.

McFARLAND, ROBERT (--1844 Hamblen Co); Md 1-Miss Barton (   ), 2-Mary Ann Scott (--1866); War of 1812 as Recruiting Off for U S on Canadian Border; U S A; Hamblen Co; Unkn.

McGAUGHEY, JOHN (7-12-1792--5-20-1874 Greene Co); Md Hannah Robinson 1812 (1-29-1792--1-12-1864); Pvt, Capt Joseph Kirk's Co, also Capt Christopher Cook's Co, Col Wm Johnson's 3rd Regt E T Drftd Mil, 9-20-1814--5-3-1815; W D & T S A; Mt Bethel Pres Cem in Greeneville, Greene Co; Pvt mkr.

McGAVOCK, JACOB (9-20-1790--12-8-1878 Davidson Co); Md Louise C Grundy 5-11-1819 (1798--1878); Pvt, Capt David S Deaderick's Co, Gen Andrew Jackson's Regt, enl 9-1813, wounded 1-21-1814; W D & T S A; Nashville, Davidson Co; Pvt mkr.

McGEE, RICHARD (1775-- 1865 Gibson Co); Md Elizabeth Gentry 1803 in Ky (1787--); Capt in War of 1812; T S A & Goodspeed Shelby Co; likely in Gibson Co; Unkn.

McGHEE, BARCLAY (8-15-1760--8-17-1819 Blount Co); Md Jane McClennahan (5-17-1767--9-8-1835); Contractor for Supplies for Gen Jackson in War of 1812; W D & T S A; New Providence Pres Cem in Maryville, Blount Co; Pvt mkr. (He gave the land for New Providence Church and Cemetery.)

McGILL, WILLIAM (--d Blount Co); Md Mary McLin 2-22-1837 (   ); Pvt, Capt James Gillespie's Co, Col Sam Wear's 1st Regt E T V, 9-23-1813--12-31-1813; W D & T S A & P D; likely at Logan's Chapel Meth Cem in Blount Co; Unkn. (Mary McGill's Pension wid #110,661.)

McGREGOR, JOHN (8-29-1794--7-4-1835 Lebanon, Wilson Co); Md Mulberry Donelson 1825 (1806--1836); Srgt, Capt Abner Pearce's Co, Creek War; T S A; Old Jefferson Cem, Rutherford Co; Pvt mkr. (There must be an error here.)

McINTURF, ISRAEL (--d Unicoi Co); Md Elizabeth Webb 10-29-1828 Carter Co (   ); Pvt, Capt Adam Winsell's Co, Col Ewen Allison's Regt E T Drftd Mil, 1-5-1814--5-28-1814; W D & T S A; Fam Cem in Unicoi Co; Unkn.

McINTURF, THOMAS Sr (8-2-1792--3-21-1881 Unicoi Co); Md Nancy Scott 6-1-1817 Carter Co (12-23-1796--4-25-1881); Pvt, Capt Adam Winsell's Co, Col Ewen Allison's Regt E T Drftd Mil, 1-5-1814--5-18-1814; W D & T S A; Peebles Fam Cem in Unicoi Co; Pvt mkr.

McINTURF, WILLIAM (--d Unicoi Co); Md   (   ); Pvt, Capt Vashon's Co, 24th Regt U S Inf, at Battle of Tohopeka, 1814, disch 3-10-1817; W D & Nelson Papers in McClung Room, Knoxville; likely in Unicoi Co; Unkn.

McKAIN, SAMUEL (--liv 1883 Hendersonville, Sumner Co); Md (   ); War of 1812 Pension #15,276; W D & P D; likely in Hendersonville, Sumner Co; Unkn.

McKAMEY, DAVID (--d 1858 aged 64 yrs Blount Co); Md Mary Simons 9-8-1812 (1791--11-29-1873); Capt, Col Wm Johnson's 3rd Regt E T Drftd Mil, 9-29-1814--5-18-1815; W D & T S A; Cecedar Pres Cem, now West Maryville, Blount Co; Pvt mkr.

McKENZIE, MALCOMB (--liv 1828 List Humphreys Co); Md (   ); War of 1812; P D & 2400 Pensioners, Armstrong; likely in Humphreys Co; Unkn.

McKINNEY, Dr CHARLES (1788 Ky --1864 Lincoln Co); Md Mary Russell 1810 (1790--1863); Surgeon in War of 1812; Goodspeed Lincoln Co; Fayetteville, Lincoln Co; Pvt mkr.

McKINNEY, JAMES (--1862 Marshall Co); Md Temperance Rowe in Lincoln Co (   ); War of 1812; Goodspeed Marshall Co; likely in Marshall Co; Unkn.

McKINNIS, JAMES (b Scotland --4-24-1868 Trousdale Co); Md (   ); served with 5 bros with Andrew Jackson, War of 1812; Goodspeed Trousdale Co; Trousdale Co; Pvt mkr.

McLEOD, ABNER (--liv 1840 List aged 44 yrs Carter Co); Md Ruth Drake 5-19-1821 Carter Co (   ); War of 1812, pensioned Carter Co; P D & 2400 Pensioners, Armstrong; likely in Carter Co; Unkn.

McLIN, BENJAMIN (--12-29-1849 Washington Co); Md Hannah Miller 9-10-1844 Washington Co (c 1808--liv 1883 at Locust Mt, Washington Co); Pvt, Capt Henry McCray's Co, Col Ewen Allison's Regt E T Drftd Mil, 1-5-1814, disch by Surgeon 1-24-1814; W D & T S A & P D; Unkn Cem near Locust Mt, Washington Co; Unkn. (McLin was likely wounded in some battle in Jan 1814, therefore discharged; Hannah McLin Wid #16,379 Pension.)

McLIN, WILLIAM (--d likely Washington Co); Md   (   ); Capt, Col Wm Lillard's 2nd Regt E T V, 10-12-1813--2-8-1814; W D & T S A; Unkn Cem in Washington Co; Unkn.

McMACKIN, JAMES (--liv 1883 Hawes Cross Rds, Washington Co); Md Peggy Lloyd 8-1-1820 (--liv 1883 Washington Co); Pvt, Capt Joseph Kirk's Co & Capt Christopher Cook's Co, Col Wm Johnson's 3rd Regt E T Drftd Mil, 9-20-1814--5-3-1815; W D & T S A & B L Wt; Cem near Milburnton, Greene Co; Unkn.

McMANUS, JOSEPH (--d 4-13-1814 in service); Md ( ); Pvt, Capt Joseph Duncan's Co, Col Sam Bunch's Regt attd to Col Ewen Allison's Regt, 1-10-1814--4-13-1814 died; W D & Blount Co Hist- Burns; likely where died; Unkn.

McMILLAN, ALEXANDER (8-12-1749 Ireland --1837 Knox Co); Md Margaret 1778 (4-2-1762--1836); Pvt, War of 1812, at N O; W D & T S A; Caledonia Pres Cem in Knox Co; Pvt mkr. (Also Rev War)

McMILLAN, DAVID (--d likely Knox Co); Md ( ); War of 1812; French Broad-Holston Hist- Rothrock; likely Knox Co; Unkn.

McMILLAN, HUGH (1784--4- 1847 Stewart Co); Md Margaret McLeod 1-30-1811 (1793--1878); Srgt, Capt Abner Pearce's Co, Maj Woodfolk's Regt W T Mil, 9-20-1814--; W D & T S A; Stewart Co; Pvt mkr.

McMINN, Gov JOSEPH (6-27-1758--11-17-1824 McMinn Co); Md 1-Hannah Cooper 5-9-1785 (6-20-1760--2-27-1811), 2-Rebecca Kinkead 1-5-1813 (10-7-1793--1-11-1815), 3-Nancy Williams (4-22-1770--); S W Terr Assmbly 1794, Constitutional Conv 1796, Hawkins Co Assm 1796, State Senate 1797-1801-03-09, Gov Tenn 1815-19; T S A; Pres Cem at Calhoun, McMinn Co; Monument erected by State of Tenn.

McMINN, JOSEPH (1790--7- 1846 Hawkins Co); Md (--liv 1846-7); Pvt, Capt Slatton's Co, E T Mil; T S A; McMinn Fam Cem near Church Hill, Hawkins Co; Unkn. (Nephew of Gov McMinn.)

McMURRY, SAMUEL (--d 2-14-1815 in service); Md ( ); Pvt, Capt Jehu Stephens' Co Mtd Gunmen, Brig Gen John Coffee's Brig, 10-6-1814--2-14-1815 died; W D & T S A; likely where died; Unkn.

McNABB, ABSALOM (1-27-1779--8-10-1858 Blount Co); Md Mary Lusk 9-28-1803 (3-25-1780--3-4-1849); Pvt, Capt Joseph Duncan's Co, Col Sam Bunch's Regt E T Drftd Mil, 1-10-1814--5-10-1814, attd to Col Ewen Allison's Regt, transfrd to Capt Edward Buchanan's Co, same Regt, 5-10-1814; W D & T S A & Blount Co Hist- Burns; Baker's Creek Pres Cem, Blount Co; Pvt mkr.

McNABB, WILLIAM S (8-3-1786--7-7-1825 Blount Co); Md Margaret Mitchell 6-3-1801 ( ); Pvt, Capt John Trimble's Co, Maj Wm Russell's Battln, Gen John Coffee's Brig; W D; Clark's Grove Cumberland Pres Cem in Blount Co; Govt mkr.

McNAIRY, JOHN (1762-- 1837 Nashville, Davidson Co); Md ( ); Terr Judge 1790 apptd by George Washington, Tenn Constitutional Conv 1796; T S A; Old City Cem in Nashville, Davidson Co; Pvt mkr.

McNEAL, JOHN (--c 11-20-1814 in camp); Md Ann Good c 1801 (--d aft 1815); Pvt & Corp, Capt Andrew Lawson's Co, Col Wm Johnson's 3rd Regt E T Drftd Mil, 9-20-1814--11-20-1814 died, Gen Nath Taylor's Brig; W D & T S A & Washington Co Ct Minutes Oct 1816, p-344 Bk 1809-17; Dep of Jacob Brown & Southey Nelson who saw him bur; likely where died; Unkn. (McNeal is bur likely in Ala, or where the Co was 11-20-1814.)

McNUTT, BENJAMIN (--c 1857 Knox Co); Md   Alexander (dau John Alexander) (   ); Repr, Greene Co, Etowah Campaign 1793 vs Cherokees; T S A & Hist Lebanon Pres Church- Ramsey; McNutt Fam Cem N bank French Broad River above Knoxville, Knox Co; Unkn.

McNUTT, GEORGE (1751 Ireland --1-5-1823 Knoxville, Knox Co); Md 1-Isabella Callison (   ), 2-Catherine Kain 11-5-1792 (   ), 3-Jean Anderson 10-10-1797 (--aft 1823); Commissioner of Knoxville 10-3-1791, and J P in 1st Knox Co Ct 1792; T S A & Knox Co Records & Hist of Lebanon Pres Church- Ramsey; McNutt Fam Cem on N side Tenn River, Knox Co; Pvt mkr.

McQUEEN, WILLIAM (McQUON) (1778--5-16-1860 Johnson Co); Md Rebecca Gwinn 9-4-1800 (11-13-1777--11-22-1852); Pvt, Capt Adam Winsell's Co, Col Ewen Allison's Regt E T Drftd Mil, 1-10-1814--5-18-1814; W D & T S A; Johnson Co; Pvt mkr.

McSPADDEN, SAMUEL (10-10-1756--8- 1844 Jefferson Co); Md 1-Sarah Keyes (1798--1850), 2-Nancy Harris (1782--); made powder for Gen Jackson for Battle of N O; Fam Hist; Dandridge Cem near Shepherd Inn, Dandridge, Jefferson Co; Unmkd.

McTEER, MONTGOMERY (--d Blount Co); Md Martha W Bogle 3-21-1835 (   ); Sub for Joseph Utter, Capt David McKamey's Co, Col Wm Johnson's 3rd Regt E T Drftd Mil, 9-29-1814--5-18-1815; W D & T S A; Clover Hill Pres Cem in Blount Co; Unkn.

McTEER, WILLIAM (6-14-1780--5-29-1862 Blount Co); Md 1-Mary McTeer 10-21-1802 (--1-6-1814), 2-Mary Bogle 9-16-1819 (   ); 1st Srgt, Capt Jehu Stephens' Co, Maj John Chiles' Regt, 10-6-1814--4-6-1815; W D & T S A & Notable Men of Tenn- Allison; Eusebia Pres Cem in Blount Co; Pvt mkr. (Maj Will A McTeer, a grandson, has given to posterity a copy of the Muster Roll of Capt Jehu Stephens' Co Mtd Gunmen, E T V.)

NAFF, JONATHAN (1771--8-15-1853 Greene Co); Md 1-Catherine Hoss 8-31-1795 (1775--c 1825), 2-Mrs Elizabeth Matthews 6-2-1828 (   ); Pvt, Capt Francis Register's Co, Col Ewen Allison's Regt E T Drftd Mil; W D & T S A & P D; likely Naff Fam Cem near Limestone in Greene Co; Unkn.

NAIL, ARCHIBALD (--9-20-1814 at Ft Williams, Ala); Md (   ); Pvt, Capt Newlin's Co, Col Philip Pipkin's Regt W T Mil, enl 6-20-1814--9-20-1814 died; W D & T S A; likely at Ft Williams, Ala; Unmkd.

NAVE, ABRAHAM (3-24-1769--11-29-1850 Carter Co); Md Mary Williams c 1794 (1778--5-3-1857); Pvt, Capt Charles Lewis' Co, Col John Brown's Regt E T V Mtd Inf, 1-1-1814--; W D & T S A; Nave (David Hess) Fam Cem near Siam, Carter Co; Govt mkr.

NAVE, JOHN (b Germany --d Knox Co); Md Mary Harrison (   ); served under Jackson in War of 1812; Goodspeed Knox Co; likely in Knox Co; Unkn.

NEELY, CHARLES LYNCH (7-22-1795--10-9-1853 in Tenn); Md Sarah E Wells 12-20-1819 (3-3-1799--7-27-1871); Pvt, Capt Matthew Johnson's Co, 1st Regt W T Mil, 12-20-1813--2-8-1814; W D & T S A; likely in Tenn; Unkn.

NEELY, GEORGE (1761--3-18-1833 Franklin, Williamson Co); Md Rebecca Green 11-15-1782 (1756--12-22-1824); Pvt, Capt James McEwen's Co, Col Thomas Hart Benton's 2nd Regt W T Mil; T S A; Franklin, Williamson Co; Pvt mkr & D A R mkr. (Also Rev War)

NEELEY, JOHN (-- 1867 Williamson Co); Md Elizabeth   1814 (--1872); War of 1812; Goodspeed Williamson Co; likely in Williamson Co; Unkn.

NEIL, JOSEPH (1774--d likely Bedford Co); Md Mary Wallace Thompson c 1796 (1775--1865); Pvt, Capt Brock's Co, Col Sam Bayless' 4th Regt E T Drftd Mil, 11-13-1814--5-18-1815; W D & T S A; likely in Bedford Co; Unkn.

NELSON, DAVID (2-11-1780--9-4-1850 Washington Co); Md (   ); Pvt, Capt Wm Walker's Co, Col John Williams' Regt E T V Mtd Inf, 12-1-1812--3-25-1813; W D; Old City Cem at Jonesboro, Washington Co; Pvt mkr.

NELSON, JOHN (--d Greene Co); Md   (   ); War of 1812; W D; Pleasant Hill Meth Cem on Horse Creek, Greene Co; Govt mkr. ("Mil War of 1812")

NELSON, MATTHEW (--liv 1850 Census in Knoxville, Knox Co); Md Patsy Cannon 8-19-1803 (   ); War of 1812; French Broad-Holston Hist- Rothrock; likely in Knoxville, Knox Co; Unkn.

NELSON, SOUTHEY (--d Knox Co aged 115 yrs); Md 1-   (   ), 2-Miss McClain (   ); Pvt, Capt Andrew Lawson's Co, Col Wm Johnson's 3rd Regt, E T Drftd Mil, 9-20-1814--5-9-1815; W D & T S A & Nelson Papers, McClung Room; Third Creek Bapt Cem, Knox Co; Govt mkr. (Also Rev War)

NELSON, WILLIAM (--d 7-18-1837 Washington Co); Md 1-
(   ), 2-Sarah   2-1828 (--aft 1837); Pvt, Capt Jacob
Tipton's Co, under Gen St Clair in 1791 at St Clair's Defeat by
Indians; Muster Roll Capt Jacob Tipton & P D Old War Invalid Roll
#48225, & Washington Co Ct Minutes; either in Nelson Fam Cem or
Fairview Meth Cem in Washington Co; Unkn.

NEVILS, JOSIAH (1794-- 1854 Williamson Co); Md Sallie Beech 1823
(1809--1852); at Battle of N O, 1815; Goodspeed Williamson Co;
Unkn.

NEWBERRY, JAMES (--liv 1828 List Sumner Co); Md   (   );
served Col Spark's Regt U S A; P D & 2400 Pensioners, Armstrong;
likely in Sumner Co; Unkn.

NEWMAN, JOHN (--liv 1828 List Robertson Co); Md   (   );
served Col Elbert's Regt Va Mil; P D & Va S A & 2400 Pensioners,
Armstrong, trans to Tenn from Va; likely Robertson Co; Unkn.

NICELY, DAVID (--liv 1883 List Meltabarger, Union Co); Md
(   ); War of 1812, Pension #17,875; W D & P D; likely
Union Co; Unkn.

NICKOLS, JOHN (1-17-1788--1879 Monroe Co); Md Elizabeth Shelton
1832 (1811--1879); Pvt, Capt L B Willis' Co, 12th Regt U S Inf;
W D; Sweetwater Cem, Monroe Co; Pvt mkr.

NOLEN, LITTLEBERRY (10-31-1777--3-13-1850 Williamson Co); Md
Rachel   (1775--); Capt, Williamson Co Mil, 1800; John Sevier
Comm Bk; McConico Ch Cem, Nolensville, Williamson Co; Pvt mkr.

NOLEN, WILLIAM (1760--5- 185 Williamson Co); Md Mary Turner
4-25-1810 (1795--); Pvt, Capt Martin's Co, Col Newton's Regt Mtd
Gunmen W T Mil; W D & T S A; Nolensville, Williamson Co; Pvt mkr.

NORWOOD, CHARLES WESLEY CURNAN (3-27-1794--3-26-1888 Blount Co);
Md Melinda George 1-17-1850 (9-1816--1-15-1863); Pvt, Capt Jehu
Stephens' Co, Maj John Chiles' Battln, E T V; 10-6-1814--5-1-1815;
W D & T S A; Baker's Creek Pres Cem, Blount Co; Govt mkr.

O'DELL, WILLIAM (1795--d Cocke Co); Md Margaret Wolfe (1802--); Pvt, Capt James Lillard's Co, Col Wm Lillard's 2nd Regt E T V, 10-13-1813--2-8-1814; W D & T S A & Cocke Co Hist- O'dell; O'dell Fam Cem on Allen Farm, Cocke Co; Unkn.

OLIVE, ISHAM (1775-- 1855 Tenn); Md   (   ); Pvt, Capt John Green's Co N C Mil 1814-15; N C S A & Texas 1812 Records; Red Mound in Tenn; Unkn.

OLIVER, HEZEKIAH (1787-- 1867 Maury Co); Md Mahala Lewis 1822 (1800--1840); War of 1812; Goodspeed Maury Co; in Maury Co; Unkn.

OLIVER, JOHN (1793--2-18-1864 Blount Co); Md Lourena Frazier 4-22-1812 Carter Co (1795--1-24-1888); Pvt, Capt Adam Winsell's Co, Col Ewen Allison's Regt E T Drftd Mil, 1-5-1814--5-26-1814; W D & T S A; Cades Cove Primitive Bapt Cem, Blount Co; Govt mkr.

O'NEAL, DARIUS (c 1764--liv 1840 List aged 76 yrs Cocke Co); Md Mary   (--liv 1852 Bradley Co); War of 1812; W D & Edwards Acct Bk & B L Wt; likely in Cocke Co; Unkn. (O'Neal was pensioned in Cocke Co, but Mary (wid) got B L Wt in 1852 for his services and was liv in Bradley Co.)

ORME, ELI Jr (1788--1-30-1875 Bledsoe (now Cumberland) Co); Md Mary Wilson 9-24-1818 (--liv 8-14-1878 when pensioned); Pvt, Capt Robt Paxton's Co, Col Parker's Regt Ky Mil, 10-12-1814--4-12-1815; P D & Ky S A; Orme Fam Cem in Bledsoe (now Cumberland) Co; Pvt mkr. (Wid got pension 8-14-1878 in Bledsoe Co.)

OVERALL, Capt WILLIAM (--killed 1-22-1793 by Indians at Dripping Spring en route to Ky); Md   (   ); killed by Indians, The Bench- Doublehead; Ramsey's Annals & Acklens Records; The Indians cut Capt Overall's flesh from the bones and carried his scalp and that of his companion, a Mr Burnett, to the Cherokee Nation and had War Dances over them; Overall left 5 children; Unmkd.

OVERHOLSER, JACOB (--bef 1852 Bradley Co); Md Hannah   (--aft 1852 when she got B L Wt in Bradley Co); War of 1812; W D & Edwards Acct Bk & B L Wt; likely in Bradley Co; Unkn.

OVERTON, Judge JOHN (4-9-1766 Va --4-12-1833 Nashville, Davidson Co); Md   (   ); Member of Tenn Supreme Ct, 1811-16; T S A; Nashville, Davidson Co; Pvt mkr.

OVERTON, THOMAS (8-15-1753--2-23-1824 Davidson Co); Md 1-Sarah Woodson in N C, 2-Penelope Holmes (--7-15-1843); served with Gen Jackson in War of 1812; W D & Fam Data; Overton Fam Cem near Bank in Old Hickory, Davidson Co; Pvt mkr. (Also Rev War, Capt in Louisa Co, Va & bro to Judge John Overton.)

OWEN, RICHARD (b England --d Hamblen Co); Md Martha Willhoit (--d in N C); War of 1812 in N C; Goodspeed E T H & N C S A; likely in Hamblen Co; Unkn.

OWINGS, SAMUEL S (1793-- 1868 Roane Co); Md Sarah Randolph (1797--1884); Pvt, Capt David McKamey's Co, Col John Brown's Regt E T V, 1-20-1814--5-20-1814; T S A & Roane Co Hist- Wells, & P D; likely in Post Oak Christian Ch Cem near Rockwood, Roane Co; Unkn. (Also in War of Cherokee Removal, Pension #5122.)

PADGETT, HENRY G (1796-- 1853 Williamson Co); Md Mary W Anderson (1797--8-2-1885 Williamson Co); War of 1812 in Va; Goodspeed Williamson Co & Va S A; Williamson Co; Unkn.

PAGE, DAVID D (b N C --d Williamson Co); Md Charity (   ); War of 1812; Goodspeed Williamson Co; likely Williamson Co; Unkn.

PALMER, WILLIAM (1777--3-12-1857 Wilson Co); Md Sarah Rankin 1803 (1781--11-4-1858); Pvt, Capt James A Black's Co, Col Roulston's 3rd Regt W T Mil, 11-13-1814--5- 1815; Acklen's Records #2; Palmer Fam Cem, near Linwood, Wilson Co; Pvt mkr.

PANKY, RILEY (--d at Ft Williams, Ala 1814); Md (   ); War of 1812; W D & T S A; at Ft Williams, Talledega Co, Ala; Unmkd.

PANNELL, JOHN (c 1791--aft 1840 Monroe Co); Md Jane McClannahan 9-17-1818 (   ); Pvt, Capt James Gillespie's Co, Col Sam Wear's 1st Regt E T V, 9-23-1813--12-31-1813; W D & P D; in Monroe Co; Unkn.

PARHAM, LEWIS (--liv 1840 List aged 55 yrs Marshall Co); Md (   ); War of 1812, pensioned Marshall Co; P D & 2400 Pensioners, Armstrong; likely in Marshall Co; Unkn.

PARKER, ALLEN (--d likely Hamilton Co); Md (   ); Creek War; Goodspeed Hamilton Co & Hamilton Co Hist- Armstrong; likely Hamilton Co; Unkn.

PARKER, ELISHA (--d in Tenn); Md (   ); War of 1812; Hamilton Co Hist- Armstrong; Unkn Cem in Tenn; Unkn.

PARKER, RICHARD (--liv 1840 List aged 55 yrs Sullivan Co); Md (   ); War of 1812, pensioned in Sullivan Co; P D & 2400 Pensioners, Armstrong; likely Sullivan Co; Unkn.

PARKINS, LEVI (9-29-1786--aft 4-28-1851 Blount Co); Md (   ); Pvt, Capt Francis Register's Co, Col Sam Bunch's Regt Mtd Gunmen, 1-6-1814--7-21-1815; W D & T S A; Friendsville Quaker Cem, Blount Co; Unkn.

PARKS, CALVIN (--d aft 1849 Blount Co); Md Viney Hickman 8-3-1849
(   ); War of 1812; W D & P D; Cem near Friendsville, Blount
Co; Unkn. (Viney Parks Pension #32,718 Blount Co)

PARKS, MARTIN L (1793--12-12-1845 Moore Co); Md Susan Smith 1818
(8-8-1803--8-11-1881); Officer in War of 1812; Goodspeed Moore Co;
likely in Lynchburg, Moore Co; Pvt mkr.

PARKS, SAMUEL (6-12-1789--6-3-1841 Bradley Co); Md Susanna Taylor
4-1814 (2-1-1798--12-12-1876); Pvt, Capt Wm Walker's Co Light
Horse, under Gen James White's Regt, Creek War, 9-20-1813; W D
& P D & Edwards Acct Bk; Henegar's Chapel Meth Cem, Bradley Co;
Pvt mkr. (Susanna Taylor was granddaughter of Nancy Ward.)

PARKS, WILLIAM (--d Blount Co); Md   (   ); Pvt, Capt
Moore's Co, Col Thomas Hart Benton's Regt 10-10-1813 also Pvt,
Capt Cavanaugh's Co, Gen John Coffee, 10-10-1812; W D & T S A;
Parks Ferry Cem below Friendsville, Blount Co; Unkn.

PARSON, ENOCH (-- either Blount Co or in Ala); Md Kitty Kain 1813
(   ); Pvt, Capt Wm Walker's Co, Col John Williams' Regt Mtd
Vol, 12-1-1812--3-25-1813; W D & T S A; Blount Co or in Ala; Unkn.

PARSON, GEORGE W (1788-- 1842 Bedford Co); Md Margaret Fisher
1809 (--1854); War of 1812; Goodspeed Bedford Co; Bedford Co; Unkn.

PARSON, PETER (--d likely Blount Co); Md Nancy Kain 1816 (   );
Pvt, Capt Wm Walker's Co, Col John Williams' Regt, 12-1-1812--3-25-
1813; W D & T S A; likely Blount Co; Unkn.

PATTEN, THOMAS (--liv Pensioned Bedford Co); Md   (   );
served in 25th U S Inf; P D & 2400 Pensioners, Armstrong; likely
Bedford Co; Unkn.

PATTERSON, ROBERT (1763-- 1848 Rhea Co); Md Rhoda Witt 1794 (--d
1853); Lieut, Tenn Mil; John Sevier Comm Bk; Patterson Fam Cem
near Sale Creek, Rhea Co; Pvt mkr.

PATTON, ISAAC (--d Franklin, Williamson Co); Md   (   );
Capt, W T Mil; T S A & Texas 1812 Records; Franklin, Williamson
Co; Unkn.

PAYNE, JACOB (1778-- 1847 Rutherford Co); Md Susan Browder (1773
--5-19-1851); 1st Srgt, Capt Nance's Co, Col John Cocke's 2nd Regt
Tenn Mil, 11-13-1814--5-13-1815; W D & T S A; Rutherford Co; Unkn.

PEARRE, JOSHUA (1777-- 1839 Williamson Co); Md Elizabeth Hulme
11-13-1823 (11-23-1803--5-12-1860); Pvt, Capt Isaac Patton's Co,
Col Thomas McCrory's 2nd Regt W T Mil, 11-14-1813--; W D & T S A;
Williamson Co; Pvt mkr.

PEARSON, Rev ABEL (9-8-1779--11-13-1856 Hamilton Co); Md
(   ); War of 1812; Hamilton Co Hist- Armstrong; Soddy Pres
Cem, Hamilton Co; Pvt mkr.

PECK, JACOB F (1-31-1793--2-18-1871 Monroe Co); Md Jane Waggoner 8-22-1815 (2-11-1795--1870); Pvt, Capt Robt Kile's Co, Col W Jones' Regt Va Vol; W D & P D & Va S A; Sink Cem near Tellico Plains, Monroe Co; Govt mkr.

PECK, MOSES LOONEY (5-2-1793--4-4-1888 Jefferson Co); Md Susan Mynatt 9-15-1819 (1-7-1792--8-26-1873); Pensioner of War of 1812; P D & W D; Westview Cem, Jefferson Co; Pvt mkr.

PEEBLES, WILLIAM Jr (10-15-1787--6-30-1875 Unicoi Co); Md Elizabeth Sheets (Shultz) 11-16-1813 in Va (9-7-1794--12-4-1886); Pvt, Capt Samuel Jones' Co, Col Cobb's Pitt Co N C Mil, 7-18-1813-- 7-23-1813; W D & N C S A; Peebles Fam Cem on Buffalo Creek, Unicoi Co; Pvt mkr.

PEERY, RANSOM (--d Blount Co); Md Catherine Martin 11-28-1817 ( ); 3rd Lieut, Capt Cummings Co, also Capt Jehu Stephens' Co, Maj Chiles' Battln, Gen John Coffee's Mtd Gunmen, 10-6-1814-- ord to Tenn 3-7-1815; W D & T S A; Unkn Cem in Blount Co; Unkn.

PENNINGTON, WILLIAM (12-13-1777--4-22-1838 Monroe Co); Md Elizabeth Eller (1776--1844); Pvt, Capt James Mahan's Co, Col Robt Dyer's Regt Mtd Gunmen, 9-28-1814--1-1-1815; W D & T S A; Monroe Co; Pvt mkr.

PERKINS, CORTNAY (--d Williamson Co); Md ( ); War of 1812; Acklen's Records; likely in Williamson Co; Unkn.

PERKINS, GEORGE (--d Williamson Co); Md ( ); War of 1812; Acklen's Records; likely in Williamson Co; Unkn.

PERKINS, NEELEY (--d Williamson Co); Md ( ); War of 1812; Acklen's Records; likely in Williamson Co; Unkn.

PERKINS, WILLIAM (--liv Hawkins Co); Md ( ); served in Hazen's Regt; P D & 2400 Pensioners, Armstrong; likely in Hawkins Co; Unkn.

PERRY, SILAS (12-9-1786 in S C --8-28-1844 Monroe Co); Md Hannah Lewis Harlan 10-4-1821 (7-22-1789--); Pvt, Capt John McLemore's Co, Col Gideon Morgan Jr's Cherokee Regt, 10-17-1813--1-6-1814, & 1-7-1814--4-11-1814; W D & T S A; Perry Fam Cem on Henderson Farm near Madisonville, Monroe Co; Pvt mkr.

PERSONS, BENJAMIN (--liv 1840 List aged 58 yrs Montgomery Co); Md ( ); served in Tenn Mil; P D & 2400 Pensioners, Armstrong; likely in Montgomery Co; Unkn.

PETERSON, JOHN (--8-18-1876 Hamilton Co); Md ( ); War of 1812; Natl Cem in Chattanooga Records; Grave #6433 Sec P - Natl Cem in Chattanooga, Hamilton Co; Govt mkr.

PETERSON, WM P (BLACKSMITH) (--d Blount Co); Md Elizabeth Brewer 11-28-1820 (Pensioned in Blount Co); War of 1812; W D & P D; likely in Myers Fam Cem, Blount Co; Unkn. (Elizabeth Brewer's Pension #27,220.)

PETERS, THOMAS (--Pensioned Bedford Co - Trans from Va); Md
(   ); served 24th U S Inf; P D & 2400 Pensioners, Armstrong;
likely Bedford Co; Unkn.

PHILLIPS, ABRAHAM (--liv 8-11-1852 Hamilton Co); Md
(   ); Pvt, Capt Howell's Co; B L Wt #33,207 Hamilton Co,
8-11-1852, Leaves from Family Tree 5-13-1934 & Ewards Acct Bk;
likely Hamilton Co; Unkn.

PHILLIPS, BENJAMIN (4-18-1766--7-2-1846 Wilson Co); Md Lydia
(--1851); Pvt, Capt Cook's Co, Col Thomas Williamson's Regt Mtd
Gunmen, Gen John Coffee's Brig; W D & T S A; Watertown, Wilson Co;
Pvt mkr.

PHILLIPS, JOSEPH (10-31-1763--5-22-1832 Davidson Co); Md Milbrey
Horn (12-4-1764--); J P Davidson Co, 1796; Davidson Co Records;
Phillips Fam Cem 6 m N Nashville, Davidson Co; Pvt mkr.

PHINK, GEORGE (--liv 5-3-1860 at Campbell's Rest, Sullivan Co);
Md   (   ); War of 1812; Nelson Papers in McClung
Room, Knoxville; likely Cem in Sullivan Co; Unkn.

PICKETT, JOHN (1778--d Dickson Co); Md   (   ); Pvt,
Capt Joseph Williams' Co, 1st Regt, W T Mtd Gunmen, 1814-15;
T S A & Texas 1812 Records; likely in Dickson Co; Unkn.

PILLOW, GIDEON Sr (6-10-1771-- 1843 Davidson Co); Md Annie Payne
1803 (1779--1864); Pvt, Capt Murray's Co, Col Wm Pillow's Regt
W T Mil; T S A; Pillow Fam Cem near Columbia, Maury Co or in Nashville, Davidson Co; Pvt mkr.

PILLOW, Col WILLIAM (c 1773-- 1873 aged 100 yrs Maury Co); Md
(   ); Early Indian Wars on Cumberland, Nickajack Expd 1794,
in 24th Regt, 6th Brig, & Col Regt, 9-26-1813--12-10-1813; W D &
T S A; Pillow Fam Cem near Columbia, Maury Co; Pvt mkr.

PLANT, JOHN (--liv 1840 List Humphreys Co); Md   (   );
War of 1812, pensioned Humphreys Co; P D & 2400 Pensioners, Armstrong; likely in Humphreys Co; Unkn.

POE, HASTINGS (--d Hamilton Co); Md   (   ); War of
1812; Natl Cem in Chattanooga Records; Natl Cem in Chattanooga,
Hamilton Co; Govt mkr.

POPE, JACOB (--d 12-3-1814 in service); Md   (   );
Pvt, Capt David McKamey's Co, Col Wm Johnson's 3rd Regt E T Drftd
Mil, 9-20-1814--12-3-1814 died; W D & T S A; likely in Ala; Unkn.

POPE, JOHN WHITAKER (10-1-1793--11-6-1839 Williamson Co); Md
Elizabeth Walker Campbell 4-29-1823 in Ala (2-12-1797--9-30-1866);
Pvt, Capt John Dalton's Co, Gen John Cocke's 2nd Regt W T Mil,
11-13-1814--5-13-1815; W D & T S A; Pope Fam Cem near Burwood,
4th Distr, Williamson Co; Pvt mkr.

PORTER, WILLIAM (9-12-1787--6-9-1854 Smith Co); Md 1-Jane Seymour 3-12-1808 (--9-5-1830), 2-Mary Handley 12-27-1832 Sevier Co (1794 --liv 1881 Smith Co); Pvt, Capt Simeon Perry's Co, Col Sam Wear's 1st Regt E T V, 9-23-1813--12-31-1813; W D & P D; Riddleton, Smith Co; Pvt mkr.

POSEY, HARRISON (--liv 1828 List Claiborne Co); Md ( ); served as Fifer, 24th Regt U S Inf; P D & 2400 Pensioners, Armstrong; likely in Claiborne Co; Unkn.

POTTS, AMOS (-- 1872-3 Bradley Co); Md (--d 1883); Pvt, in War of 1812 in S C Regt; S C S A & Edwards Acct Bk; Potts Fam Cem 1 m S Tucker Springs, Bradley Co; Unmkd.

POWELL, DAVID (1784-- 1852 Smith Co); Md Hannah Baird ( ); War of 1812; Goodspeed Smith Co; likely in Smith Co; Unkn.

POWELL, JOSEPH (7-7-1785--8-4-1854 Giles Co); Md 1-Jane Massey (1790 in S C --10-1853 Giles Co), 2-Rebecca York 1854 ( ); Ensign, Capt Jonathan Graves' Co, Col Peter Perkins' Regt Miss Terr; W D; Powell Fam Cem near Minor Hill, Giles Co; Pvt mkr.

POWELL, Judge SAMUEL (7-10-1776--8-2-1841 Hawkins Co); Md Mary C ( ); Est 1st Law School in Tenn, Sullivan Co, 1800 & Judge 1st Circuit Ct 1812-13; T S A; Old Pres Cem, Rogersville, Hawkins Co; Pvt mkr.

PRIDE, ALLEN (9-26-1795--12-12-1855 Roane Co); Md Martha H (2-26-1792--10-16-1864); Lieut, 14th Cav, U S A, 9-16-1814--; W D & T S A; Winton's Chapel Meth Cem near Rockwood, Roane Co; Pvt mkr.

PRIGMORE, THOMAS (1789--aft 1860 McMinn Co); Md Keziah Murray ( ); Lieut, Capt Allen Bacon's Co, Col John Brown's Regt Mtd Gunmen, 8-3-1813--11-1-1813, Gunner & Capt, Gen James White's Brig, 11-1-1813; T S A; McMinn Co; Unkn.

PRYOR, GREEN (4-7-1789 N C --6-4-1862 Marion Co); Md Obedience Holloway 1815 (1799--1858); Pvt, Capt Wm White's Co, Col John Brown's 2nd Regt Mtd Gunmen, 1-20-1814--5-20-1814; W D & T S A; Marion Co; Pvt mkr.

PYOTT, JAMES (came to Roane Co 1825 --d Roane Co); Md ( ); War of 1812, likely in Va; Roane Co Hist- Wells; likely in Roane Co; Unkn.

RADER, ADAM (b in Va --d Washington Co); Md 1-Elizabeth Dover
(   ), 2-Anna   (   ); Srgt, Capt Abraham Hamilton's
Co, Coleman's 6th Regt Va Mil, 8-29-1814--11-30-1814 at Ellicott
Mills, Rockingham Co, Va; W D & Va S A; Rader-Hice Fam Cem on
Southern R R, bet Johnson City & Jonesboro, Washington Co; Govt
mkr.

RAINEY, WILLIAM (--d 1830 Bledsoe Co); Md   (   );
Capt Home Guards in 1812; Goodspeed Bledsoe Co; likely Bledsoe
Co; Unkn.

RAINS, Capt JOHN (--d likely near Nashville, Davidson Co); Md
(   ); One of "Long Hunters" who went from Va to the "Bluffs",
1779, enforted at Bluffs 1780 for 4 yrs; Capt of Scouts & early
Indian battles; Capt S W Terr 1793; Ramsey's Annals, T S A;
likely in old Cem near Nashville, Davidson Co; Unkn. (One John
Rains, 5-2-1796--7-4-1879, bur Old City Cem in Nashville, could
have been son of Capt John Rains.)

RAMBO, PETER (--d Sevier Co); Md Frances Marshall (1798--1875);
served as Spy for Gen Hull, betrayed his soldiers into hands of
enemy, imprisoned in Canada; W D & Goodspeed E T H; Shiloh Meth
Cem in Sevier Co; Unkn.

RAMSEY, FRANCIS ALEXANDER (5-31-1764--11-5-1820 Knox Co); Md 1-
Peggy Alexander 4-7-1789 (4-3-1766--7-9-1805), 2-Mrs Ann Fleming
Agnew 1806 (--d 1816), 3-Mrs Margaret Russell Cowan Humes 1820
(   ); Commissioner for Ct House Knox Co, 1792, furnished
forage & provisions for Tellico Blockhouse, 1798; W D & Hist of
Knoxville; Old Lebanon-in-the-Fork Pres Cem; Pvt mkr. (Father
of James M G Ramsey, Historian)

RANDOLPH, HENRY (1778-- 1849 Jefferson Co); Md   (   );
War of 1812; Burnett's Bapt Preachers; Friendship Bapt Cem in
Jefferson Co; Pvt mkr. (Randolph was a Bapt preacher.)

RANKIN, ANTHONY (1794-- 1872 Greene Co); Md Margaret
(1796--1863); War of 1812; W D & P D & Nelson Papers, McClung
Room; Timber Ridge Pres Cem, Greene Co; Pvt mkr.

RAULSTON, GEORGE (--d Blount Co); Md Julia   (Pension
#10,855 Blount Co); Pvt, Capt James Gillespie's Co, Col Sam Wear's
1st Regt E T V, 9-23-1813--12-31-1813; W D & P D; Liberty Christian Ch Cem in Blount Co; Unkn.

RAWLINGS, LENIT ASHEL (1778-- 1840 Hamilton Co); Md Phebe Thurman (6-25-1780--8-17-1810); Lieut, mustered into War at Dallas,
6-27- ; Hamilton Co Hist- Armstrong; Jackson's Chapel Cem near
Old Dallas, Hamilton Co; Pvt mkr.

READ, SAMUEL (--d likely Bradley Co); Md Jane   (   );
5th Corp, Capt Jehu Stephens' Co, Col John Chiles' Mtd Gunmen,
10-6-1814--4-6-1815; W D & T S A; likely in Bradley Co; Unkn.

READ, SION SPENCER (4-22-1791-- 1845 Rutherford Co); Md Hardenia Jefferson Spencer 1819 (1804--1889); Srgt, Capt ---, Col John Coffee's Regt, enl 12-12-1812--4-27-1815; T S A; Read Fam Cem near Smyrna, Rutherford Co; Pvt mkr. (One list says bur Old McMinnville Cem, Warren Co.)

REAGAN, JAMES (--d likely Bradley Co); Md Elizabeth H Bates 11-26-1818 (   ); Srgt, Capt John Houk's Co, Col Sam Bunch's Regt E T Drftd Mil, 1-8-1814--5-17-1814; W D & B L Wt & Edwards Acct Bk; likely Bradley Co; Unkn.

REAGAN, JOHN (10-27-1788--8-7-1872 Blount Co); Md   (   ); 6th Corp, Capt Jehu Stephens' Co, Col Sam Wear's Mtd Gunmen, 10-6-1814--4-7-1815; W D & T S A; Walkers Chapel Meth Cem, Blount Co; Pvt mkr.

REECE, CHARLES C (--liv 1828 List Davidson Co --d 1830 Davidson Co); Md   (   ); served Tenn Vol; P D & 2400 Pensioners, Armstrong; likely Davidson Co, Unkn.

REED, JESSE EMMERSON (1794--7-21-1851 Overton Co); Md Mary Andrews 4-1-1818 (1803--1886); Pvt, Capt Evans' Co, Col Stephen Copeland's 3rd Regt Tenn Mil, 1-28-1814--5-10-1815; W D & T S A; Reed Fam Cem, Overton Co; Official 1812 mkr.

REES, CHARLES (--d likely Hamilton Co); Md   (   ); served Creek War under Col Gideon Morgan; Hamilton Co Hist- Armstrong; likely Hamilton Co; Unkn.

REGISTER, FRANCIS (--bet 1834-53 Washington Co); Md Jemima Glascock 9-11-1814 Washington Co (1-8-1795--4-24-1863); Capt, Col Sam Bunch's Regt, attd Col Ewen Allison's E T Mil, 1-10-1814--7-21-1814; W D & T S A; Old Milton English Fam Cem bet Green Shed & Geraldstown in Greene Co; Unmkd.

REYNOLDS, HUMPHREYS (--aft 1852 likely Bradley Co); Md (   ); War of 1812; B L Wt in 1852 Bradley Co; W D & Edwards Acct Bk & B L Wt; likely Bradley Co; Unkn.

REYNOLDS, JACOB (1793--liv 1840 aged 47 yrs Franklin Co); Md (   ); Pvt, Col John Williams' 39th Regt U S Inf; P D & 2400 Pensioners, Armstrong; likely Franklin Co; Unkn.

REYNOLDS, JETHRO (--d in service); Md   (   ); heirs listed were Alfred, Nancy, Polly, Calvin, Keziah, Cynthia & Jacob Reynolds in Roane Co; P D & 2400 Pensioners, Armstrong; Pvt, 1st Regt Rifles, Roane Co; likely where died; Unkn.

REYNOLDS, JOHN (b Ireland --7-27-1835 Bearden, Knox Co); Md Barbara Frazier (   ); War of 1812, Col John Williams' Regt; French Broad-Holston Hist- Rothrock; Reynolds Fam Cem at Bearden, Knox Co; Pvt mkr.

REYNOLDS, THOMAS (--liv 1828 List Williamson Co); Md (   ); Pvt, Col Wm Johnson's 3rd Regt E T Drftd Mil, P D & 2400 Pensioners, Armstrong; likely Williamson Co; Unkn.

RHEA, JOHN (--d 12-9-1813 in service); Md   (   );
Pvt, 24th Regt U S Inf; P D & 2400 Pensioners, Armstrong; likely
where died; Unmkd. (Heirs in Rhea Co were Jenny, Sarah, Elizabeth & Nancy Rhea.)

RHEA, JOHN (1753--5-27-1832 Sullivan Co); Single; Del to Constitutional Conv 1796, U S Congress 1803--1815, U S Comm to Choctaws 1816; T S A & Dir of Congress; Blountville Pres Cem, Sullivan Co; Pvt mkr.

RHEA, JOSEPH M (--d likely Sullivan Co); Md   (   );
Ord Srgt, Capt James Rogers Co, Col Wm Johnson's 3rd Regt E T Drftd Mil, 9-15-1814--5-3-1815; W D & T S A & Nelson Papers in McClung Room; likely in Sullivan Co; Unkn.

RHEA, ROBERT (--liv 1828 List Monroe Co); Md   (   );
Pvt, Col Wm Johnson's 3rd Regt E T Drftd Mil; P D & 2400 Pensioners, Armstrong; likely Monroe Co; Unkn.

RHEA, Maj ROBERT (--d 8-23-1841 aged 65 yrs Sullivan Co); Md Elizabeth Rhea (1767--3-13-1821); Maj, Tenn Mil; T S A; Weavers Union Cem, Sullivan Co; Pvt mkr.

RHEA, ROBERT (--d 1850 Blount Co); Md   (   ); Pvt,
Capt Joseph Duncan's Co, Col Sam Bunch's Mtd Regt, 1-10-1814--7-21-1814, wounded at Tohopeka 3-27-1814 & carried to Blount Co on bier, then Pvt, Capt David McKamey's Co, Col Wm Johnson's 3rd Regt E T Drftd Mil, 9-29-1814--5-18-1815; W D & T S A & Tenn Legislative Petitions; Red Top Primitive Bapt Cem, Happy Valley, Blount Co; Govt mkr. (Also Rev War, Marker says "Pvt, Col Crockett's Va Regt)

RICE, WILLIAM (1780--11-29-1859 Wilson Co); Md Sarah Harper c 1805 (4-6-1783--3-1864); Pvt, Capt McCulley's Co, 3rd Regt, 1st Battln, & Pvt, Capt Ezekiel Bass' Co, Maj Woodfolk's Regt; Wilson Co; Pvt mkr.

RICHARDS, JAMES (--liv 1828 List Wilson Co); Md   (   );
Pvt, Tenn Vol; P D & 2400 Pensioners, Armstrong; likely in Wilson Co; Unkn.

RIDEOUT, THOMAS (11-25-1795--1-8-1875 Rutherford Co); Md
(   ); Pvt, Capt John B Rice's Co Light Inf, 1st Regt Va Mil; W D & Va S A; Rideout Fam Cem near Murfreesboro, Rutherford Co; Official 1812 mkr.

RIDER, JOHN Jr (--d Blount Co); Md Dorcas Thompson 3-8-1821
(   ); Pvt, Capt James Gillespie's Co, Col Sam Wear's 1st Regt E T V, 9-23-1813--12-31-1813, also Spy under Gen James White in Cherokee Wars; W D & P D & B L Wt in Bradley Co; Cem near Morganton, Loudon Co; Unkn.

RIDLEY, GEORGE (--liv 1828 List Williamson Co); Md
(   ); Pvt, Tenn Vol; P D & 2400 Pensioners, Armstrong; likely Williamson Co; Unkn.

RIGGS, JESSE (8-22-1792--1-27-1869 Sullivan Co); Md 1-Mary Ann Barron 8-12-1813 (--d 10-1852), 2-Hannah Humphreys 11-4-1858 (--liv 1883 Washington Co); Pvt, Capt Amon Barron's Co, Col Ewen Allison's Regt E T Mil, 1-1-1814; W D & T S A; Double Springs Bapt Cem (Kendricks Creek), Sullivan Co; Pvt mkr.

RIPLEY, Gen E W (--d likely in Tenn); Md ( ); Gen in War of 1812; Beginnings of West Tenn- Williams; Unkn Cem in unkn Co; Unkn. (Ripley, county seat of Lauderdale Co, named for Gen E W Ripley.)

RITCHIE, THOMAS (--d at Ft Williams, Ala in 1814); Md ( ); Pvt, Capt Cowan's Co, Maj Wm Russell's Regt Mtd Gunmen, enl 9-28-1814; W D & T S A; at Ft Williams, Talledega Co, Ala; Unmkd.

ROADMAN, WILLIAM CHESNEY (10-6-1784--8-28-1849 Cocke Co); Md Sarah Muse Sanford 11-12-1807 ( ); Comm Maj Battln of Tenn Mil, got to N O one day late; Hist of Cocke Co- O'Dell; Roadman Fam Cem, Oldport, Cocke Co; Pvt mkr.

ROANE, Gov ARCHIBALD (1759--1-4-1819 Knox Co); Md Mary Ann Campbell 1788 ( ); Gov of Tenn 1801-1803; Atty Gen, Hamilton Distr, Sup Ct Judge; T S A; Pleasant Forest Pres Cem near Campbell Station, Knox Co; Monument erected by State of Tenn in 1918.

ROBERSON, JAMES (11-11-1784--7-31-1852 Bledsoe Co); Md 1-Margaret Worthington 1-11-1804 (10-26-1786--1-8-1827), 2-Sarah Hutcheson 1828 ( ); 1st Maj, 31st Regt Bledsoe Co Mil, 9-11-1812 & Pvt, Capt I S McMeans' Co, E T V from Rhea Co, 1-8-1814--6-18-1814 & Pvt, Col Wm Johnson's 3rd Regt E T Drftd Mil, at N O 1-8-1815; W D & T S A; Bledsoe Co; Pvt mkr.

ROBERSON, WILLIAM (11-7-1759--1-20-1816 Bledsoe Co); Md Rhoda Sartain ( ); Ensign in Bledsoe Co Vol Mil, 5-3-1813; John Sevier Comm Bk & T S A; Roberson Fam Cem near Pikeville, Bledsoe Co; Pvt mkr. (Also Rev War)

ROBERTS, Maj ANDREW (1795-- 1860 Knox Co); Md Jane Kelley 6-20-1820 (2-18-1801--1876); Maj of Mil under Gen Andrew Jackson; W D; Washington Pres Cem, Knox Co; Pvt mkr.

ROBERTS, ISAAC (3-1-1761--2-19-1816 Maury Co); Md Mary ( ); 1st Maj & Lieut Col Davidson Co Mil, Brig Gen 5th Brig, Member Assmbly from Davidson Co & Brig Gen W T Mil, 10-4-1813--1-4-1814 Creek War; W D & T S A; Roberts Fam Cem east Nashville Hiway near Columbia, Maury Co; Pvt mkr.

ROBERTS, JAMES (--d Warren Co); Md ( ); War of 1812, at N O; T S A; Roberts Fam Cem in Warren Co; Unkn.

ROBERTS, JOZEDIC (1791--10-3-1838 Knox Co); Md Mary Luttrell 10-22-1818 (1797--9-26-1838); Pvt, Capt Daniel Price's Co, Col Sam Wear's 1st Regt E T V, 9-23-1813--1-1-1814; T S A; Roberts Fam Cem near Knoxville, Knox Co; Pvt mkr.

ROBERTS, MARK R (--liv 1828 List Hardeman Co); Md ( ); Pvt, Tenn Vol; P D & 2400 Pensioners, Armstrong; likely Hardeman Co; Unkn.

ROBERTSON, CHARLES (3-17-1788--10-3-1841 Hardeman Co); Md Elizabeth Sevier (1792--1868); Pvt, Capt Miles Vernon's Co, Col Edwin Boothe's 5th Regt E T Drftd Mil, 11-13-1814--5-13-1815; W D; Moore Fam Cem 2 m S Pocahontas, Hardeman Co; Pvt mkr. (Grandson of Col Charles Robertson 1740-1798 of Washington Co)

ROBERTSON, GEORGE (6-15-1786--10-17-1876 Greene Co); Md Deborah Register 6-1-1809 (3-21-1791--3-22-1871); Pvt, Capt Francis Register's Co, Col Sam Bunch's Regt E T Drftd Mil, 1-10-1814--7-21-1814; W D & T S A; Bethesda Pres Cem near Cedar Lane, Greene Co; Pvt mkr.

ROBERTSON, Maj JAMES (11-11-1784--7-31-1852 Bledsoe Co); Md Margaret Worthington 11-1-1804 (10-26-1786--1-8-1827); Pvt, Capt Isaac S McMeans' Co, Mtd Vol, at Tohopeka & N O; W D & T S A; Bledsoe Co; Pvt mkr.

ROBERTSON, JOSEPH (--d likely in Greene Co); Md ( ); Pvt, disch same time as bro George Robertson in Capt Francis Register's Co, Col Sam Bunch's Regt E T Drftd Mil; W D & Letter of J R Smith, Jeraldstown, Greene Co, 1935; likely in Greene Co; Unkn.

ROBERTSON, JOHN (1781-- 1858 Roane Co); Md ( ); Pvt, Capt Joseph Hale's Co, Col Sam Bayless' 4th Regt E T Drftd Mil, 11-23-1814--; T S A & Texas 1812 Records; likely in Roane Co; Unkn.

ROBINSON, JACOB (12-3-1773--2-19-1840 Washington Co); Md Elizabeth (12-16-1777--5-7-1856); Pvt, Capt James R Rogers Co, Col Wm Johnson's 3rd Regt E T Drftd Mil, 9-15-1814--5-3-1815; W D & T S A; Double Springs (Kendricks' Creek) Bapt Cem, Sullivan Co; Pvt mkr.

ROBINSON, STEPHEN (1778--1845-6 Dekalb Co (Wilson); Md 1-Martha Meadors ( ), 2-Mary Lancaster (6-6-1798--1846); Pvt, Capt Kennedy's Co, Col Wm Hall's Regt W T Mil; T S A; Robinson Fam Cem near Liberty, Dekalb Co; Pvt mkr.

ROBINSON, THOMAS (5-10-1789 Va --7-22-1864 Loudon, Loudon Co); Md Sarah King 7-28-1811 Hawkins Co (12-28-1788--5-7-1865); War of 1812 from Hawkins Co; Goodspeed E T H Hawkins Co; likely in Loudon, Loudon Co; Unkn.

ROBINSON, WILLIAM L (--d Nashville, Davidson Co); Md ( ); Lieut, War of 1812; Acklens Records; Cem in Nashville, Davidson Co; Unkn.

RODDYE, JAMES (1742--bet 1821-23 Hawkins Co); Md 1-Catherine Chase ( ), 2-Lydia Russell (--d 1825); Lieut Col Mil in 1788, Member Gen Assmbly Tenn; T S A; Bent Creek Bapt Cem near Russellville, Hamblen Co; Pvt mkr. (Also Rev War, at Boyds Creek & Kings Mt, Capt)

RODDYE, JESSE (1-5-1775--2-16-1861 Rhea Co); Md Jennie Mahaffe 12-8-1797 (   ); Pvt, Capt John Trimble's Co, Col John Brown's 2nd Regt Mtd Gunmen; T S A & Leaves from the Family Tree; Roddye Fam Cem at Roddye Station, Rhea Co; Pvt mkr.

RODGERS, JAMES (1750-- 1820 Knox Co); Md Rhoda Alexander (   ); Cherokee Expd 1793 & War of 1812; T S A & Texas 1812 Records; likely Knox Co; Unkn.

RODGERS, WILLIAM (2-13-1794--1-29-1866 Knox Co); Md Elizabeth Donaldson (1767--1847); Pvt & Lieut, Maj John Chiles' Battln; W D & T S A & Armstrong Notable Families; Concord Cem in Knox Co; Pvt mkr.

ROGERS, CHARLES (--d 10-6-1824 Davidson Co); Md   (   ); Pvt, Tenn Mil; P D & 2400 Pensioners, Armstrong; likely Davidson Co; Unkn.

ROGERS, DAVID (10-3-1779--9-14-1871 Claiborne Co); Md Polly Lewis May 1800 (1-1-1781--2-13-1880); Maj, Col Wm Lillard's 2nd Regt E T V, Gen White's Brig, 10-15-1813--1-14-1814; W D & P D; Rogers Fam Cem near Speedwell, Claiborne Co; Pvt mkr.

ROGERS, ELIJAH (1774-- 1841 Sevier Co); Md Catherine Clack (   ); War of 1812; Burnett's Bapt Preachers; Forks of Pigeon Bapt Cem in Sevierville, Sevier Co; Pvt mkr.

ROGERS, ELISHA (12-4-1787--3-27-1858 Hamilton Co); Md Sarah Thurman 1809 (3-24-1790--4-8-1862); Lieut, 31st Regt Tenn Mil, 1808 Bledsoe Co; John Sevier Comm Bk; Hamilton Co; Pvt mkr.

ROGERS, ROBERT (--7-15-1815 Montgomery Co); Md Elizabeth Moore (md 2-Nathan Ragan); War of 1812; W D & T S A; Montgomery Co; Unkn.

ROGERS, VINCENT (1787--4-29-1867 Blount Co); Md Abigail Hardin 1816 (1798--5-21-1884); Pvt, Capt Alexander Biggs' Co, Col Edwin Boothe's 5th Regt E T Drftd Mil, 11-13-1814--5-18-1815; W D & P D; Ellijoy Bapt Cem, Blount Co; Pvt mkr. (Pension Cl #13536, Cert 7,735)

ROGERS, WILLIAM (6-28-1779--8-11-1857 Shelby Co); Md Ann Brown 4-1-1799 (8-25-1777--7-22-1841); Pvt, Capt John McClure's Co, Lieut Elijah Dean's N C Mil, 2-16-1815--3-13-1815; W D & N C S A; Cem near Cordova, Shelby Co; Pvt mkr.

ROPER, JOHN (3-3-1782--2-22-1858 Jefferson Co); Md Margaret Franklin 3-9-1803 (5-11-1789--10-25-1861); Capt, Col Wm Lillard's 2nd Regt E T V, 10-8-1813--2-8-1814; W D & T S A; Branner Fam Cem in Jefferson City, Jefferson Co; Pvt mkr.

ROSS, JAMES (--d Roane Co); Md 1-Mrs Stover (   ), 2-Mary Martin (   ); served as officer, Col Kirkpatrick in Va Mil; Va S A; likely Roane Co; Unkn.

ROSS, NATHANIEL (4-12-1795--7-31-1882 Bradley Co); Md
(   ); Pvt, York Distr Co, in S C Mil; Edwards Acct Bk &
S C S A; Henegar's Chapel Meth Cem near Charleston, Bradley Co;
Pvt mkr.

ROULSTON, Col JAMES (RAULSTON) (6-16-1772--8-7-1844 Marion Co);
Md Jane Simmons 1796 (3-27-1783--); Col, 3rd Regt W T Inf Vol,
11-13-1814--5-13-1815; W D & T S A; Roulston Fam Cem near South
Pittsburg-Whitwell, Marion Co; Official 1812 mkr.

ROUTH, STEPHEN (--d Sevier Co); Md Sarah McClusky (   );
War of 1812; Burnett's Bapt Preachers; Unkn Cem in Sevier Co; Unkn.
(Stephen Routh was a Bapt preacher.)

ROYSTER, DAVID (--d Shelby Co); Md   (   ); Pvt, Capt
Thomas Davenport's Co, 5th Regt Va Mil, 1813-14; Va S A & Texas
1812 Records; likely Shelby Co; Unkn.

RUCKER, JAMES (9-4-1758--9-10-1819 Rutherford Co); Md 1-Ephraim
Tate (   ), 2-Nancy Ann Read 1-31-1788 (5-12-1765--11-3-1845);
Pvt, Capt Yardley's Co, Col Newton Cannon's Regt Mtd Riflemen,
9-24-1813--; W D & T S A; Vet Admr Cem at Murfreesboro, Rutherford Co; Govt mkr.

RUFFIN, WILLIAM (1797-- 1857 Shelby Co); Md   (   );
Maj in War of 1812; Elmwood Cem Record Bk, Memphis; Elmwood Cem in
Memphis, Shelby Co; Govt mkr.

RULE, MICHAEL (9- 1788--6- 1855 Knox Co); Md Elizabeth Dill (7-27
-1790--12-9-1849); War of 1812 in Va, Rockbridge Co; Va S A & Rule
Fam Hist 1941; Rule Fam Cem, Knox Co; Pvt mkr.

RUSSELL, JOHN (--liv 1840 List aged 55 yrs Jefferson Co); Md
(   ); served 22nd Regt U S Inf; P D & 2400 Pensioners, Armstrong; likely Jefferson Co; Unkn.

RUSSEY, JAMES (1755--3-30-1835 Franklin Co); Md Sarah   1774
(   ); Early Indian Wars; Goodspeed Franklin Co; in Winchester,
Franklin Co; Pvt mkr. (Also Rev War)

SADLER, BENJAMIN (--liv 1828 List Sumner Co, trans from Va); Md ( ); served 1st Regt U S Inf, Va; P D & 2400 Pensioners, Armstrong & Va S A; likely Sumner Co; Unkn.

SANDERS, JOHN (--d 2-8-1815, wounded at N O); Md (wid got Pension); War of 1812, reported killed at N O, wounded, died 2-8-1815; W D & P D, Bowen letters; Cem at N O; Unkn.

SARTIN, ELI (--liv 1840 List aged 55 yrs Jefferson Co); Md ( ); served 1st Regt U S Riflemen; P D & 2400 Pensioners, Armstrong; likely Jefferson Co; Unkn.

SAVAGE, GEORGE (1786--2-8-1873 Warren Co); Md Elizabeth Kenner 12-3-1811 (5-25-1791--7-22-1889); Corp, Capt James Cummings' Co, Col Sam Bunch's Regt E T V, 10-17-1813--1-17-1814; W D & T S A & P D; Riverside Cem in McMinnville, Warren Co; Pvt mkr.

SAWYER, DEMPSEY (3-1-1776--10-9-1860 Williamson Co); Md Courtnay Kennedy 1815 (7-1795--7-19-1880); Pvt, Capt Ezekiel Ross' Co, 9-24-1813 & Capt Robertson's Co, Col Philip Pipkin's Regt W T Mil, & Capt Mullins' Co, Col Wm Metcalf's 1st Regt W T Mil, 1-28-1814--; W D & T S A; likely Williamson Co; Pvt mkr.

SAWYER, ELI (--liv 1828 List Sumner Co); Md ( ); served 1st Regt U S Inf; P D & 2400 Pensioners, Armstrong; likely Sumner Co; Unkn.

SAWYERS,-Col JOHN (1745--11-20-1831 Knox Co); Md Rebecca Crawford 1-30-1776 (2-17-1753--2-25-1841); J P in S W Terr, Knox Co; W D & S W Terr Papers; Washington Pres Cem, Knox Co; Pvt mkr. (Also Col in Rev War)

SAWYERS, SMILY (--d 7-22-1816 Greene Co); Md ( ); "Disch 3 mos tower in Militia" by Andrew Smily, John Glascock; Inv Bk 1810-1843 Greene Co; likely Greene Co; Unkn.

SAWYERS, WILLIAM (5-18-1791--4-9-1870 Knox Co); Md Elizabeth Casady 2-26-1821 (3-14-1802--10-13-1865); Pvt, Capt John Bayless' Co, Col Sam Wear's 1st Regt E T V, 9-23-1813--12-31-1813; W D & T S A; Washington Pres Cem on Washington Pike, Knox Co; Pvt mkr.

SCOTT, Capt JAMES (--d Sullivan Co); Md Mary Allison ( ); Capt, War of 1812; Kings Mt Men- White; likely in New Bethel Pres Cem, Sullivan Co; Unmkd.

SCOTT, EDWARD (-- 1844 Knox Co); Md Sarah C Haines 1-17-1799 ( ); Registrar Land Office E T, 1808-1815; French Broad-Holston Hist- Rothrock & T S A; likely in Knoxville, Knox Co; Unkn.

SCOTT, JAMES (1760--8-30-1823 Knoxville, Knox Co); Md Jane Adams (1760--8-10-1837); Indian Wars 1790-1793 & Capt, Blount Co Mil, 1801; T S A & John Sevier's Comm Bk; First Pres Cem, Knoxville, Knox Co; Pvt mkr.

SCOTT, REUBEN (--liv 1850 aged 54 yrs Knox Co); Md Polly (--liv 1850 aged 54 yrs); War of 1812; French Broad-Holston Hist-Rothrock; likely Knox Co; Unkn.

SCOTT, WILLIAM (1780-- 1855 Blount Co); Md Phebe Lamar (1780-- 1866); Pvt, Capt James Allen's Co, Col Ewen Allison's Regt E T Drftd Mil, 1-17-1814, transfd ; W D & T S A; Myers Fam Cem at Townsend, Blount Co; Pvt mkr.

SCOTT, Capt WILLIAM (--d likely Knox Co); Md Isabelle ( ); served in 24th Regt U S Inf; W D & P D; likely in Knox Co; Unkn.

SCRUGGS, EDWARD (--c 1846-7 Williamson Co); Md Althea Hassell 8-1-1818 (6-7-1800--6-23-1888); Pvt, Capt James Randall's Co, Col Robt Steele's 4th Regt W T Mil, 3-15-1814--5-23-1814; W D & T S A; Williamson Co; Pvt mkr.

SCUDDER, MATHIAS (--liv 1828 List Wilson Co); Md ( ); served Tenn Mil; P D & 2400 Pensioners, Armstrong; likely Wilson Co; Unkn.

SEAY, JOHN (4-29-1764--9-13-1830 Smith Co); Md Sarah McCarty (--10-6-1831); War of 1812; ; Seay Fam Cem in Smith Co; Unkn.

SEEHORN, JACOB (1773-- 1871 Dandridge, Jefferson Co); Md ( ); Pvt, Capt Thomas McCuiston's Co, Col Wm Lillard's 2nd Regt E T V, 10-13-1813--2-8-1814; W D & T S A & Texas 1812 Records; Dandridge Cem, Jefferson Co; Pvt mkr.

SENTER, JOHN (--liv 1883 Bathpage, Sumner Co); Md ( ); War of 1812; P D, Pension #13,171 Sumner Co; likely Bathpage, Sumner Co; Unkn.

SEVIER, Maj ALEXANDER GREENE (--5-9-1827 Greene Co); Md Elizabeth Hunter (--Pensioner); Maj, U S Marine Corps, Battle of Bladensburg, 1814, Commdr Barney; W D & T S A & P D; Greeneville Cem, Greene Co; Pvt mkr. (A G Sevier was son of Valentine & Naomi Douglas Sevier.)

SEVIER, Col GEORGE WASHINGTON (2-1-1782--2-9-1849 Overton Co); Md Catherine Weatherly Chambers ( ); Ensign & Lieut, 1804-5-7, Capt Rifle Co, 1808, Lieut, 7-6-1812 & Col, 1-24-1814; W D & T S A; Garrett Cem, Overton Co; Pvt mkr.

SEVIER, Gov JOHN (9-23-1745--9-4-1815 in Ala); Md 1-Sarah Hawkins c 1762 in Va (--d 1-1780), 2-Catherine Sherrill 8-1780 (--d 10-7-1836 in Ala); Indian Wars, 1784--1794 & Gov Tenn, 1796--1801, 1803--09; W D & T S A; Court House Lawn, Knoxville, Knox Co; Monuments by State of Tenn & D A R; (Both John Sevier & his 2nd wife died in Ala, & their remains were later moved to Knoxville.)

SEVIER, JOHN ("Devil Jack") (9- 1769--6- 1815 bur at sea near Charleston, S C); Md Susanna Conway 1800 (6-9-1776--5-4-1816); Corp, 6th U S Inf, 1-25-1812, 7th U S Inf, 6-14-1813 & Q M 6-23-1813, Srgt Maj, 7-16-1813, Ensign 12-22-1814 at N O, Capt White's Co, wounded, disch 6-15-1815; W D & T S A; bur at sea; Unmkd. (He was too ill from his wound to get home overland aft battle of N O, so took a ship & died off coast of Charleston & was bur at sea. He was son of Valentine & Naomi Douglas Sevier.)

SEVIER, JOHN (--1876 Clay Co); Md   (   ); Pvt, Capt Penny's Co, Col Sam Bunch's Regt E T V, 10-12-1813--1-21-1814; W D & T S A & P D; likely Clay Co; Unkn.

SEVIER, JOHN F (--d 1858 Johnson Co); Md Susan Rector 10-6-1853 (--d aft 1858); Pvt, Capt Benjamin King's Co, Col Wm Lillard's 2nd Regt E T V, 10-12-1813--2-8-1814; W D & T S A; likely Johnson Co; Unkn.

SEVIER, WILLIAM (--3-10-1830 Overton Co); Md   (   ); Enl 12-1812, Capt John Kennedy's Co, Tenn Mil; W D & T S A; Overton Co; Unkn.

SHANE, MORRIS (--likely Davidson Co); Md Phoebe Castleman (9-2-1787--6-4-1852); at Ft Buchanan 9-30-1792; T S A; likely in Davidson Co; Unkn.

SHANNON, ARCHIBALD B (--liv 1828 List Wilson Co, 1840 List aged 48 yrs Shelby Co); Md   (   ); served Tenn Vol; P D & 2400 Pensioners, Armstrong; likely Shelby Co; Unkn.

SHARP, ALEXANDER--(7-10-1793--7-17-1839 Blount Co); Md Susannah Maxwell 9-10-1816 (   ); 4th Srgt, Capt Jehu Stephens' Co, Col Sam Wear's Regt, Mtd Gunmen, 10-6-1814--4-6-1815; W D & T S A; Clark's Grove Cumberland Pres Cem, Blount Co; Pvt mkr.

SHARP, JOHN (--d Union Co); Md   (   ); War of 1812; W D; Sharp Fam Cem near Luttrell, Union Co; Govt mkr. (Nearby grave is Sam L Sharp, Govt mkr, with Rev War on it.)

SHARP, NICHOLAS (c 1795--2-6-1844 Anderson Co); Md Sarah Jones 4-22-1814 (--liv 3-18-1871 Anderson Co); Pvt, Capt James Tunnell's Co, Col Wm Johnson's 3rd Regt E T Drftd Mil, 11-13-1814--5-4-1815, disch 7-24-1815; W D & T S A; Anderson Co; Pvt mkr.

SHAW, JAMES (--liv 1828 List Bedford Co, 1840 List aged 69 yrs Marshall Co); Md   (   ); served Mtd Gunmen Regt; P D & 2400 Pensioners, Armstrong; likely Marshall Co; Unkn.

SHAW, JOHN LYLE (1780 Va --1852 Warren Co); Md Sarah Davidson (   ); War of 1812; Acklen's Records; Old McMinnville Cem, Warren Co; Pvt mkr.

SHELBY, DAVID (--d Sumner Co); Md   (   ); War of 1812;   ; likely Sumner Co; Unkn. (He built the stone house, "Spencer's Choice", near Gallatin, Sumner Co.)

SHELL, JOHN (--liv 1850 aged 61 yrs Knox Co); Md Nancy Pursley 12-4-1815 Knox Co (--liv 1850 aged 54 yrs); War of 1812; French Broad-Holston Hist- Rothrock; likely Knox Co; Unkn.

SHELL, LEWIS (--d likely Knox Co); Md Nancy Solust 3-8-1818 Knox Co (   ); War of 1812; French Broad-Holston Hist- Rothrock; likely Knox Co; Unkn.

SHIELDS, JOHN (--10-2-1829 aged 37 yrs likely Greene Co); Md Mary Gill (   ); War of 1812; Notable Men of Tenn- Allison; likely Greene Co; Unkn.

SHINPAUGH, HENRY (--d Knox Co); Md Elizabeth McDaniel (   ); War of 1812; Goodspeed Knox Co; likely Knox Co; Unkn. (Also Rev War)

SHIPE, HENRY (11-8-1789--11-8-1879 Knox Co); Md Deborah Skeggs 10-7-1819 (12-12-1796--5-22-1871); Pvt, Capt Daniel Pierce's Co, Maj John Chiles' Batln, Mtd Gunmen, 9-20-1814--5-1-1815; W D & T S A; Union Bapt Cem, Knox Co; Pvt mkr.

SHIVERS, THOMAS (--d Davidson Co aged 86 yrs); Md   (   ); War of 1812; Notable Men of Tenn- Allison, p-285; likely Davidson Co; Unkn. (A son, Jonas Shivers md Elizabeth McCasland)

SHOEMAKER, WILLIAM (--liv 1883 Chestnut Mound, Smith Co); Md (   ); War of 1812; P D; likely at Chestnut Mound, Smith Co; Unkn. (Pension #5,391)

SHUMATE, Lieut W J (--liv 1828 List Williamson Co); Md (   ); served Col Williamson's Regt Mil; P D & 2400 Pensioners, Armstrong; likely Williamson Co; Unkn.

SIEVERS, FREDERICK (SEAVERS) (--1-27-1815 Clinton, Anderson Co); Md   (--Pensioner aft 1815); Pvt, Col Edwin Boothe's 5th Regt E T Mil; Clinton, Anderson Co; Unkn.

SIMMONS, JAMES (--liv 1840 List Washington Co); Md (   ); War of 1812; P D & 2400 Pensioners, Armstrong; likely Washington Co; Unkn. (He was pensioned in Washington Co.)

SIMMONS, THOMAS A (1793 Va --d Robertson Co); Md Mary Clayton (   ); War of 1812; W D; likely Robertson Co; Unkn.

SIMPSON, Col JOHN W (2-20-1789--3- 1862 White Co); Md Jane Montgomery 9-19-1819 (   ); Maj & Lieut Col, Col Wm Metcalf's Regt W T Mil, 11-13-1814--5-13-1815; T S A; Bethlehem Ch Cem near Sparta, White Co; Pvt mkr.

SIMPSON, LACKEY (LOCKEY) (--liv 1828 List Unkn Co); Md (   ); War of 1812, papers destroyed in fire in War Office; P D & 2400 Pensioners, Armstrong; likely in Tenn, unkn Co; Unkn.

SIMPSON, SANFORD (1790-- 1868 Knox Co); Md Hope Poston (--2-28-1880); Pvt, Capt Jesse Carter's Co, Va Mil, 8-11-1814--2-15-1815; W D & Va S A; Island Home Bapt Cem, Knoxville, Knox Co; Pvt mkr.

SLAUGHTER, BERNARD (--liv 1828 List Williamson Co); Md (   ); served 1st Regt U S Riflemen; P D & 2400 Pensioners, Armstrong; likely Williamson Co; Unkn.

SLEEKER, GEORGE (--liv 1828 List Williamson Co); Md (   ); served 2nd Regt Tenn Mil; P D & 2400 Pensioners, Armstrong; likely Williamson Co; Unkn.

SLEEPING G RABBIT (--d 1836 Bradley Co); Md   (   );
War of 1812; W D; bur near Council Spring, Bradley Co; Govt mkr.
(He was grandfather of Jesse Bushyhead, Indian.)

SLOAN, JAMES (--d Monroe Co); Md   (   ); Pvt, Capt
John Trimble's Co, Maj Wm Russell's Batln Gen John Coffee's Regt,
10-6-1814--4-6-1815; W D & T S A; Monroe Co; Unkn.

SMALLWOOD, ELISHA (--liv 1828 List Sullivan Co); Md
(   ); served 24th Regt U S Inf; P D & 2400 Pensioners, Armstrong; likely Sullivan Co; Unkn.

SMARTT, ALEXANDER (--d 12- 1813 in service); Md   (   );
heirs were Nancy, Sally, Joseph & Samuel Smartt in Cocke Co; War
of 1812; P D & 2400 Pensioners, Armstrong; likely where died; Unkn.

SMARTT, WILLIAM CHEEK (11-13-1785--6-18-1865 McMinnville, Warren
Co); Md 1-Margaret Colville 9-13-1804 (3-23-1787--2-22-1827),
2-Mrs Elizabeth Hackett Waterhouse 11-16-1827 (   ); Maj,
2nd Regt 9-20-1814, & Lieut Commander 29th Regt 11-9-1815, &
later Gen in Tenn Mil; T S A; Liberty Ch Cem in McMinnville,
Warren Co; Pvt mkr.

SMILEY, H B (b Ky --bef 1887 aged 75 yrs Marshall Co); Md Sarah
Lowry (b S C --bef 1887 aged 93 yrs); War of 1812; Goodspeed Marshall Co; likely Marshall Co; Unkn.

SMITH, ALEXANDER Sr (1766--5-8-1824 Cocke Co); Md Mary Dewitt
3-30-1803 (   ); Maj, Tohopeka, 3-27-1814; T S A & Cocke Co
Hist- O'Dell; Green Lawn Fam Cem in Cocke Co; Pvt mkr.

SMITH, ANTHONY (1787-- 1847 aged 60 yrs Roane Co); Md Ann Bailey
(1797--1887 aged 90 yrs); War of 1812 from Roane Co; Goodspeed
E T H & Wells List 1812 Soldiers; likely Roane Co; Unkn.

SMITH, DANIEL (2-13-1788--1-4-1871 Carter Co); Md Hyliah
(2-28-1825--7-8-1894); Srgt, Capt Adam Winsell's Co, Col Ewen
Allison's Regt E T Drftd Mil; W D; Rittertown-Fish Springs Bapt
Cem, Carter Co; Pvt mkr. (Bur in Smith Fam Cem near Fish Springs,
Carter Co; moved by T V A, Watauga Dam)

SMITH, DANIEL (10-29-1748--6-16-1818 Sumner Co); Md Sarah Ann
Michie (   ); Sec S W Terr 1790 under Gov Blount, Constitutional Conv 1796, & U S Senate 1798, 1805-09; T S A; Smith Fam
Cem at "Rockcastle", Sumner Co; Monument erected by State of
Tenn. (Also Rev War, as Maj Gen of Mil, a noted surveyor, made
first map of state of Tenn)

SMITH, EZEKIEL (9-17-1789--5-4-1863 Carter Co); Md Nancy G Doran
(9-17-1789--); Pvt, Capt Joseph Everett's Co, Col Ewen Allison's
Regt E T Drftd Mil, 1-7-1814--trans 4-27-1814 to Capt Jones
Griffin's Co, Col Sam Bunch's Regt; W D; Smith Fam Cem near
Fish Springs, Carter Co; Pvt mkr.

SMITH, Col GEORGE (5-12-1776-- 1849 Davidson Co); Md Tabitha
Donelson (7-17-1781--); War of 1812; W D & T S A; likely in
Donelson Cem, Davidson Co; Unkn.

SMITH, GEORGE (-- 1827 Hawkins Co); Md Elizabeth White c 1818 (10-22-1795--2-8-1873); War of 1812; Goodspeed E T H p-1213; likely Bent Creek Bapt Cem near Whitesburg, Hamblen Co; Unmkd.

SMITH, JACOB (1784-- 1866 Robertson Co); Md ( ); Pvt, Co Mtd Gunmen, Tenn Mil; T S A & Texas 1812 Records; Robertson Co; Unkn.

SMITH, JAMES M (--d Mechanicsville, Rutherford Co); Md Martha Page ( ); War of 1812, at N O; Vol State- Moore; Rutherford Co; Pvt mkr.

SMITH, JOHN JAMES (c 1765-- 1859 Humphreys Co); Md Elizabeth Self 1795 (--1816); Lieut, under Gen Andrew Jackson at N O; T S A; Smith Fam Cem in Humphreys Co; Unmkd.

SMITH, JOHN (10-18-1780--3-10-1829 Sullivan Co); Md Catherine Humphreys 8-14-1808 Sullivan Co (3-17-1787--7-3-1881); Pvt, Capt Wm King's Co, Col Ewen Allison's Regt E T Drftd Mil, 1-6-1814--5-2-1814; W D & T S A; Smith Fam Cem on Holston River, Sullivan Co; Pvt mkr.

SMITH, JOHN M (--Will 12-12-1812, Prob May 1814; Did he fall at Battle of Tohopeka 3-27-1814?); Single; Pvt, --- Co, Col John Williams' Regt; W D & Will Bk #1 p-102 Washington Co; Bur site unkn; Unkn.

SMITH, JOSEPH (12-21-1792--2-5-1875 Union Co); Md ( ); War of 1812; W D; Baker's Forge Cem in Union Co; Govt mkr. (Data found in T V A Records of graves removed by Norris Dam)

SMITH, JOSIAH (12-12-1781--4-21-1837 Union Co); Md Nancy Stonely Condry 10-9-1813 (1784--11-17-1848); Pvt, Capt Thomas Sharp's Co, Col Wm Lillard's 2nd Regt E T V, 10-14-1813--2-8-1814; W D & T S A; Butcher Fam Cem, Union Co; Pvt mkr. (Near Norris Dam)

SMITH, JOSIAH (--liv 1883 New Middleton, Smith Co); Md ( ); War of 1812; P D, Pension #16,033; likely at New Middleton, Smith Co; Unkn.

SMITH, NATHANIEL (--liv 1828 List Wilson Co); Md ( ); served 39th Regt U S Inf; P D & 2400 Pensioners, Armstrong; likely Wilson Co; Unkn.

SMITH, PHILLIP (2-12-1789--8-24-1882 Knox Co); Md 1-Polly McCampbell (--d 4-14-1842), 2-Jeanette McKinley ( ); Pvt, Capt James Anderson's Co, Maj James P H Porter's Vol Cav, 9-23-1813--12-21-1813; W D & T S A; McCampbell Fam Cem, Knox Co; Pvt mkr.

SMITH, STARLING (--9-20-1839 Knox Co); Md Martha B Rudder 6-28-1807 (--d 1871 aged 85 yrs); Pvt, Capt Solomon Hendrix' Co, Col Sam Bayless' 4th Regt E T Drftd Mil, 11-13-1814--5-26-1815; W D & P D; likely Mt Olive Bapt Cem in Knox Co; Pvt mkr. (Martha R Smith got Pension)

SMITH, TURNER (--1875 Washington Co); Md Mary Ruble 2-21-1809
(   ); War of 1812; W D & Reminescenses of Old Timer- Smith;
Old Smith Fam Cem on Southern R R east Jonesboro, Washington Co;
Pvt mkr.

SMITH, WILLIAM (--liv 1828 List Bedford Co); Md   (   );
Pvt, 2nd Regt Tenn Mil; P D & 2400 Pensioners, Armstrong; likely
Bedford Co; Unkn.

SMITH, WILLIAM (--liv 1828 List Lincoln Co); Md   (   );
Pvt, W T Mil; P D & 2400 Pensioners, Armstrong; likely in Lincoln
Co; Unkn.

SMITH, Maj WILLIAM (--d Sullivan Co); Md   (   ); War
of 1812; Fam Records; Boy Fam Cem at Rockhold Campground near
Bluff City, Sullivan Co; Pvt mkr.

SMITHART, JOHN (--killed 3-27-1814 Tohopeka); Md   (   );
War of 1812, killed at Tohopeka; Hamilton Co Hist- Armstrong;
likely in Ala; Unkn.

SNAPP, JACOB K (12-4-1791--8-6-1852 Blountville, Sullivan Co); Md
Eleanor   (1802--8-21-1850); Ensign, Col John Williams' 39th
Regt U S Inf, 12-1-1812--disch 10-17-1814; W D & T S A; Blountville
Pres Cem, Sullivan Co; Pvt mkr & Ft Chiswell Ch D A R. (Why did
the D A R mark this soldier of War of 1812?)

SNEED, CONSTANTINE P (11-29-1790--8-12-1864 Davidson Co); Md Susannah Hardeman (4-26-1807--5-19-1859); Pvt & Srgt, Capt Robt Ed-
miston's Co, Col Robt H Dyer's 1st Regt Mtd Gunmen, 9-28-1814--
4-27-1815; T S A; Davidson Co; Pvt mkr.

SNEED, TAYLOR (--d Monroe Co); Md   (   ); Corp, Capt
Cleutche's Co 7th U S Inf; W D & P D & B L Wt; in Monroe Co; Unkn.
(He sold B L Wt in Terr of Arkansas)

SNODGRASS, Maj WILLIAM (5-10-1760--12-18-1849 Sullivan Co); Md
Mary   (1-22-1761--1-28-1828); Early Indian Wars, Commander
Cherokee Indians at Ft Armstrong, & Lieut Col, Col Wm Lillard's
22nd Regt E T V, 1-4-1814--2-8-1814; W D & T S A; Snodgrass Fam
Cem bet Blountville & Bristol, Sullivan Co; Pvt mkr & D A R mkr.
(Also Rev War, at Kings Mt)

SOMERVILLE, Lieut (--killed 3-27-1814 at Tohopeka); Md
(   ); Lieut, Col John Williams' 39th Regt U S Inf; W D &
T S A & Vol State- Moore; likely in Ala; Unkn.

SOMMERS, JAMES (1790-- 1862 Weakley Co); Md   (   );
Pvt, Capt John Jones' Co, Col John Williams' 39th Regt U S Inf;
T S A & Texas 1812 Records; Dresden Cem, Weakley Co; Unkn.

SPAIN, THOMAS PETERSON (10-1-1786--12-21-1836 Robertson Co); Md
Catherine Mayes 5-8-1828 (12-28-1798--12-16-1877); Pvt, Capt
Wood's Co, Va Mil; W D & Va S A; Robertson Co; Pvt mkr.

SPENCER, THOMAS SHARPE (--killed 4-1-1794 Spencer's Hill, Van Buren Co); Single; Early Indian Wars; Ramsey's Annals & T S A; Spencer's Hill, Van Buren Co; D A R mkr 1927. (Also Rev War)

SPINKS, JOHN (1742-- 1833 Wilson Co); Md Sally Crawford (   ); Chaplain with Jackson & Lieut Col, Col John K Wynn's 17th Regt U S Inf; W D & T S A; Gladesville Cem near Lebanon, Wilson Co; Pvt mkr.

SPROTT, BLYTHE (SPRATT) (12-29-1790--6-15-1868 Williamson Co); Md Elizabeth Blythe (1800--1840); Pvt, Lieut Berry's Co, Col Robt H Dyer's 1st Regt W T Mil, 3-11-1814--5-16-1814; T S A; Williamson Co; Pvt mkr.

SPURLOCK, JOSIAH (--d Cannon Co); Md   (   ); War of 1812 aged 18 yrs in 41st Regt; Cannon Co Hist- Brown; likely Cannon Co; Unkn.

STANDIFER, JAMES (--d Bledsoe Co); Md   (   ); Capt, Rifle Co, attd 31st Regt Mil, 9-11-1812--; W D & T S A; Standifer Fam Cem near Tine, lower Bledsoe or upper Sequatchie Co; Unkn.

STEWART, SIMEON (--d 9-17-1814 in service); Md   (   ); heirs were Alexander, Isaac, James & Rachel Stewart in Warren Co; Pvt, 1st Regt Riflemen; P D & 2400 Pensioners, Armstrong; likely where died; Unkn.

STEELE, ROBERT G (--d Franklin Co); Md Sarah Y Graves (   ); War of 1812; Goodspeed Franklin Co; likely Franklin Co; Unkn.

STEELE, SAMUEL (5-13-1782--3-7-1864 Davidson Co); Md Patience Shane 4-19-1805 (9-7-1787--6-4-1852); Capt, Brig Gen Robt Porterfield's Regt, Va Mil; Va S A; Davidson Co, near Hermitage; Pvt mkr.

STEPHENS, Capt JEHU (--d Monroe Co); Md Anne Tipton 11-27-1831 (   ); Capt, Co Mtd Gunmen, Col Sam Wear's E T V, 9-23-1813--12-31-1813, later a Co Mtd Gunmen from E T under Brig Gen John Coffee, 10-6-1814--4-6-1815; W D & T S A; Unkn Cem in Monroe Co; Unkn. (This Batln & others fromed into Regt & sent to Florida Coast for protection vs invasion by the British. David Crockett was a member of this company. Anne Tipton was dau Wm Tipton, Rev War & War of 1812.)

STEPHENS, JOHN (1776-- 1831 Bedford Co); Md Martha A Gully (1796--1879); War of 1812; B L Wt & Goodspeed Bedford Co; Bedford Co; Unkn.

STEWART, WILLIAM (b Scotland --d near Hermitage, Davidson Co); Md   (   ); War of 1812 under Jackson; Goodspeed Wilson Co; Davidson Co, likely Hermitage Ch Cem; Unkn. (He was an elder in Hermitage Church.)

STINSON, (STEPHENSON) William Sr (1744--10-29-1796 Washington Co); Md   (   ); Registrar Washington Co, 1789; Washington Co Records; Old Salem Pres Cem at Washington College, Washington Co; Pvt mkr. (Also Rev War)

STOKELEY, THOMAS (--liv 1828 List Haywood Co); Md
(   ); Pvt, Col Gray's Regt Riflemen; P D & 2400 Pensioners,
Armstrong; likely Haywood Co; Unkn.

STONE, JOHN (--d 11-6-1813 in service Ala); Md   (   );
Cornet, Capt Wm Locke's Co, Col John Allcorn's Regt, W T V Cav,
9-24-1813--11-6-1813 died; W D & T S A; likely Ala; Unkn.

STONE, WILLIAM (--2-18-1853 Marion Co or Sequatchie Co); Md Mary
Randles 6-15-1809 Sevier Co (1793--liv 1871 Sequatchie Co); Srgt,
Capt Jesse G Raney's Co, Col John Brown's 2nd Regt Mtd Gunmen,
Ensign 3-11-1814, disch 5-20-1814; W D & P D; Stone Fam Cem at
Davis, Sequatchie Co; Pvt mkr. (Stone was commissioned Brig Gen
3-27-1814 at Tohopeka.)

STONE, Capt WILLIAM (11-1-1775 Va --10-3-1854 Marshall Co); Md
Nancy Allen Daniel 1807 Va (1790--1838); War of 1812; Miss Susie
Gentry's Records & U S D 1812 Tenn Records; Stone Fam Cem near
Mooresville, Marshall Co; Pvt mkr. (Mrs Mary Jane Stone Dickerson, dau Wm Stone, was Real Daughter Tenn U S D of 1812.)

STOUT, DAVID D (11-11-1790--4-11-1888 Johnson Co); Md 1-Elizabeth
Howard 7-14-1818 Carter Co (--6-19-1857), 2-Anne Martin 3-20-1870
(--1-1906); Pvt, Capt Henry Hunter's Co, Col Wm Johnson's 3rd Regt
E T Drftd Mil, 9-13-1814--5-3-1815; W D & T S A & P D; Stout Fam
Cem near Butler, Johnson Co; Pvt mkr. (Mrs Dicey Stout Garland
was Real Daughter, Tenn U S D of 1812.)

STOVALL, JAMES (c 1800--aft 1854 Sumner Co); Md Polly (Mary)
Dephrest 3-5-1817 (   ); Pvt, Capt Martin's Co, Col Williamson's Regt W T Mtd Gunmen, 9-28-1814--; T S A; in Sumner, now
Trousdale Co; Unkn.

STOVER, DANIEL (4-10-1775--8-10-1849 Carter Co); Md 1-Phoebe Ward
1794 (--bef 1810), 2-Antoinette Williams 3-4-1810 (--1884 in Ind);
Srgt, Capt Jesse Cole's Co, Col Sam Wear's 1st Regt E T V, 10-18-1813--1-17-1814; W D & T S A; Stover Fam Cem at Siam, Carter Co;
Official 1812 mkr, 10-18-1932.

STOVER, JACOB (--d 1-20-1815 Ft Deposit, Ala); Md Elizabeth
(--liv 7-29-1853 aged 65 yrs); Pvt, Capt Wm Henderson's Co, 44th
Regt, Gen Nath Taylor's Brig, 9-1814--1-20-1815; T S A & P D;
likely at Ft Deposit, Ala; Unkn.

STRAIN, ROBERT (11-6-1790--4-26-1870 Limestone, Washington Co);
Md Nancy Biddle 6-8-1815 (3-15-1791--aft 1883); Ensign, Capt Wm
McLin's Co, Col Wm Lillard's 2nd Regt E T V, 10-12-1813--2-8-1814;
W D & T S A & P D; Urbana Meth Cem, Limestone, Washington Co; Pvt
mkr.

STRINGFIELD, Rev THOMAS (2-13-1797--6-12-1858 Jefferson Co); Md
Sarah Williams 1826 (   ); Battles of Camp Lookout & Emuckfau,
where wounded in skull & thought dead, revived by Gen Jackson,
1814; Price's Holston Methodism & W D; Stringfield Fam Cem at
Strawberry Plains, Jefferson Co; Unmkd. (Meth preacher)

STRONG, Dr JOSEPH CHURCHILL (10-3-1775-- 1844 Knoxville, Knox Co); Md 1-Catherine Neilson 1804 (1785--1810), 2-Jane Kain 1811 (1788--1846); Asst Surgeon U S N until 1801, M D for examining recruits in East Tenn; W D & J Hartsell "Memora", E T H S Publications, 1939-40; First Pres Cem in Knoxville, Knox Co; Pvt mkr. (Dr Strong was native of Boston.)

STUART, Capt JAMES Sr (--d Knoxville, Knox Co); Md (   );.Capt, Col Wm Johnson's 3rd Regt E T Drftd Mil, 9-20-1814--5-3-1815; T S A & Nelson Papers, p-75, wrote letter for pension; likely in Knoxville Cem, Knox Co; Unkn.

STUART, Capt JAMES Jr (--d Knox Co); Md (   ); Ensign, later Capt 2nd U S Inf, 9-1812, 1st Lieut, 24th U S Inf, July 1812, in Garrison at Ft Niagara, 12-19-1813 when assaulted; W D & T S A & Nelson Papers in McClung Room, p-432; likely in Knox Co; Unkn.

STUART, Capt THOMAS (--d likely Washington Co); Md (   ); Capt, Col John Williams' 39th Regt U S Inf, 1814; W D; likely in Washington Co; Unkn.

SUSONG, ANDREW (10-6-1792--10-1-1877 Greene Co); Md Susan Ball 1818 (5-23-1799--4-18-1881 Greene Co); Pvt, Capt George Keyes Co, Col Wm Lillard's 2nd Regt, E T V, 10-12-1813--2-8-1814; W D & T S A; Susong Memorial Bapt Cem near Greeneville, Greene Co; Pvt mkr.

SUTTON, EDMOND (1780--4- 1825 Rutherford Co); Md Mary Pierce (   ); Pvt, Capt Butler's Co, Col John K Wynne's 1st Regt Tenn Vol, 10-4-1813--1-4-1814; W D & T S A; Rutherford Co; Pvt mkr.

SWANSON, EDWARD (--d Williamson Co); Md (   ); War of 1812; W D; Williamson Co; Official 1812 mkr. (Also Rev War)

SWANSON, RICHARD (12-8-1790--8-13-1873 Williamson Co); Md Deborah Tarkington 1809 (9-10-1790--3-1876); Pvt, Capt George Mebane's Co, 1st Regt Tenn Inf, 6-20-1814--12-20-1814; T S A; Williamson Co; Pvt mkr.

SWISHER, MICHAEL (--d likely Hamilton Co); Md Anna   (--liv 6-10-1852 B L Wt Hamilton Co); Pvt, Capt Short's Co, --- ; P D & B L Wt, Edwards Acct Bk, Leaves from Family Tree- Allen, 5-13-1934; likely in Hamilton Co; Unkn.

SYPERT, LAWRENCE (1778--aft 1868 Lebanon, Wilson Co); Md Mary Lambeth (   ); Pvt, Capt Charles Wade's Co, also Capt John Hayes' Co, Wilson Co, 6-24-1814--; T S A; Lebanon Cem, Wilson Co; Unkn.

SYPERT, WILLIAM L (--liv 1840 List aged 45 yrs Wilson Co); Md (   ); Pvt, Capt Thomas Williamson's Co, Col Pillow's Regt W T Mil; P D & 2400 Pensioners, Armstrong; likely Wilson Co; Unkn.

TALIAFERRO, ZACHARIAH (1799-- 1875 Wilson Co); Md (   ); Pvt, Capt Tate's Co, Gen John Coffee's Brig W T; T S A & Texas 1812 Records; likely in Lebanon, Wilson Co; Unkn. ("Extra pay for youngest soldier")

TALLEY, HOP (--d Lewis Co); Md (   ); War of 1812 & Mr Bandy Data, V A, Mountain Home, Tenn; Unkn Cem near Hickman, Lewis Co; Unkn.

TALLEY, WILLIAM (--d Hamilton Co); Md (   ); War of 1812; Hamilton Co Hist- Armstrong; in Hamilton Co; Unkn.

TANKERSLEY, WILLIAM (--10- 1814 in service); Md (   ); Pvt, 3rd Regt, U S Inf; W D & P D & 2400 Pensioners, Armstrong; likely where died; Unkn.

TATE, DAVID III (1789-- 1860 May Spring, Grainger Co); Md Mrs Mary Chamberlain Masengill 2-25-1816 (   ); War of 1812; Leaves from Family Tree- Allen, 12-6-1936; Chamberlain Fam Cem near May Spring, Grainger Co; Pvt mkr.

TATE, EDWARD (7-19-1785-- 1870 Grainger Co); Md Lucy Moody (3-13-1792--1853); Promoted to Maj in War of 1812; Goodspeed E T H Grainger Co; Tate Fam Cem in Grainger Co; Pvt mkr.

TATE, JOHN KNOX (1792--12-20-1853 Marion Co); Md Rachel Carmichael 12-5-1816 (1790--3-4-1870 Battle Creek, Marion Co); Creek War; T S A & Leaves from Family Tree- Allen, 12-13-1936; Tate Fam Cem on Battle Creek, Marion Co; Pvt mkr.

TATUM, Maj HOWELL (1753-- 1828 Nashville, Davidson Co); Md (   ); Treas, W T Distr 1794-96, Judge Supreme Ct 1797-98 & War of 1812; T S A & Texas 1812 Records; Nashville, Davidson Co; Unkn.

TAYLOR, ANDREW (b Ireland --bet 5 & 11- 1787 Washington Co); Md 1-Elizabeth Wilson (--bef 1770), 2-Anne Wilson c 1770 (--aft 1787); Member of Constitutional Conv State Franklin, 1784 & J P Washington Co; W D & T S A; Taylor Fam Cem on hill above Powder Branch near Watauga Point, Carter Co; Unmkd. (Also Rev War)

TAYLOR, BENJAMIN (8-11-1788--10-3-1856 Blount Co); Md Letitia Upton (8-1788--8-1-1844); Pvt, Capt Edward Buchanan's Co, Col Sam Wear's Regt E T Drftd Mil, 1-10-1814--5-20-1814; W D & T S A; Centenary Bapt Cem, Blount Co; Pvt mkr.

TAYLOR, CHARLES (--d likely Hamilton Co); Md (   ); Corp, Capt Edward Buchanan's Co, Col Sam Wear's Regt E T Drftd Mil, 1-10-1814--5-20-1814; W D & T S A; likely in Hamilton Co; Unkn.

TAYLOR, CHARLES FOX (--likely Hamilton Co); Md (   ); Pvt, Col Gideon Morgan Jr Regt in Creek War; T S A & Hamilton Co Hist- Armstrong; Hamilton Co; Unkn.

TAYLOR, JAMES (--d 1-22-1815 in service); Md ( ); Pvt, Capt Jehu Stephens Co Vol Mtd Gunmen, Brig Gen John Coffee's Brig, 10-6-1814--1-22-1815 died; W D & T S A; likely where died; Unkn.

TAYLOR, LARKIN C (b N C -- 1847 Bradley Co); Md Martha Reed, McMinn Co (--aft 1887 Bradley Co); Capt, War of 1812; Goodspeed E T H Bradley Co; Bradley Co; Unkn.

TAYLOR, LEEROY (--6-22-1836 near Madisonville, Monroe Co); Md Keziah Reasoner (1797--aft 1860); Pvt, Capt Adam Winsell's Co, Col Ewen Allison's 1st Regt E T Drftd Mil, 1-1-1814--6-1-1814; W D & T S A & B L Wt; Taylor Fam Cem near Madisonville, Monroe Co; Unkn. (Leeroy Taylor md Keziah Reasoner 6-1-1815 Carter Co)

TAYLOR, LEEROY (1758--3-24-1834 Washington Co); Md 1-Mary Bradford 1774 ( ), 2-Nellie (--bef 1834); Indian Wars & Constitutional Conv from Washington Co, 1796; W D & T S A; Fairview Meth Cem, Washington Co; Govt mkr & Pvt mkr. (Also Rev War)

TAYLOR, Gen NATHANIEL (2-24-1772--2-20-1816 Carter Co); Md Mary Patton 11-15-1791 (--bef 9-1853); Capt Co vs Indians 1799 & Brig Gen, War of 1812, 9-20-1814--6-20-1815, stat at Ft Claiborne, 1-8-1815 during Battle of N O; W D & T S A; Taylor Fam Cem on Powder Branch, Carter Co; Pvt mkr - flat slab with inscription illegible.

TAYLOR, PARMENAS (4-4-1753--2-28-1827 Jefferson Co); Md Patty White 1779 (1760--1838); Indian Wars, Col of Jefferson Co Mil, Jefferson Co Records; likely Jefferson Co; Unkn. (Also Rev War)

TAYLOR, Capt RICHARD (--d Tenn); Md ( ); Capt, Col Gideon Morgan Jr at Tohopeka, 3-27-1814; T S A & Old Frontiers- Brown; likely in Tenn; Unkn.

TAYLOR, THOMAS (--killed 11-9-1813 Talledega, Ala); Md ( ); Pvt, Capt John Baskerville's Co Vol Cav, Col John Allcorn's Regt W T V, 9-24-1813--11-9-1813 killed; W D & T S A; likely in Ala; Unkn.

TAYLOR, WILLIAM (--d Tenn); Md Martha ( ); 2nd Corp, Capt Jehu Stephens' Co, Mtd Gunmen, Col Sam Wear's Regt E T V, 9-23-1813--12-31-1813; W D & P D; likely in Tenn; Unkn. (Widow had Pension)

TAYLOR, Dr WILLIAM VANNAH (1790-- 1873 Shelby Co); Md Fannie McCoy Henderson aft 1815 ( ); Surgeon on Ship Constitution; Elmwood Cem Records; Elmwood Cem in Memphis, Shelby Co; Govt mkr.

TEDDER, JAMES A (--d Roane Co); Md Elizabeth Todd 2-21-1821 ( ); Lieut, War of 1812, enl 8-31-1813--; T S A; Tedder Fam Cem 2 m N Rockwood, Roane Co; Unmkd.

TEDDER, JOHN BROWN (1789-- 1862 Roane Co); Md Mary Robinson 2-4-1819 (1796--1872 Roane Co); Srgt, Capt James Standifer's Co, Mtd Inf; T S A; Tedder Fam Cem 2 m N Rockwood, Roane Co; Unmkd.

TEFFETELLER, JOSEPH (--d Blount Co); Md ( ); Pvt, Capt Edward Buchanan's Co, Col Sam Wear's Regt E T Drftd Mil, 1-10-1814--5-20-1814; W D & T S A & P D; Blount Co; Unkn. (Pension #3,633)

TEMPLE, JESSE (12-20-1790--7-4-1873 Hickman Co); Md Tabitha Tinsley 9-22-1814 (7-28-1793--2-7-1883); Pvt, Capt Thomas Sterritt's Co, Col Sam Parker's Regt Ky Mil; Ky S A; Cem in 13th District, Hickman Co; Pvt mkr.

THOMAS, ABRAHAM (--d Hamilton Co); Md ( ); War of 1812; Hamilton Co Hist- Armstrong; likely Hamilton Co; Unkn.

THOMAS, Dr ARCHIE (1780--d Robertson Co); Md ( ); War of 1812 with Jackson; W D; Springfield, Robertson Co; Unkn.

THOMAS, ENOCH (8-24-1791--10-22-1855 Bradley Co); Md Marthena (12-15-1809--9-14-1878); Pvt, Capt Casper's Co, Col --- ; Edwards Acct Bk; Henegar's Chapel Meth Cem near Cleveland, Bradley Co; Pvt mkr.

THOMAS, ISAAC (1735-- 1818 Sevier Co); Md Elizabeth Timothy Masengill c 1782 (--d aft 1818); Early Indian Wars, Trader, Comm of Sevierville, 1799; T S A; Thomas Fam Cem at Sevierville, Sevier Co; Unmkd. (Also Rev War)

THOMAS, ISAAC (1792--aft 1878 Claiborne Co); Md Rebecca Barr 1-6-1817 ( ); Pvt, Capt Benjamin H King's Co, Col Wm Lillard's 2nd Regt E T V, 10-12-1813--2-8-1814; W D & T S A & P D; likely near Old Town (Old Tazewell), Claiborne Co; Unkn.

THOMAS, JOHN (1798--d Blount Co); Md Elizabeth Daniels 8-3-1822 (8-9-1802--); Pvt, War of 1812; W D & P D; Logan's Chapel Meth Cem at Wildwood, Blount Co; Official 1812 mkr. (Widow's Pension #22,039)

THOMAS, WILLIAM (--4-12-1848 Sevier Co); Md Catherine Houk 9-7-1810 Sevier Co (1789--liv 1850); Pvt, Capt Isaac Williams' Co, Col Sam Bunch's 2nd Regt E T Drftd Mil, 1-10-1814--1-24-1814 disch; W D & P D; in Sevier Co; Unkn.

THOMPSON, JAMES P (--liv 1883 Warren Co); Md ( ); War of 1812; P D & Liv 1883 at McMinnville, Warren Co; likely in Warren Co; Unkn. (Pension #23,336)

THOMPSON, MOSES (--d 9-24-1814 at Ft Williams, Ala); Md ( ); Pvt, Capt Nowlin's Co, Col Philip Pipkin's Regt, enl 6-20-1814--; W D & T S A; at Ft Williams, Talledega Co, Ala; Unmkd.

THOMPSON, SAMUEL (--liv 1832 List aged 80 yrs Blount Co); Md ( ); Pvt, Capt Edwin Boothe's 5th Regt E T Drftd Mil, 11-13-1814--5-15-1815; W D & P D; Thompson Fam Cem near Thompson Bridge, Blount Co; Unmkd.

THOMPSON, THOMAS (1767-- 1837 Davidson Co); Md Nancy
(   ); Signer of Cumberland Compact 5-1-1780, J P Davidson
Co, 1799; T S A & 2400 Pensioners, Armstrong; Thompson Fam Cem
4 m S Nashville, Davidson Co; Pvt mkr. (Also Rev War Pensioner)

THORNBURG, JOHN (--liv 1840 List aged 61 yrs Washington Co);
Md   (   ); Pvt, 24th Regt Riflemen; P D & 2400 Pensioners, Armstrong; likely in Washington Co; Unkn.

THORPE, JOHN (--liv 1840 List aged 63 yrs Hardin Co); Md
(   ); Pvt, 5th Regt U S Inf; P D & 2400 Pensioners, Armstrong;
in 5th District, Hardin Co; Unkn.

TILSON, JOHN (--12-24-1855 18th Distr, Washington Co); Md Mary
Erwin 12-2-1812 (c 1794--liv 1872 aged 78 yrs Unicoi Co); Pvt,
Capt Jacob Hartsell's Co, Col Wm Lillard's 2nd Regt E T V, 10-13-1813--2-8-1814, under Maj Wm Snodgrass; W D & T S A & P D; Unkn
Cem in 18th Distr, Washington Co (now Unicoi); Unkn. (Mary Tilson's Pension #2960)

TILSON, THOMAS (--liv 1860 Washington Co (now Unicoi); Md
(   ); War of 1812; Nelson Papers in McClung Room, Knoxville;
likely in Unicoi Co; Unkn.

TILTON, PHILIP (TITLOW) (---liv 1828 List & 1840 List aged 57 yrs
Knox Co); Md   (   ); Pvt, 1st Regt Riflemen; P D &
2400 Pensioners, Armstrong; likely Knox Co; Unkn.

TIPTON, ABRAHAM (8-27-1794--7-3-1868 Carter Co); Md Martha Lacey
3-8-1817 (8-27-1798--10-13-1875 Carter Co); Srgt, Capt Jesse Cole's
Co, Col Sam Wear's 1st Regt E T V, 10-18-1813--1-17-1814; W D &
T S A; Johnson Fam Cem in eastern Elizabethton, Carter Co; Pvt mkr.

TIPTON, ABRAHAM BUTLER (3-3-1783--11-15-1831 Knox Co); Md Jane
Roddy 4-29-1806 (12-16-1789--12-26-1852); Pvt, Capt Wm Walker's
Co, Col John Williams' Co, 12-12-1812--3-25-1813; W D & T S A;
Woodlawn Cem, Knoxville, Knox Co; Pvt mkr.

TIPTON, ABRAM BUTLER (10-8-1794--3-2-1865 Sullivan Co); Md Margaret Snapp (11-21-1793--8-10-1886 Sullivan Co); 3rd Srgt, Capt
Wm King's Co, Col Ewen Allison's E T Drftd Mil, 1-6-1814--5-18-1814; W D & T S A; Blountville Cem, Sullivan Co; Pvt mkr.

TIPTON, BENJAMIN (c 1787-- 1865 Blount Co); Md 1-Nancy Brooks
10-28-1824 (   ), 2-Polly   (   ); Pvt, Capt Callaway's Co, Col Sam Wear's 1st Regt Mtd Vol, 9-23-1813--12-31-1813;
W D & T S A; Ellijoy Bapt Cem, Blount Co; Unmkd.

TIPTON, EDWARD (--killed 1-22-1814 Emuckfau, Ala); Md
(   ); Pvt, Capt Philip Pipkin's Co, Col Perkins' Regt Mtd
Riflemen, 12-19-1813--1-22-1814; W D & T S A; likely at Emuckfau,
where killed; Unmkd.

TIPTON, ISAAC (1791--d likely Knox Co); Md Frances White (   );
Pvt, Capt Reuben Tipton's Co, Maj John Chiles' Regt Mtd Gunmen,
9-20-1814--5-1-1815; W D & Blount Co Hist- Burns; likely Knox Co;
Unkn. (Also served Pvt, Capt Callaway's Co, Col Sam Wear's 1st
Regt E T V, 9-23-1813--12-31-1813, W D)

TIPTON, JACOB (--d in Tenn); Md   (   ); Pvt, Capt Adam Winsell's Co, Col Ewen Allison's Regt E T Drftd Mil, 1-5-1814--on command at Ft Williams 4-27-1814, & trans from Capt Francis Register's Co, Col Sam Bunch's Regt; W D & T S A; likely in Tenn; Unkn.

TIPTON, JACOB (11-5-1790--9-17-1839 Tipton Co); Md Lorina Taylor 1-1-1818 (5-3-1800--3-12-1874 Tipton Co); Ensign & 2nd & 1st Lieut in 1st Regt Rifle Corp U S A, Register Land Office for East Tenn & Brig Gen 14th Regt Tenn Mil; W D & T S A; Tipton Fam Cem near Covington, Tipton Co; Pvt mkr.

TIPTON, Capt JACOB (c 1765--11-4-1791 at St Clair's Defeat); Md Mary Bradford (--aft 1791); Capt, Maj Rhea's Regt to Ft Washington near Cincinnati, July 19, 1791; W D & Canadian Archives; likely at site of death; Unmkd.

TIPTON, Col JOHN (1732--Md --8-1813 Washington Co); Md 1-Mary Butler c 1750 (--d 6-8-1776 in Va), 2-Martha Denton Moore (wid) 7-22-1777 Va (--d aft 1813); Constitutional Conv 1796 from Washington Co, Senator 1796, Chicamauga Expd vs Indians 1788; W D & T S A; Tipton-Haynes-Gifford Fam Cem on Sinking Creek, Washington Co; Govt mkr & Monument erected by Tenn Hist Commission & Patriotic Societies, Sesquicentennial Tenn, 1946. (Also Capt, Rev War in Va)

TIPTON, JOHN II (4-21-1769--10-8-1831 Nashville, Davidson Co); Md Elizabeth Snapp 10-28-1791 in Va (--d bef 1831); on Gen Jackson's Staff at N O & Tenn Legislature; W D & T S A; Old City Cem in Nashville, Davidson Co; Mkd by 49th Gen Assmbly of Tenn, Monument. (Col Tipton died while in Legislature)

TIPTON, JOHN (1791--11-23-1871 Blount Co); Single; Pvt, Capt Reuben Tipton's Co, Maj John Chiles' Regt E T V Mtd Gunmen, 9-20-1814--5-1-1815; W D & T S A & Blount Co Hist- Burns; likely at Ellijoy Bapt Cem, Blount Co; Unkn. (He was in brother's Co.)

TIPTON, JONATHAN (12-1-1796--3-16-1840 Blount Co); Md 1-Margaret Watson c 1817 (5-20-1798--12-20-1827), 2-Elizabeth Johnson 11-6-1829 (   ); Pvt, Capt Reuben Tipton's Co, Maj John Chiles' Regt E T Mtd Gunmen, 9-20-1814--5-1-1815; W D & T S A & Blount Co Hist- Burns; Tipton Fam Cem on Badgett Farm, Blount Co, near Knox Co line; Govt mkr.

TIPTON, Capt REUBEN (1781--d Knox Co); Md 1-   (   ), 2-Ailcey Childress (   ); Srgt, Capt Sam Bunch's Co, Col John Williams' Regt Mtd Vol, 12-1-1812--3-25-1813, & 3rd Lieut, Capt Callaway's Co, Col Sam Wear's 1st Regt E T Mtd V, 9-23-1813--12-31-1813, & Pvt, Capt John Chiles' Co, Col John Brown's 2nd Regt Mtd Gunmen, 1-10-1814-- & Capt, Maj Chiles' Regt Mtd Gunmen, 9-20-1814--5-1-1815; W D & T S A; Cem in Knox Co; Unkn.

TIPTON, SAMUEL (11-14-1767 Va --7-21-1833 Elizabethton, Carter Co); Md 1-Jemima Little (6-1776--   ), 2-Susanna Reneau c 1783 (11-14-1767 Va --2-10-1853 aged 85-3-26 dys); Tenn Legislature 1801 & 1803 from Carter Co; T S A; Samuel Tipton Fam Cem S of Elizabethton, Carter Co; Pvt mkr. (1st Court Carter Co held in his house, Elizabethton laid out on his land; also Rev War in Va)

TIPTON, SAMUEL (--d likely Carter Co); Md   (   );
Pvt, Capt Solomon Hendrix' Co, Col Sam Bayless' 4th Regt, E T
Drftd Mil, 11-14-1814-- ; W D & T S A; likely in Carter Co; Unkn.
(Can this be the son of Samuel & Susanna Reneau Tipton? Fam
Tradition says he served in War of 1812.)

TIPTON, WILLIAM Sr (2-13-1761--11-3-1849 Knox-Blount Co); Md
Phoebe Moore (--d aft 1840 Blount Co); Pvt, Capt Callaway's Co,
Col Sam Wear's 1st Regt Mtd Vol Inf, 10-5-1813-- 1814, Battles
of Pensacola, Talledega, Enochopco, Tohopeka; W D & T S A; Tip-
ton Fam Cem on Badgett Farm, Blount Co-Knox Co line; Govt mkr.
(Also Rev War; in War of 1812 when almost 60 yrs of age)

NOTE: There were over 30 members of this Tipton family in the
      War of 1812 from East Tenn.

TOLLETT, JOHN (--d Bledsoe Co); Md   (   ); Comm to
select County Seat Bledsoe Co in 1807, also J P; T S A; Cem near
Tollett's Mill, N Bledsoe Co; Unkn.

TONEY, WILLIAM (--liv 1828 List Carter Co); Md   (   );
Pvt, 5th U S Inf from Va, trans to Carter Co; P D & 2400 Pensioners, Armstrong & Va S A; likely Carter Co; Unkn.

TOOLE, WILLIAM (1-4-1791--5-16-1860 Blount Co); Md 1-Elizabeth
       (3-30-1794--10-30-1823), 2-Elizabeth Wallace 2-22-1825
(   ); Pvt, Capt James Gillespie's Co, Col Sam Wear's 1st Regt
E T V, 9-23-1813--12-31-1813; W D & T S A; New Providence Pres
Cem, Maryville, Blount Co; Pvt mkr.

TOWNSEND, JOHN (--liv 1828 List Carroll Co); Md   (   );
Pvt, Capt Washington's Cav; P D & 2400 Pensioners, Armstrong;
likely in Carroll Co; Unkn.

TOWNSLEY, GEORGE (--d 1841 Blount Co); Md Jane   (   );
Pvt, Capt John Tedford's Co, 1793 Indian Wars; W D; Townsley Fam
Cem near Norwood Inn, Blount Co; Hiway #411 cut thru Cem; Unmkd.

TOWNSLEY, JAMES (--d Blount Co); Md   (   ); Pvt,
Capt James Gillespie's Co, Col Sam Wear's 1st Regt E T V, 9-23-
1813--12-31-1813; W D & Blount Co Hist- Burns; Townsend Fam Cem
near Norwood Inn, Blount Co; Hiway #411 cut thru Cem; Unmkd.

TRACEY, PARIS (--d 9-20-1814 at Ft Williams, Ala); Md   --
(   ); Pvt, Capt Nowlin's Co, Col Pipkin's Regt, enl 6-20-
1814; W D & T S A; at Ft Williams, Talledega Co, Ala; Unmkd.

TREZAVANT, Col JAMES (2-14-1783 Va --8-5-1841 Shelby Co); Md Mary
Blount (10-19-1789--3-4-1852); Commanded Regt in War of 1812 to
protect Va Coast; Va S A; Elmwood Cem, Memphis, Shelby Co; Govt
mkr.

TRIBBETT, ROBERT (TRIPLETT) (--liv 1840 List aged 57 yrs Sullivan Co); Md   (   ); War of 1812; P D & 2400 Pensioners, Armstrong; likely Sullivan Co; Unkn.

TROUSDALE, WILLIAM (9-23-1790 N C --3-27-1872 aged 82 yrs Sumner Co); Md Mary Bugg (1808--1883); Col in Creek War aged 23, with Jackson at Talledega, Tallushatchie, Pensacola & N O; W D & T S A; Gallatin, Sumner Co; Monument by State of Tenn. (Also in Seminole & Mexican Wars; & Gov of Tenn)

TUCK, MOSES (--d Loudon Co); Md 1- (   ), 2-Polly Black (   ); War of 1812; W D; McCollam Fam Cem near Greenback, Loudon Co; Govt mkr, by 1812 Chapter.

TUCKER, JONATHAN (--d 1-14-1828 Washington Co); Md Mary Hartman 3-6-1800 (--liv 1-17-1852 aged 75 yrs Washington Co & liv 4-12-1855 in Yancey Co, N C); Pvt, Capt Jacob Hartsell's Co, Col Wm Lillard's 2nd Regt E T V, 10-12-1813--2-8-1814; W D & T S A & B L Wt & P D; Beals Fam Cem on Jump Hill bet Embreeville & Erwin, Unicoi Co; Pvt mkr. (Will dated 1-14-1828, prob July 1828)

TUNNELL, ROBERT (12-4-1782 Va --d Hamilton Co); Md Elizabeth Johnson 1802 (   ); Early Indian Wars & in 7 Battles War of 1812; Hamilton Co Hist- Armstrong; Harrison Fam Cem in Hamilton Co; Unkn.

TURNER, WILEY (4-14-1796--1-18-1860 Humphreys Co); Md Maria Thompson 11-13-1817 (11-10-1797--3-6-1874); 3rd Corp, Capt Blair's Co, Col James Roulstone's 3rd Regt W T Mil, 11-13-1814--5-13-1815; W D & T S A; Humphreys Co; Pvt mkr.

TURNLEY, GEORGE (--liv 1840 List aged 78 yrs Jefferson Co); Md (   ); War of 1812; P D & 2400 Pensioners, Armstrong; likely Jefferson Co; Unkn. (Also Rev War)

TYLER, JOHN B (b Va -- 1860 Montgomery Co); Md (   ); Capt, Cav in N C War of 1812; N C S A; likely Montgomery Co; Unkn.

TYREE, THOMAS I (--d Tenn); Md Charlotte Ellison 4-27-1819 (   ); Pvt, Capt Archer's Co, Va Mil; P D & Va S A; Unkn Co in Tenn; Unkn.

UPTON, WILLIAM (--d Monroe Co); Md Mrs   Jones Ballard
(   ); 1st Lieut, Capt Jehu Stephens' Co, Col Sam Wear's
Regt Drftd Mil, 10-6-1814--4-6-1815; W D & T S A; Unkn Cem in
Monroe Co; Unkn.

USHER, JOHN (--d at Ft Williams, Ala in 1814); Md
(   ); Pvt, Capt Lunsford's Co, Col John Brown's 2nd Regt Mtd
Gunmen; W D & T S A; at Ft Williams, Talledega Co, Ala; Unmkd.

VAN HOOSEN, (VAN HOUSER) JOHN (--liv 1883 List McMinnville,
Warren Co); Md   (   ); War of 1812; P D, Pension
#8729; likely McMinnville, Warren Co; Unkn.

VAN HUSS, MATTHIAS (1778--c 1860 Carter Co); Md Louvenia Dugger
(   ); War of 1812; Goodspeed E T H Carter Co; Van Huss Fam
Cem, Carter Co; Unkn.

VAN DYKE, THOMAS J (1777 Del --12-27-1814 at Ft Claiborne, Ala);
Md Penelope S Campbell, dau Judge David Campbell 1798 (1784--d
Ala); at Tellico Blockhouse 1797, 1803, Kingston, S W Point, Hi-
wassee Garrison 1807, & Surgeon in Col Wm Lillard's 2nd Regt E T V,
Gen Doherty's Brig, 10-14-1813--3-1-1814, & Surgeon in Col Wm John-
son's 3rd Regt E T Drftd Mil, 9-18-1814--12-27-1814 d Ft Claiborne,
Ala; W D & T S A & Leaves from the Family Tree- Allen; Campbell
Fam Cem, Rhea Co; Pvt mkr.

VANCE, DAVID G (--d 1823-4 Washington Co); Md   (--aft
1824); Capt, Col Sam Bunch's Regt Mtd Gunmen, 10-16-1813--1-22-
1814; W D & T S A; likely in Washington or Greene Co; Unkn. (Inv
filed Oct 17, 1823 Washington Co, Tenn)

VINCENT, GEORGE (1753-- 1832 Sullivan Co); Md Eleanor Acuff (1761
--1-23-1849); Capt Mil Co vs Chicamauga Indians, 1788, Col Robert
Love & Gen Joseph Martin; T S A; Vincent Fam Cem, Sullivan Co;
Pvt mkr.

VINCENT, THOMAS (2-20-1790--1-20-1864 Washington Co); Md Sarah Em-
bree (4-1-1811--8-5-1843); Pvt, Capt Hugh Martin's Co, Col Wm Lillard's 2nd Regt E T V, 10-12-1813--2-8-1814; W D & T S A; Hunt Fam
Cem 1 m E Johnson City on Hiway #19, Washington Co; Pvt mkr.

WADDELL, ELIAS (WADDLE) (--killed 3-27-1814 Tohopeka, Ala); Md ( ); 2nd Lieut; Capt Jonas Laughmiller's Co, Col Ewen Allison's E T Drftd Mil, 1-10-1814--3-27-1814 killed; W D & T S A; likely Ala; Unmkd.

WADDELL, JACOB (WADDLE) (--captured at Ft Niagara); Md ( ); heirs were Polly, Parmelia, Henry, Jacob & Harman of Sullivan Co; Pvt, 24th Regt U S Inf; P D & 2400 Pensioners, Armstrong; likely at Ft Niagara; Unkn.

WADDELL, JONATHAN (WADDLE) (3-3-1779--3-11-1836 Washington Co); Md Hannah Greenway 12-17-1803 (5-8-1785--12-19-1822); Capt, Col Sam Bayless' 4th Regt E T Drftd Mil under Gen Wm Carroll, 11-13-1814--5-18-1815, mustered out at Knoxville 5-18-1815 & got pay to Washington Co; W D & T S A; Waddell Fam Cem on Nolachucky River, Washington Co; Unkn.

WAGONER, JOHN (b N C --d Williamson Co); Md Sarah ( ); War of 1812; Goodspeed Williamson Co; likely Williamson Co; Unkn.

WALKER, EDWARD Jr (9-7-1795--4-8-1860 Claiborne Co); Md 1-Mahala Tussey (--d 12-28-1842), 2-Sarah Crumley 6-25-1848 Hancock Co (1818--); Pvt, Capt John Slatter's Co, Col Edwin Boothe's 5th Regt E T Drftd Mil, 11-13-1814--6-2-1815; W D & P D & T S A; Mulberry Gap Cem in Hancock Co; Pvt mkr.

WALKER, JAMES (--liv 1828 List Henry Co); Md ( ); Pvt, Tenn Vol; P D & 2400 Pensioners, Armstrong; likely Henry Co; Unkn.

WALKER, JOEL (1764-- 1834 Maury Co); Md Mary B c 1800 ( ); Pvt, Capt McKamey's Co, Col John Brown's 2nd Regt E T Mil, 1-1-1814--5-20-1814; W D & T S A; Maury Co; Pvt mkr.

WALKER, Maj JOHN Jr (--killed 8- 1834); Md Emily S Meigs 1-10-1824 ( ); served in Battle of Talledega & Tohopeka; W D & Old Frontiers- Brown; Walker Fam Cem 3 m N E Cleveland, Bradley Co; D A R mkr. (Emily S Meigs was granddaughter of Col Return J Meigs)

WALKER, JOHN (1791--liv 11-9-1850 Sevier Co); Md ( ); Ord Srgt, Capt Simeon Perry's Co, Mtd Inf, Col Sam Bunch's Regt, 9-20-1813--12-1813; W D & P D; likely in Sevier Co; Unkn.

WALKER, JOHN S (1-1-1787--6-4-1869 Meigs Co); Md Elizabeth (10-10-1789--5-17-1869); Pvt, Capt Jacob Hartsell's Co, Col Wm Lillard's 2nd Regt E T V, 10-13-1813--2-8-1814; W D & T S A; Ten Mile Cem in Meigs Co; Govt mkr by a descendant c 1957.

WALKER, WILLIAM (-- Blount Co); Md ( ); Pvt, Capt John McNair's Co, Col Sam Bunch's Mtd Mil, 1-10-1814 & Pvt, Capt David McKamey's Co, Col Wm Johnson's 3rd Regt E T Drftd Mil, 9-29-1814--5-18-1815; W D & T S A; likely Big Springs Pres Cem, Blount Co; Unkn.

WALKER, WILLIAM (7-16-1786--3-27-1868 Blount Co); Md Elizabeth Culbertson 12-24-1810 (4-29-1792--3-12-1870); Capt, Col John Williams' Vol, 12-1-1812--3-25-1813, & Capt, Light Horse Co, Col John Williams' 39th Regt at Tohopeka, 3-27-1814; W D & T S A; Burns Fam Cem near Townsend, Blount Co; Govt mkr.

WALKER, WILLIAM (11-16-1791--6-26-1863 Bledsoe Co); Md Rachel Eden 1-20-1814 (1-28-1798--5-2-1864 Bledsoe Co); Pvt, Capt Stewart's Co, Col Wm Johnson's 3rd Regt E T Drftd Mil, 9-20-1814--5-3-1815; W D & T S A; Walker Fam Cem in Bledsoe Co; Pvt mkr. (Bur beside his father who has Rev War mkr)

WALKER, WILLIAM W (--liv 1840 List aged 25 yrs (?) Robertson Co); Md ( ); War of 1812; P D & 2400 Pensioners, Armstrong; likely Robertson Co; Unkn. (The "aged 25 yrs" must be error)

WALLACE, WILLIAM (9-8-1794--4-21-1864 Blount Co); Md Margaret Chamberlain 10-16-1816 (8-17-1792--10-8-1844); Pvt, Capt Samuel Cowan's Co, Maj James P H Porter's Sqdrn E T Mil, under Gen James White, enl 9-23-1813-- ; W D & T S A; New Providence Pres Cem at Maryville, Blount Co; Granite monument, cost $1,000.

WALTON, ISAAC (2-1-1763--8-21-1840 Sumner Co); Md Catherine Perry 1783 (1765--9-6-1824); Member of Tenn Constitutional Conv, 1796 & Repr from Sumner Co; T S A; Sumner Co; Pvt mkr.

WARNER, RICHARD (8-26-1794--3-8-1876 Bedford Co); Md Lucy Brown 11-28-1826 (3-1-1806--4-2-1860); Pvt, Capt Ephraim D Dickson's Co, Col Robt H Dyer's 1st Regt Mtd Gunmen, 9-28-1814--4-27-1815; W D & T S A; Warner Fam Cem 5 m W Shelbyville, Bedford Co; Pvt mkr.

WATERHOUSE, RICHARD GREEN (4-11-1775 in N J --3-6-1827 Rhea Co); Md 1-Polly Tipton 1803 ( ), 2-Elizabeth Hackett 1-1-1816 (--wid md aft 1827 to Gen Wm C Smartt of Warren Co, Tenn); Pvt, Capt Wm Walker's Co, Col John Williams' Regt, 12-1-1812--3-25-1813; W D & T S A; Waterhouse Fam Cem near Spring City, Rhea Co; Pvt mkr. (Waterhouse was divorced from his 1st wife, Polly Tipton)

WATKINS, Maj (--d Nashville, Davidson Co); Md ( ); Maj, War of 1812; Old City Cem, Nashville, Davidson Co; Pvt mkr.

WATKINS, THOMAS W (1794-- 1877 Wilson Co); Md Nancy S 1814 (1796--1880); Pvt, Capt Wm Lock's Co, Cav, Col John Allcorn's Regt W T Mil, 9-24-1813--12-10-1813; W D & T S A & Tenn Soldiers in War of 1812-Vol 1- Allen; Lebanon, Wilson Co; Pvt mkr.

WATKINS, PHILIP (--d likely Hamilton Co); Md Mary (--liv 2-21-1852 B L Wt); War of 1812; P D #42,420 & Leaves from Family Tree, 5-13-1934, Edwards Acct Bk; likely Hamilton Co; Unkn. (Wid Mary Watkins got 40 acres 2-21-1852 B L Wt, liv Hamilton Co)

WATSON, JONATHAN (--enl 1809 & died 18); Md ( ); Data from Nelson Papers, McClung Room, Knoxville & Washington Co Records, Inv Bk 00 p-367, 1815; likely Washington Co; Unkn.

WAUGH, JOHN (b Penn -- 1855 aged 77 yrs Ashe Co, N C); Md Ruth Piper (1780--1848 near Madisonville, Monroe Co); Comm Agent at Tellico Blockhouse under Jackson, War of 1812; Goodspeed E T H Monroe Co; likely in Monroe Co; Unkn.

WEAKLEY, ROBERT (7-20-1764--2-4-1845 Lakeland, Davidson Co); Md   (   ); Member Constitutional Conv 1787 & U S Congress 1809-11; N C S A & Congressional Dir; Weakley Fam Cem at Lakeland, Davidson Co; Pvt mkr. (Also Rev War)

WEAR, JOHN (1793-- 1868 Sevier Co); Md 1-Susan Mullendore (1796 --1837), 2-Sarah A M Patty 9-26-1839 (--liv 4-26-1878 Sevier Co); Waggoner & Pvt, Capt Simeon Perry's Co, Col Sam Wear's 1st Regt E T V, 9-23-1813--12-31-1813, & Lieut, Capt John Houk's Co, Col Sam Bunch's E T Drftd Mil, 1-8-1814--5-16-1814 & Waggoner, Capt Jehu Stephens' Co, Col Sam Wear's Regt Mtd Gunmen, 10-6-1814 --4-6-1815; W D & T S A & Henderson & McGhee Store Accts, Maryville, Blount Co; Shiloh Meth Cem, Sevier Co; Pvt mkr.

WEAR, ROBERT (11-4-1781--8-4-1846 Loudon Co); Md 1-Lucretia Thomas (8-1-1784--2-21-1830), 2-Margaret Wilkinson 4-4-1831 (   ); Capt, Col Sam Wear's 1st Regt E T V, 9-23-1813--12-31-1813, & Districk Surveyor Blount Co, 1815; W D & T S A & Blount Co Records; Wear Fam Cem near Morganton, Loudon Co; Pvt mkr.

WEAR, Col SAMUEL (1753--4-13-1817 Sevier Co); Md 1-Mary Thompson 1779 (1757--1797), 2-Mary Gilleland c 1800 (1758--1843); Capt, Co vs Indians at Tallassee, 6-19-1793 & Col, 1st Regt E T V, 9-23-1813--1-1-1814, & later Col, Regt Mtd Gunmen Drftd Mil, 1814-1815; W D & T S A; Wear Fam Cem at Wear's Cove, near Sevierville, Sevier Co; Pvt mkr & D A R mkr. (Also Rev War, Capt)

WEBB, JESSE (--liv 1840 List aged 63 yrs Claiborne Co); Md (   ); Pvt, Tenn Mil; P D & 2400 Pensioners, Armstrong; likely Claiborne Co; Unkn.

WEBB, JOHN (--liv 1828 List Lincoln Co); Md   (   ); Pvt, 44th Regt U S Inf; P D & 2400 Pensioners, Armstrong; likely Lincoln Co; Unkn.

WEIR, JAMES (WEAR) (--9-13-1845 Blount Co); Md Patsy Rankin 7-13-1797 (1784--liv 4-10-1858 McMinn Co); Pvt, Capt Nath Evans' Co vs Cherokees 1794 for 3 mos; W D & P D; likely Blount Co; Unkn.

WEITZELL, ADAM (WINSELL) (1749 Penn -- 1827 Johnson Co, then Carter); Md Mary Davis 1773 (1750--1822); Capt, Col Ewen Allison's Regt E T Drftd Mil, 1-10-1814--5-18-1815; W D & T S A; Wills Fam Cem near Mountain City, Johnson Co; Pvt mkr. (Also Rev War in Penn)

WENDELL, DAVID (1777-- 1842 Murfreesboro, Rutherford Co); Md Sarah Hale Neilson (   ); War of 1812; Acklen's Records; Old City Cem in Murfreesboro, Rutherford Co; Pvt mkr.

WEST, THOMAS (5-28-1792--6-6-1870 Grainger Co); Md Rachel Oliphant 3-23-1815 (9-13-1794--1-4-1872); Pvt, Col John Williams' Regt U S Inf, & Pvt, Capt Francis Register's Co, Col Sam Bayless' 4th Regt E T Drftd Mil, 1-14-1814--7-21-1814, & in Col Sam Bunch's Regt, under Maj Lemuel P Montgomery at Tohopeka, 3-27-1814; W D & T S A; Shiloh Cem near Rutledge, Grainger Co; Pvt mkr.

WESTER, DANIEL (12-23-1786--8-2-1857 Roane Co); Md 1-Elizabeth Lloyd 5-1-1804 (12-5-1789--11-7-1845), 2-Mary Ann Breedlove (   ); Pvt, Capt Uriah Allison's Co, 8th U S Inf, enl at Kingston 8-31-1812 for 5 yrs; Bethel Pres Cem in Kingston, Roane Co; Pvt mkr.

WHARTON, JESSE (7-29-1782--7-22-1833 Nashville, Davidson Co); Md (   ); Member of Congress 1807--1809 Davidson Co, in U S Senate 1814-1815; Congressional Dir; Mt Olivet Cem in Nashville, Davidson Co; Pvt mkr.

WHITAKER, THOMAS (--likely Greene Co); Md (   ); Pvt, War of 1812; Data from J R Smith, Jeraldstown, Greene Co, 1935; Cem near Fall Branch, Washington Co; Unkn.

WHITE, HUGH LAWSON (10-29-1773--4-10-1840 Knoxville, Knox Co); Md 1-Elizabeth Carrick 12-13-1798 (1783--3-25-1831), 2-Mrs Anne E Payton 11-30-1832 (--4-1847 Wash, D C); Judge Knox Co, Laison Off bet Col John Williams & Gen Andrew Jackson at Tohopeka, 1814; W D & T S A & Goodspeed Knox Co; First Pres Cem in Knoxville, Knox Co; Pvt mkr.

WHITE, Gen JAMES (1747 in N C --8-14-1821 Knoxville, Knox Co); Md Mary Lawson 4-14-1770 (1742--3-10-1819); Gen of Tenn Mil, 1813 E T Mil, joined Gen John Cocke during Creek War at Hillabees; W D & T S A; First Pres Cem in Knoxville, Knox Co; Monument & D A R mkr 1932, James White D A R. (Also Rev War)

WHITE, MOSES (4-22-1775--5-30-1830 Knox Co); Md Isabella McNutt 1799 (1781--3-26-1842); Pvt, Capt Thomas Gillespie's Co, Gen John Sevier's Expd 1793, 9-27-1793--10-27-1793; Col David Henley's Waste Book, copy in Lawson McGhee Library, Knoxville; White Fam Cem on N T James Farm, Knox Co; Pvt mkr.

WHITEHEAD, THOMAS (--likely Blount Co); Md (   ); Pvt, Capt Adam Winsell's Co, Col Ewen Allison's Regt E T Drftd Mil, 1-10-1814--5-18-1814; W D & T S A; Unkn Cem in Blount Co; Unkn.

WHITEHEAD, WILLIAM (--likely Blount Co); Md Hannah   (Pensioner); Pvt, Capt Adam Winsell's Co, Col Ewen Allison's Regt E T Drftd Mil, 1-10-1814--5-18-1814; W D & P D; Unkn Cem in Blount Co; Unkn.

WHITESIDE, JENKINS (1782--9-22-1822 Nashville, Davidson Co); Md (   ); Comm of Knoxville, 1801-02, U S Senate 1809--1811; Hist of Knoxville & Congressional Dir; Old Cem in West Nashville, at Sulphur Springs, Davidson Co; Pvt mkr.

WHITSETT, ABSOLEM (--d 1814 in service, Huntsville, Ala); Md Elizabeth Kidd bef 1814 (   ); Pvt, Col John K Wynne's Regt, enl 10-4-1813 in Marshall Co; T S A; likely in Ala; Unkn.

WHITSON, JOHN (--likely Bradley Co); Md   (   ); Pvt, Capt Ross' Co; W D & Edwards Acct Bk; likely Bradley Co; Unkn.

WHITTLE, JOHN (--11-12-1864 Sevier Co); Md Mary Keener 8-31-1820 Knox Co (1801--liv 5-8-1878 9th Distr, Sevier Co); Pvt, Capt Simeon Perry's Co, Col Sam Wear's 1st Regt E T V, 9-23-1813-- 12-31-1813; W D & T S A; in Sevier Co; Unkn.

WILCOXSON, DAVID (--d likely in Hamilton Co); Md Elizabeth Harris 11-1-1805 Sevier Co (1785--liv 1851 Hamilton Co); Pvt, Capt Simeon Perry's Co, Col Sam Wear's 1st Regt E T V, & Pvt, Capt Wm Henderson's Co, Spies, Gen Nathaniel Taylor's Brig; W D & T S A & P D; likely in Hamilton Co; Unkn.

WILHOITE, PHILLIP (WILHITE) (--5- 1877 Unicoi Co); Md 1-Margaret Farnsworth 7-20-1808 (--d bef 1844), 2-Mary Tucker 5-28-1844 (   ); Pvt, Capt Robt McAlphin's Co, Col Wm Lillard's 2nd Regt E T V, 10-14-1813--2-8-1814; W D & T S A; Beals Fam Cem at Jump Hill bet Embreeville & Erwin, in Unicoi Co; Official 1812 mkr 1928.

WILLIAMS, ARCHIBALD (c 1774-- 1838 Carter Co); Md Rhoda Taylor 12-28-1796 Carter Co (c 1775--bef 1830 Census); Capt in Carter Co Mil, 1796 & Sheriff Carter Co, 1808-1810; T S A & Carter Co Records; Williams Fam Cem on Buffalo Creek, Carter Co; Unmkd.

WILLIAMS, BEVERLEY (--liv 1840 List aged 57 yrs Gibson Co); Md   (   ); served Capt Thos Williamson's Co, W T Mil; P D & 2400 Pensioners, Armstrong; likely Gibson Co; Unkn.

WILLIAMS, EDMOND (--bet 9 & 11- 1795 Carter Co, then Washington); Md Lucretia Adams in Mass c 1759 (--aft 1795); Sheriff Washington Co N C & State of Franklin 1788, Gen Assmbly 1784; N C S A & T S A; Williams Fam Cem on Buffalo Creek, Carter Co; Govt mkr. (Also Rev War)

WILLIAMS, ETHELRED (1792-- 1818 Nashville, Davidson Co); Md (   ); War of 1812; W D; Old City Cem in Nashville, Davidson Co; Official 1812 mkr.

WILLIAMS, FRANCIS (b Penn -- 1862 near Morristown, Hamblen Co); Md Catherine Hodges 1810 (b S C -- 1858 Hamblen Co); War of 1812 under Jackson; Goodspeed E T H Hamblen Co; likely Williams Fam Cem in Hamblen Co; Unkn.

WILLIAMS, JOHN (b Va --d likely Carter Co); Md   (   ); War of 1812; Goodspeed E T H; likely Carter Co; Unkn.

WILLIAMS, Col JOHN (1-29-1778 in N C --8-10-1873 Knox Co); Md Malinda White c 1807 (2-15-1789--3-2-1838); Col, Regt on Natchez Expd 12-1-1812 & later Col 39th Regt U S A Inf, 6-1813--6-15-1815; W D & T S A; First Pres Cem in Knoxville, Knox Co; Pvt mkr. (His portrait done by Miss Eleanor Wiley has just been presented to State of Tenn)

WILLIAMS, JOSHUA (9-14-1762--9-22-1831 Maury Co); Md Sarah Davidson (7-30-1773--12-8-1853 Maury Co); Sheriff Buncombe Co, N C & Senate from N C 1800-1803; Asstd in formation of Maury Co 1807, J P; N C S A & T S A; Williams Fam Cem on Snow Creek, near Sante Fe, Maury Co; Pvt mkr.

WILLIAMS, MATTHEW (--liv 1828 List Davidson Co, --d 2-14-1820); Md ( ); Pvt, Capt Thos Williamson's Co, Col Wm Pillow's Regt W T Mil; P D & 2400 Pensioners, Armstrong; likely Davidson Co; Unkn.

WILLIAMS, SAMUEL HUMPHREYS (6-27-1768--4-24-1835 Maury Co); Md Ruth Davidson (11-7-1777--5-23-1849); Sheriff Buncombe Co N C 1804 & Surveyor Gen 7th District & Col 2nd Div Maury Co Mil, asst in forming of Maury Co, 1807; N C S A & T S A; Zion Pres Cem near Columbia, Maury Co; Pvt mkr - large flat mkr.

WILLIAMS, SILAS (--d likely Claiborne Co); Md Catherine 8-1-1842 ( ); Corp, Capt Wm Hamilton's Co, Col Wm Lillard's 2nd Regt E T V, 10-19-1813 for 3 mos; W D & P D; likely Claiborne Co; Unkn.

WILLIAMS, THOMAS (2-1-1786--12-2-1856 Nashville, Davidson Co); Md Polly Lawson McClung 8-5-1811 Knox Co ( ); Pvt, Capt Wm Walker's Co, Col John Williams' Regt E T Mil, 12-1-1812--3-25-1813; W D & T S A; likely in Knoxville Cem, Knox Co; Pvt mkr.

WILLIAMSON, JOHN (--d 10-3-1813 in service); Md ( ); heirs were Nancy, Elizabeth, Nelson & Reuben Williamson in Cocke Co; Pvt, 1st Regt Riflemen; P D & 2400 Pensioners, Armstrong; likely where died; Unkn.

WILLIAMSON, JOHN (12-16-1764--8-7-1829 Wilson Co); Md Margaret Scott Cloyd 3-4-1781 (1-24-1766--10-8-1845); Capt, 17th Regt Wilson Co Mil; John Sevier's Comm Bk; Cem in Lebanon, Wilson Co; Pvt mkr.

WILLIAMSON, SAMUEL (1786 N C -- 1860 Maury Co); Md Judith Woodfin (1790--1873); War of 1812; Goodspeed Maury Co; in Maury Co; Unkn.

WILLIS, JAMES (5-20-1800--10-6-1858 Hawkins Co); Md Sallie Stapleton 1829 (8-10-1811--8-19-1867); Pvt, Capt Joseph Williams' Co, Lieut Col Robt H Dyer's Regt Mtd Gunmen; W D & T S A; Bethesda Cem in Hamblen Co; Pvt mkr.

WILLIS, LARKIN (8-3-1777--1-15-1859 Hawkins Co); Md Mary 1-20-1799 (7-19-1782--8-23-1813); Pvt, Capt Samuel Bunch's Co, Col John Williams' Regt, 12-1-1812--3-25-1813; W D & T S A & P D; Bethesda Cem in Hamblen Co; Pvt mkr.

WILLOUGHBY, WALLACE (1774-- 1850 in Tenn); Md ( ); Pvt, Capt Dixon's Co Riflemen, Va Mil, 1814; Va S A & Texas 1812 Records; Unkn Cem in Tenn; Unkn.

WILLS, DAVID (--liv 1828 List Davidson Co); Md ( ); Pvt, 1st Regt Tenn Mil; P D & 2400 Pensioners, Armstrong; likely Davidson Co; Unkn.

WILSON, Capt DAVID (--d likely Sumner Co); Md   (   ); Spker House 1794 from Sumner Co; T S A; likely Sumner Co; Unkn.

WILSON, JOHN (1799-- 1852 in Tenn); Md   (   ); Pvt, N C Mil War of 1812; N C S A & Texas 1812 Records; Unkn Cem in Tenn; Unkn.

WILSON, ROBERT (--d Blount Co); Md Esther Carreuthers 2-22-1814 (   ); Pvt, Capt Joseph Duncan's Co, Col Sam Bunch's Regt Mtd Inf, 1-10-1814--7-21-1814; W D & Blount Co Hist- Burns; likely Big Springs Pres Cem, Blount Co; Unkn. (Edwards Acct Bk gives Nancy Wilson as wid of Robert Wilson - Was she a 2nd wife?)

WILSON, SAMUEL (--wounded 11-9-1813 at Talledega, --d 12-8-1813); Md   (   ); Pvt, Capt Robt Jetton's Co, Col John Allcorn's Regt W T Cav, 9-24-1813--12-8-1813; W D & T S A & Tenn Soldiers in War of 1812-Vol 1- Allen; likely in Ala; Unkn.

WILSON, SAMUEL (1-27-1794--1-19-1854 McMinn Co); Md (   ); War of 1812; Goodspeed E T H; Clear Springs Cem near Englewood, McMinn Co; Pvt mkr.

WINCHESTER, GEORGE (3-6-1757--killed 7-9-1794 Sumner Co); Single; Deputy Surveyor under Armstrong, 2nd Maj Mero Distr, 1790, early Indian Wars in Mero Distr; T S A; Waylaid & shot, then scalped by Indians 7-9-1794 & bur at Cragfont, Sumner Co; Pvt mkr. (Also Rev War in Va with bro Gen James Winchester)

WINCHESTER, Gen JAMES (2-6-1752--7-26-1826 Sumner Co); Md Susan Black (   ); Mil Insp Mero Distr 1789, early Indian Wars in Mero Distr, apptd by Pres Madison Brig Gen U S Army 4-8-1812, Prisoner of War near Quebec until April 1814, later at N O & Mobile; U S & T S A; Cragfont Fam Cem, Sumner Co; Pvt mkr. (Rev War in Va under Gen George Washington)

WINGFIELD, JOSEPH (--d in Tenn); Md   (   ); Pvt, Capt John Jackson's Co, W T Mil; T S A & Texas 1812 Records; Unkn Cem in Tenn; Unkn.

WOLFE, JAMES (--d Blount Co); Md 1-Isabella Russell 3-12-1853 (--d bef 1858), 2-Margaret Brooks 11-10-1858 (-); Pvt, Capt Jehu Stephens' Co, Col Sam Wear's Mtd Gunmen, 10-6-1814--4-6-1815; W D & Blount Co Hist- Burns & P D; Logans Chapel Meth Cem, Blount Co; Govt mkr.

WOLFE, JOSEPH (c 1797--4-30-1884 near Johnson City, Washington Co); Single; Pvt, Capt Jonathan Waddle's Co, Col Sam Bayless' 4th Regt E T Drftd Mil, 11-13-1814--5-28-1815; W D & T S A & P D, survivors Cl# 7205, Cert 3856, & Washington Co Records; Unkn Cem near Johnson City, Washington Co; Unkn. (J C Comet, 5-10-1884, "Old Capt Joe Wolfe died - Vet of War of 1812 - 90 yrs")

WOOD, JOHN (--d 10 or 11- 1813 in service); Md   (   ); heirs were Franklin, John, Lucinda, Jesse, Thomas & Owen Wood in Rutherford Co; War of 1812; P D & 2400 Pensioners, Armstrong; likely where died; Unkn.

WOODS, JOHN (1751-- 1815 Franklin Co); Md Abigail Estill 4-30-1778 (11-22-1762--8-19-1840); Early Indian Wars & 2nd Lieut Vol Co Franklin Co; W D & T S A; Woods Fam Cem near Belvedere, Franklin Co; Unmkd. (Also Rev War)

WORLEY, JOHN (--d Sullivan Co); Md Nancy Henry 1772 (   ); Pvt, Capt Adam Winsell's Co, Col Ewen Allison's Regt E T Drftd Mil, 1-5-1814--5-26-1814; T S A & W D; Worley Fam Cem, Sullivan Co; Unkn.

WRIGHT, JOHN A (1796--7-23-1861 Monroe Co); Md Secelia Cook (1800--7-18-1861); War of 1812; Goodspeed E T H Monroe Co; likely Monroe Co; Unkn.

WRIGHT, JOHN (1-7-1790--6-22-1876 Johnson City, Washington Co); Md 1-Barbara Range 12-14-1817 (1787--12-15-1847), 2-Mrs Margaret White Beagles 11-20-1849 (c 1810--liv 1883 Washington Co); Pvt, Capt Jesse Cole's Co, Col Sam Wear's 1st Regt E T V, 10-18-1813--1-17-1814; W D & T S A & P D; Oak Hill Cem in Johnson City, Washington Co; Pvt mkr & Official mkr, 1928. (John Wright was an early Christian minister)

WRIGHT, NELSON S (1-30-1790--7-8-1862 Maryville, Blount Co); Md Jane   (8-31-1793--2-9-1856); 2nd Srgt, Capt Jehu Stephens' Co, Col Sam Wear's Regt Mtd Gunmen, 10-6-1814--4-6-1815; W D & T S A & Blount Co Hist- Burns; New Providence Pres Cem, Maryville, Blount Co; Pvt mkr.

WRIGHT, WILLIAM (--liv 1828 List Knox Co, 1850 Census, aged 61 yrs Knox Co); Md   (   ); Pvt, Col Ramsey's 1st Regt U S Inf; P D & 2400 Pensioners, Armstrong; likely Knox Co; Unkn.

WYATT, Capt JAMES (11-25-1797 S C --12-1-1829 Lincoln Co); Single; Capt, Col Robt H Dyer's 1st Regt W T Cav, 9-28-1814--3-28-1815, enl Fayetteville, Lincoln Co; W D & T S A; Old Lebanon Pres Cem near Fayetteville, Lincoln Co; Pvt mkr.

WYN, HENRY (--wounded 11-9-1813 at Talledega, --d 11-12-1813 Ala); Md   (   ); Pvt, Capt John W Byrn's Co, Col John Allcorn's Regt W T Mtd Mil, 9-24-1813--11-12-1813 died; W D & T S A & Tenn Soldiers in War of 1812-Vol 1- Allen; likely in Ala; Unkn.

WYNNE, Col JOHN K (1-16-1765--1-7-1847 Wilson Co); Md Lucy Mabry 9-29-1789 (10-13-1777--6-29-1853); Col, 1st Regt W T Mil, Creek War, 10-4-1813--1-4-1814; W D & T S A & Acklen's Records; Wynne Fam Cem ½ m N-Hickory Rd, 4 m W Lebanon, Wilson Co; Pvt mkr. ("Traveled 286 m from Ft Strother in Ala to Fayetteville, and on to Lebanon, Wilson Co")

WYRICK, PHILLIP (--d Union Co); Md   (   ); War of 1812; W D; Dyer Fam Cem near Luttrell, Union Co; Govt mkr. (One of graves found near Norris Dam)

YATES, ROBERT (--d Ft Williams, Ala in 1814); Md
(   ); War of 1812; W D & T S A; at Ft Williams, Talledega
Co, Ala; Unmkd.

YEAROUT, JOHN (10-26-1795--3-9-1872 Blount Co); Md Martha Raulston
10-10-1816 (3-8-1799--11-9-1872); Pvt, Capt Joseph Duncan's Co,
Col Sam Bunch's Regt Mtd Inf, 1-10-1814--7-21-1814; W D & Blount
Co Hist- Burns; Cecedar Cumberland Pres Cem, Blount Co; Pvt mkr.

YEARWOOD, WILLIAM III (1-8-1780--8-5-1865 McMinn Co); Md 1-
(-   ), 2-Mrs Martha Dickson Neely 1-24-1809 (10-24-1789--2-14-
1867); Pvt, Capt Sublett's Co, Col Wm Henderson's Regt in N C;
Hist of Sweetwater Valley- Lenoir; Mt Harmony Ch Cem, McMinn Co;
Pvt mkr.

YELL, JAMES (1791--11-20-1839 Coffee Co); Md Jerusha Barton
(1797--); War of 1812, at N O; Goodspeed Bedford Co; likely in
Coffee Co; Unkn.

YOUNG, JAMES (1788 S C -- 1860 Jackson Co); Md Elizabeth Draper
(   ); Adj, Maj Gen Wm Carroll at N O, 1815; Goodspeed Jackson Co; Jackson Co; Unkn.

YOUNT, JACOB (--d 3-29-1814 in service); Md   (   );
Pvt, Capt Edward Buchanan's Co, Col Sam Wear's Regt E T Drftd Mil,
1-10-1814--5-20-1814; W D & T S A; likely in Ala; Unmkd.

YOUNT, PETER (--d Blount Co); Md Nancy Shook 9-23-1819 (   );
Pvt, Capt Joseph Duncan's Co, Col Sam Bunch's Regt Mtd Inf, 1-10-
1814--trans Capt Edward Buchanan's Co, 4-27-1814, on command at
Ft Williams, 5-20-1814; W D & Hist of Blount Co- Burns; Unkn Cem
in Blount Co; Unkn.

The following list of Soldiers of the War of 1812 are buried in other states, but had descendants who were members of the Tenn Society, or were of sufficient military importance to warrant their being listed.

ALEXANDER, ANDREW (2-1-1773--2-19-1850); Md Phoebe Bracken 1805 (1783--8-9-1869); Pvt, Capt John Rockwell's Co Inf, 7th Regt, Gray's Va Mil, 7-30-1814--10-20-1814, when he got sub, Alexander McClure; W D & Va S A; Cem in Mercer Co, W Va; Pvt mkr.

ALLEN, WILLIAM (6-16-1790--9-29-1846); Md Mary Morgan (   ); Capt Louisiana Vol Artillery, 11-1-1812--for 2 yrs; La S A; Cem in La; Unkn.

ANDERSON, JOSEPH McNAIR (11-5-1757--4-17-1837); Md Only Patience Outlaw 1792 (   ); Tenn Constitutional Conv 1796 from Jefferson Co, & Member Tenn Assmbly; T S A; Congressional Cem, Washington, D C; Govt mkr. (Also Rev War)

AYRES, JOHN (1790--7-25-1871); Md Sarah Ann Ward 8-9-1813 (1797--2-11-1878); Pvt, Capt Alexander Gibson's Co, Ohio Mil; P D & O S A; Cem in Paris, Jennings Co, Ind; Unmkd.

AYRES, MATTHIAS (8-31-1781--5-8-1851); Md Nancy G Howell 1-19-1814 (9-1-1797--3-4-1884); 1st Lieut, Capt Jesse B Keys' Co, Col Yancey's Va Mil; P D & Va S A; Saline Co, Mo; Pvt mkr.

BELL, PETER (1776-- 1832); Md Margaret Orr (   ); Ohio Legislature 1808--1815, Hamilton Co; Ohio S A; East of Montgomery, Hamilton Co, Ohio; Pvt mkr.

BENSON, PETER (1764--3-23-1838); Md Azubah   (1764--10-25-1801); Pvt, Capt White Young's Co, 15th Regt Vermont Inf; W D & Vt S A; Brookline, Orange Co, Vermont; Pvt mkr.

BENTON, Col THOMAS HART (3-14-1782-- 1858); Md Elizabeth McDowell of Va c 1820 (   ); Col, Tenn Mil, 12-1-1812--4-25-1813, Lieut Col, Col John Williams' 39th Regt U S Inf, 6-18-1813--1-15-1815 & later Col; W D & T S A; Bellefontaine Cem, St Louis, Mo; Pvt mkr.

BISHOP, ELI (--liv 10-24-1850); Md   (   ); Pvt, Capt Andrew Lawson's Co, Col Wm Johnson's 3rd Regt E T Drftd Mil; W D & P D; likely Madison Co, Ala; Unkn.

BLACKBURN, Rev GIDEON (8-27-1772--8-23-1838); Md Grizzell Blackburn 10-3-1793 (   ); Chaplain under Andrew Jackson & raised Co of Vol during Creek War; T S A & E T H S Publications; Carlinville, Ill; Pvt mkr.

BOTTS, SETH (1787-- 1872); Md   (   ); Lieut, Capt Wm Hamilton's Co, Col Wm Lillard's 2nd Regt E T V, 10-12-1813--2-8-1814; W D & T S A & P D; Cem near Meadeville, Linn Co, Mo; Pvt mkr.

BOWEN, HENRY (3-18-1770--4-18-1850); Md Eleanor Stewart Tate 8-3-1797 (5-5-1778--10-1-1833); Col 2nd Battln, 112th Regt Va Mil; Tazewell Co Va Annals; Bowen's Cove, Tazewell Co, Va; Pvt mkr.

BRANDON, CARTER (1793-- 1861); Md   (   ); War of 1812; W D; Frazier Cem in Jackson Co, Ala; Govt mkr.

BROWN, JOHN (--d 5-11-1846); Md Sally Ayres 3-22-1810 Va (1789 --aft 1871 Pensioner); Pvt, Capt Jonathan Waddle's Co, Col Sam Bayless' 4th Regt E T Drftd Mil, 11-13-1814--5-18-1815; W D & P D; Tazewell Co, Va; Pvt mkr.

BRYAN, THOMAS (11-12-1793--7-25-1878); Md 1-Mary Dooley (1795-- 7-23-1844), 2-Thomasin Grogan (2-23-1821--9-13-1910); War of 1812; W D; Bryan Fam Cem in Walker Co, Ga; Official 1812 mkr 1957.

BUCKNER, THOMAS (--4-19-1852); Md Nancy Carr 5-12-1810 (--liv 4-7-1865 aged 68 yrs Sevier Co); Pvt, Capt Andrew Lawson's Co, Col Wm Johnson's 3rd Regt E T Drftd Mil, 9-18-1814--4-5-1815; W D & T S A & P D; Madison Co, Mo; Unkn.

CASEY, Gen WILLIAM (1754-- 1820); Md Jane Montgomery (   ); Kentucky Convention 1792; Hist of Ky- Collins & Allen; Casey Fam Cem, Adair Co, Ky; Pvt mkr.

CHURCH, GEORGE (--5-23-1823); Md Milly Berry 12-4-1822 Ky (1800 --aft 1855); Pvt, Capt James Cummings' Co, Maj John Chiles' Batln, 10-13-1813--1-17-1814; T S A & B L Wt; Barren Co, Ky; Unkn.

CLABAUGH, JOHN (1778--aft 1850); Md Elizabeth Haggard c 1801 (1783--aft 1850); Pvt, Capt John Roper's Co, Col Wm Lillard's 2nd Regt E T V, 10-8-1813--2-8-1814; W D & T S A; Walker Co, Texas; Unkn.

COCKE, Col WILLIAM (1748--8-22-1828); Md 1-Mary McLin 1-3-1772 Va (1756--d Hawkins Co), 2-Kissiah Simms, wid (   ); Pvt, Col John Williams' 39th Regt U S Inf, & 1814, Agent Chickasaw Indians, apptd by Pres Madison; T S A & U S A; Columbus, Miss; Monument erected by State of Miss. (Also Rev War)

COFFEE, Gen JOHN (6-2-1772 Va --7-7-1833); Md Mary Donelson 10-3- 1809 (6-13-1793--); Enl 1812, raised troops to Natchez 1-19-1812 --2-16-1812, later Gen W T Troops War of 1812; W D & T S A; Florence, Ala; Monument - (Epitaph by Andrew Jackson).

COX, ISHAM (--d Ala); Md   (   ); Srgt, Capt James McKamey's Co, Col John Brown's 2nd Regt Mtd Gunmen, also Pvt, Capt Wm White's Co, Col John Brown's Regt; T S A; bur in Ala; Unkn.

CROCKETT, DAVID (8-17-1786 Greene Co --3-3-1836); Md 1-Polly Finley 1804 Jefferson Co (--d 1815), 2-Elizabeth Patton, wid, 1816 Franklin Co (5-22-1788--d Texas); Enl Pvt, 9-13-1813 Maj John Gibson's Regt, 2-Srgt, Capt John Cowan's Com Maj Wm Russell's Spies Mtd Gunmen, 9-27-1814--3-27-1815; T S A; bur Texas, at the Alamo; Monument.

DONALD, WILLIAM BLAIR (1780-- 1851); Md Mary Campbell 1813 (1787 --1862); Capt in War of 1812; Lyle Fam Hist; bur in Va; Unkn.

DORSEY, JOHN (1780-- 1825-30); Md Elizabeth Dorsey 1810 (1782--1873); Pvt, Capt Sam McClure's Co, Col Woods' Va Mil; W D & Va S A; Jefferson Co, Va (now W Va); Unkn.

DUNBAR, RICHARD GILLIAM (1793-- 1847); Md Mary Louiza Winn aft 1840 (   ); Capt, Cav Co at Mobile, Pensacola & N O; W D & Knox Co Hist; bur N O, La; Unkn.

EARLY, WILLIAM (1776--11-30-1813); Md Hannah Laughlin 6-13-1802 Sullivan Co (1780--1857 in Ky); Ensign, Capt James McNeil's Co, & George W Craig's Co, Col Jennings Regt Ky Vol, & Col Taul's 7th Regt Ky Mtd Vol; Ky S A & Ky Soldiers of War of 1812 p-64; Whitley Co, Ky; Pvt mkr.

FARRAGUT, DAVID G (7-15-1801--8-14-1870); Md Susan Machant 9-24-1823 at Norfolk, Va (   ); Mdshipman aged 9½ yrs on Essex with Capt Porter, brought Barkley into port as prize, 1814; Natl Archives & Tenn, Vol State- Moore; bur 9-30-1870 Woodlawn Cem, N Y City, N Y; Monument.

FORT, WILLIAM (--d Mo); Md   (   ); Pvt, Capt David Smith's Co, Col Robt H Dyer's 1st Regt W T Mil, 9-24-1813--12-10-1813, & Pvt, Capt David Smith's Co, Col John Coffee's Regt, 10-10-1812--4-27-1813; W D & T S A; Randolph Co, Mo; Unkn.

FRISTOE, RICHARD M (1789-- 1845); Md   (   ); 1st Lieut, Capt Daniel Price's Co, 1st Regt Mtd Gunmen; W D & T S A; Woodlawn Cem, Independence, Mo; Official 1812 mkr.

FRISTOE, Rev THOMAS (1795-- 1872); Md   (   ); Ensign, Capt Daniel Price's Co, 1st Regt Tenn Mtd Gunmen; W D & T S A; Cem near Glasgow, Howard Co, Mo; Govt mkr. (U S D 1812 chapter in Mo named for him)

GAINES, EDMUND PENDLETON (3-20-1777 Va --6- 1849); Md 1-Barbara Blount 1-8-1815 (9-14-1792--), 2-Myra Clark (   ); 2nd Lieut, 1799, Brig Gen 3-9-1814, at Lake Erie, 8-15-1814--thru War; W D & T S A; likely at N O, La; Pvt mkr.

GILLENWATERS, WILLIAM TERRELL (4-30-1795--6-18-1865); Md Elizabeth Roddye 1819 in Rhea Co (--d 1851 Mo); Capt, Col Wm Lillard's 2nd Regt E T V, 10-2-1813--2-8-1814; W D & T S A; Masonic Cem in Dallas, Texas; Pvt mkr.

GIST, GEORGE (GUESS) (SEQUOYAH) (c 1773-75 Tuskegee near Ft Loudon --1845); Md Sallie   1815 Cherokee Nation (1789--1855 aged 66 yrs); Pvt, Capt John McLemore's Co, Col Gideon Morgan, Jr Regt Cherokee Indians, 10-7-1813--1-6-1814, & 1-1814 thru 3-27-1814 at Tohopeka; W D & T S A; bur in Mexico; Monument in Statuary Hall, Washington, D C.

GIST, JOHN (1792--aft 1855); Md   (   ); Pvt, Capt Laskin Terrill's Co under Gen Jackson, also 3 mos Vol in Jackson Co; W D & Gist Fam Gen- Dorsey; likely Cook Co, Texas; Unkn.

GIST, JOSEPH (c 1789 N C --2-9-1846); Md Sinnia Hollis 5-24-1818 Lawrence Co (1800--12-23-1853 Ala); Pvt, Capt John Jackson's Co, Col Wm Metcalf's Regt W T Mil, 11-13-1814--5-13-1815 at Nashville; W D & T S A; Lauderdale Co, Ala; Pvt mkr.

GIST, JOSHUA (3-17-1793 N C --8-8-1873); Md Susannah Grooms 4-17-1817 Shelbyville, Bedford Co (3-17-1793--2-26-1863 Ala); Pvt, Capt John Jackson's Co, Col Wm Metcalf's Regt W T Mil, 11-13-1814 --5-16-1815; W D & T S A; Cherokee, Colvert Co, Ala; Pvt mkr.

GRANT, CHARLES (b N Y --d likely Mich); Md Hannah Hines (   ); War of 1812; Goodspeed E T H; St John, Clinton Co, Mich; Pvt mkr.

GUINN, ANDREW (8-22-1788--6-11-1863); Md Mary Newsome 4-30-1812 (7-4-1794--3-10-1866); Ensign, Capt Solomon Taylor's Co, Gen Bridges, 9-19-1812--4-1-1813, promoted Lieut 3-1-1813; W D; Guinn Fam Cem in Summers Co, W Va; Unkn.

HART, THOMAS (10-26-1791--7-28-1865); Md Elizabeth Duncan 12-15-1814 (12-17-1796--7-7-1818); Pvt, Capt James Gillespie's Co, Col Sam Wear's 1st Regt E T V, 9-23-1813--12-31-1813; W D & T S A; Bartholomew Co, Ind; Pvt mkr.

HENLEY, Col DAVID (2-1-1749--1-1-1823); Md Lady Sally Heselrigge in Boston 3-12-1782 (1762--10-1785 Boston); Agent of War for Terr S W River Ohio 1792--1801, & Clerk in W D, Washington, D C 1812--1823; U S A; Georgetown Cem, Md; Pvt mkr. (Also Rev War, Col under Gen Lincoln & Gen Scott's Regt in Mass; one of 3 Comm for settling Va Rev War Claims & Boundary Dispute)

HILL, Rev JOAB (1795 in N C -- 1847); Md Elizabeth Lane 1802 (   ); Lieut Col, Col Sam Bayless' 4th Regt & in Col Edwin Boothe's 5th Regt E T Drftd Mil, 11-13-1814--5-15-1815; T S A; Bennington Cem, S W Athens, Clark Co, Mo; Pvt mkr.

HILL, WILLIAM KEENAN (3-18-1794 N C --8-1-1841); Md Rebecca K Harris 5-11-1818 (10-7-1801--12-29-1860 Columbia, Tenn); Pvt, Capt John Looney's Co, Col Lowry's 2nd Regt W T Mil, 9-20-1814 --3-20-1815; W D; Velasco (now Columbia) Brazoria Co, Texas; Unkn.

HOUSTON, SAMUEL (--d Ala); Md Nancy Gillespie 1792 (   ); Wagon Master, Capt Edward Buchanan's Co, Col Sam Wear's Regt E T Mtd Mil, 1-10-1814--5-20-1814; T S A; 20 m from Huntsville, Ala; Unkn.

HOUSTON, SAMUEL (3-2-1793--7-26-1863); Md 1-Eliza Allen 1-1829 (   ), 2-Margaret Lea c 1849-50 (--d aft 1863); Pvt, Ensign & Lieut, 7th U S Inf, & 39th Regt Col John Williams, 3-24-1813 Maryville; W D & T S A; Oakwood Cem, Huntsville, Texas; Mkd by State of Texas.

HUDSON, ROBERT (10-10-1774--2-24-1847); Md Elizabeth Jones (6-8-1783--5-16-1859); Pvt, Capt Moore's Co Riflemen, 52nd Regt Va Mil; W D & Va S A; Hudson Fam Cem, Rappahannock Co, Va; Pvt mkr.

JENKINS, DRURY (--d likely in Mo); Md ( ); War of 1812; B L Wt for land in Mo; Blount Co Deed records; likely in Mo; Unkn.

JOBE, JOSHUA (5-15-1795--5-8-1868); Md Ruth Tipton (8-27-1791--5-26-1864); Pvt, Capt Adam Winsell's Co, Col Ewen Allison's Regt E T Drftd Mil, 1-5-1814--3-6-1814; W D & T S A; Little Stone Pres Cem near Ringgold, Ga; Pvt mkr.

KEYES, WILLIAM (1778-- 1864); Md Margaret Donald (1775--1849); Col, Ohio Regt, Gen Wm Harrison; W D & Lyle Fam Hist; in Ohio; Unkn.

LANE, Col TIDENCE III (9-1-1788--9-4-1851); Md Abigail Hewes Thomas 1-1-1811 ( ); Pvt, Capt Hill's Co, Gen Wm Metcalf's 1st Regt W T Mil, promoted Lieut Q M & Lieut Col, 11-11-1814--5-13-1815; T S A; Brandon Cem, Hines Co, Miss; Pvt mkr.

LEA, LUKE (1-21-1783--6-17-1851 killed by fall from horse); Md Susan Wells McCormick 2-28-1810 (--7-8-1848); Pvt, Capt Wm Walker's Co, Col John Williams, later was Col, Regt under Gen Jackson; W D & Edwards Acct Bk; Leavenworth, Kansas; Pvt mkr. (One reference said Mo)

LEA, PRYOR (8-31-1794--9-14-1879); Md 1-Mariah Kennedy 10-6-1818 Knox Co ( ), 2- ( ), 3- ( ); Creek War with Jackson; Knox Co Hist; likely in Texas; Unkn.

LOONEY, Col ABSOLOM (--1782-- 1860); Md 1-Nancy Long (--1818), 2-Eleanor Wilson (1796--1859); War of 1812; T S A; Bienville Parish, La; Pvt mkr.

LYLE, ARCHIBALD (1771-- 1857); Single; Raised & Commd Cav Co in Va; Lyle Fam Hist; likely in Va; Unkn.

McCLAUGHERTY, JAMES (3-21-1780--4-12-1854); Md Sallie Mullins 8-5-1802 (1781--1-8-1859); Srgt, Capt Andrew Johnston's Co, 86th Regt Giles Co, Va Mil, 2-17-1815--3-2-1815; Va S A; McClaugherty Fam Cem 3½ m GlenLynn on New River, Giles Co, Va; Pvt mkr.

McDOWELL, JAMES (1760--); Md Mary Patton 1779 ( ); Col, War of 1812; Lyle Fam Hist; Mason Co, Ky; Unkn. (Also Rev War, Maj)

McDOWELL, JOHN LYLE (1794-- 1878); Md Nancy Vance 1817 (1797--1868); Col, War of 1812 in Ky; Lyle Fam Hist; Mason Co, Ky; Unkn.

McDOWELL, SAMUEL (1780--d Ky); Md ( ); Srgt, Capt Trotter's Co, in Ky; Lyle Fam Hist; likely Jessamine Co, Ky; Unkn.

MARTIN, Gen JOSEPH (1740-- 1808 Va); Md 1-Sarah Lucas (   ), 2-Susannah Chiles (   ); Battle of Lookout Mt, 1788, Col Washington Co Mil, 1788; T S A & Ramsey's Annals; likely Martin Fam Cem in Va; Unkn. (Also Rev War)

MASENGILL, GEORGE (1791--d Texas); Md Miss Gann (   ); Pvt, Capt Gann's Co; W D & P D & Masengill Hist; Nacogdoches, Texas; Unkn.

MASSEY, JAMES (1779-- 1863); Md   (   ); Pvt, Capt James Lillard's Co, Col Wm Lillard's 2nd Regt E T V, 10-12-1813--2-8-1814; W D & T S A; Cem 4 m E Springfield, Green Co, Mo; Pvt mkr.

MATLOCK, WILLIAM (1798 N C -- 1864); Md Susan Manafee 1844 White Co (   ); Pvt, Capt Jesse Cole's Co, Col Sam Wear's 1st Regt E T V, 9-12-1813--12-31-1813; W D & T S A; bur in Ga; Unkn.

MILLION, JACOB (12-26-1782--9-5-1852); Md 1-Mary May 1-2-1809 (5-28-1787--4-22-1842), 2-Sophia Kaw 2-23-1845 (--5-14-1864); Pvt, Capt Henry McCray's Co, Capt McPherson's Co & Capt John Hampton's Co, Col Ewen Allison's Regt E T Drftd Mil, 5-24-1814--7-26-1814; W D & T S A; Wheelock Cem near Nashville, Miami Co, Ohio; Pvt mkr.

MORRISSETT, JOHN (1793--5-6-1851); Md Miss Gaines (   ); War of 1812; T S A; Moved to Ala & to Texas, bur Texas; Unkn.

MULKEY, JAMES BOLIN (1-19-1795--9-22-1851); Md Elizabeth Wyman 8-25-1814 (1-18-1798--5-13-1866); Pvt, Capt Dudley Farris' Co, 13th Ky Mil, 3-29-1813--9-28-1813; W D & Ky S A; Old Mulkey Fam Cem near Bloomington, Monroe Co, Ind; Pvt mkr.

NELSON, DAVID (9-24-1793--10-17-1844); Md Amanda Frances Thompson Deaderick 5-15-1816 (8-30-1799--12-3-1886); Surgeon, Col Sam Bayless' 4th Regt E T Drftd Mil, 11-13-1814--5-18-1815; W D & T S A; Oakland Cem in Ill; Pvt mkr. (Also served with Ky Regt in Canada Campaign, 1812)

O'DELL, JEREMIAH (b Va --d Mo, Marshall Co); Md   (   ); War of 1812, wounded 11-9-1813; Cocke Co Hist- O'Dell; bur in Mo; Unkn.

OTEY, JOHN W (1771 --d Ala); Md Mary Walton 7-15-1800 (   ); Capt, War of 1812;   ; Green Lawn Cem near Huntsville, Ala; Pvt mkr.

PIERCE, SETH (3-22-1780-- 1824 Steuben Co, N Y); Md Anna Turner Cushing 11-21-1802 (3-15-1784--12-7-1849); Pvt, Capt E Warren's Co, Lieut Col C Thomas' Regt Vermont Vol Mil; Vt S A; Painted Post Cem, Steuben Co, N Y; Pvt mkr.

PIERCE, WILLIAM (6-1-1758--11-5-1812); Md Lydia Perry N Y (7-22-1760--); Pvt, died in service from exposure 1812; New Eng Gen Records; Painted Post Cem, Steuben Co, N Y; Pvt mkr.

PIERSON JOHN BLAIR (1787-- 1865 Mo); Md ( ); Srgt, Capt Edward Buchanan's Co, Col Sam Wear's E T Drftd Mil, 1-10-1814--5-20-1814; W D & T S A; Kahoka, Clark Co, Mo; Pvt mkr.

POINDEXTER, JOHN (1793-- 1877); Md Elizabeth Graves 1815 ( ); Lieut 8th Regt Va Mil; W D & Va S A; Garrettsburg, Ky Cem; Pvt mkr.

RAMSEY, JOHN L (1787--d Ohio); Md Martha Town 1816 ( ); War of 1812; Lyle Fam Hist; likely Highland Co, Ohio; Unkn.

REID, Maj JOHN (1784 Va --1-18-1816 at father's); Md Miss Maury (--aft 1816); enl 4-21-1806 1st Inf, 12-9-1807 2nd Lieut, 7-15-1814 Capt 44th Inf Regt, 5-17-1815 1st Inf, 12-23-1814 1st Maj, gallant conduct at N O with Jackson; W D & T S A; Reid Fam Cem in Bedford Co, Va; Pvt mkr. (Maj Reid's wife was dau of Abram Maury)

RENO, FLEMING (--d Ill); Md Sarah Jane Walters ( ); Pvt, Capt George Gregory's Co, Col Sam Bunch's Mtd Vol; W D & T S A; Temple Cem in Fulton Co, Ill; Official 1812 mkr.

ROBERTSON, ANDREW (1796-- 1873); Md ( ); Corp, Capt John Wade's Co, Col James Raulston's 3rd Regt W T Mil, under Gen Wm Carroll, 11-13-1814--5-13-1815; W D & T S A; Robertson Fam Cem near Liberty, Clay Co, Mo; Official 1812 mkr.

ROGERS, JOHN ALEXANDER (12-15-1789-- 1873); Md 1-Margaret Forgey 1-28-1812 (2-4-1794--6-2-1817), 2-her sister, Ellen Forgey 12-25-1817 (6-17-1798--8-20-1837), 3-Lucretia Ann Coates 1842 (4-3-1811--12-1875); Capt, 24th U S Inf, 3-12-1812--6-15-1815; on Canadian Campaign; T S A; Center Point, Kerr Co, Texas; Pvt mkr.

ROSS, JOHN (10-3-1790--8-1-1866); Md 1-Quatie Brown Henley (1791--2-1-1839), 2-Mary Brown Stapler 9-2-1844 (--7-1865); Adj, Col Gideon Morgan Jr's Cherokee Regt, 1813-1814; W D & T S A; Park Hill, Okla; Pvt mkr.

SEVIER, Maj CHARLES ROBERTSON (1778-- 1855); Md Elizabeth Witt 1802 Green Co (1786--1855 Texas); 2nd Maj, Overton Co, 1806, Maj, Col Thomas McCrory's 2nd Regt W T Mil, 10-4-1813--1-4-1814; T S A; Milford, Ellis Co, Texas; Pvt mkr.

SHUMATE, LOUIS (LOUIS de La SHUMATE) (1770-- 1861); Md Mary Chadwell 1792 (1772--1812); Pvt, Capt Seth Combs' Inf, 83rd Regt Va Mil, attd to 41st, 7-30-1814--8-2-1815; Va S A & W D; Cem in Fauquier Co, Va; Pvt mkr.

SLOAN, ARCHIBALD (--d Ala); Md Susan Snyder 12-19-1820 ( ); Pvt & Corp, Capt Cavanaugh's Co, Col John Coffee's Regt; W D & T S A; likely in Ala; Unkn.

SMITH, Gen NATHANIEL (--d in Texas); Md ( ); Lieut, War of 1812; W D & T S A; in Texas; Unkn. (Also Gen in Cherokee Removal, 1827)

STINSON, Capt JAMES (STEPHENSON) (--d Ind); Md ( ); Capt in War of 1812; Col Washington Distr, 1796; T S A; Wayne Co, Ind; Pvt mkr.

STRINGFIELD, JOHN (2-13-1762--1-5-1822); Md Sarah Boylston ( ); Capt in Creek War with 3 sons, Thomas, William & James from Ala; W D & Ala S A; in Ill; Unkn.

STROTHER, Capt JOHN (--d 8-17-1815); Md - (-); Chief Topographer for Jackson in Creek War, 9-26-1813--2-26-1814, & Capt, Col Philip Pipkin's 1st Regt Inf, 6-20-1814--12-21-1814, mustered out Fayetteville 1-21-1815, & set out for Ala with Gen John Sevier in June 1815 to run Creek Indian Boundary Line; W D & T S A & Andrew Jackson & Early Tenn Hist- Heiskell; bur 8-18-1815 in Ala; Unmkd. (Ft Strother, built on Coosa River near Ten Islands, named for him; used during Creek War. John Sevier died just one month later, also in Ala.)

TEDFORD, JOHN (--d Iowa); Md ( ); 2nd Lieut, Capt James Tedford's Co, Col Sam Wear's 1st Regt E T V, 9-23-1813--12-31-1813; W D & T S A; likely in Iowa; Unkn.

TIPTON, JACOB (1790--d Mo); Md Anna Watson ( ); Ensign, Capt Reuben Tipton's Co, Maj John Chiles' & Col Sam Wear's Regt Mtd Gunmen, 9-20-1814--5-1-1815, also Pvt, Capt Callaway's Co, Col Sam Wear's 1st Regt E T V, 9-23-1813--12-31-1813; W D & T S A; Cem in Mo; Unkn.

TIPTON, JOSEPH (c 1795--d Ga); Md Martha Ingram 1-25-1825 ( ); Pvt, Capt Edward Buchanan's Co, Col Sam Wear's Mtd Mil, 1-10-1814-- ; W D & T S A; Unkn Cem in Ga; Unkn.

TIPTON, SAMUEL (c 1795-- 1869); Md Jane Ilks 1816 Carter Co (1798 --aft 1850 Census); Pvt, Capt Solomon Hendrix Co, Col Sam Bayless' 4th Regt E T Drftd Mil, 11-13-1814--5-26-1815; W D & P D; Cem in Cherokee Co, Texas; Unkn.

TOWNSEND, HORACE (1782-- 1839); Md Rebecca Cornell 1801 (6-7-1778--1862); Srgt, Capt Samuel C Kennedy's Co 76th N Y Mil, 9-8-1812; W D; Townsendville Meth Cem, Seneca Co, N Y; Pvt mkr.

TROTTER, WILLIAM (1792--d Ind); Md Elizabeth Hart 10-4-1821 ( ); Pvt, Capt Jehu Stephens' Co, Col Sam Wear's Mtd Gunmen, 10-6-1814--4-6-1815; W D & T S A & Blount Co Hist- Burns; likely in Ind; Unkn.

VANCE, DAVID G (--likely Buncombe Co, N C); Md Theodicia ( ); Capt, Mtd Vol Co, Col John Williams' 24th Regt U S Inf, 12-1-1812--for 2 yrs--3-1815; W D & T S A & Charlotte Obsr, 7-10-1937; Vance Fam Cem, Buncombe Co, N C; Govt mkr. (There is some confusion re the 2 David G Vances; see List of Soldiers bur in Tenn for the one who died 1823-4 in Washington Co.)

WARNER, SAMUEL (3-26-1800--10- 1887); Md Martha A Mosley 1828 (--1-17-1884); War of 1812 under Jackson; Goodspeed N E Ark Hist p-361; Cem in Jonesboro, Ark; Pvt mkr.

WELLS, COLEMAN (1781-- 1833); Md Elizabeth Phillips (1786--1882); War of 1812; Goodspeed Williamson Co; likely in Va; Unkn.

WHITSETT, ABSOLOM (--d Ala); Md ( ); Color Bearer at Battle of N O; Acklen's Records; Huntsville, Ala; Pvt mkr.

WHITE, BENJAMIN (--1830); Md Martha Jobe (--1812 drown in Holston River); Pvt, Capt John Williams Expd vs Seminoles in Fla, 12-2-1812--3-1813; W D & T S A & Forgotten Campaign- Williams; Cem in Decatur, Ala; Pvt mkr. (Also Rev War)

WILLIAMS, MOSES (1802-- 1877); Md Nancy Wilder (1800--liv 1877 in Ark); War of 1812; W D & P D, Nancy Williams a Pensioner; likely in Ark; Unkn.

ZENOR, DAVID (5-16-1797--1-5-1877); Md Phoebe Baker (7-31-1801--5-5-1818); Pvt, Capt Zeba Holt's Co, Ky Mil, at N O; W D & Ky S A; Zenor Fam Cem, Paris, Jefferson Co, Ind; Pvt mkr.

GENERAL ENTRY BOOK
PRISONERS OF WAR at QUEBEC, CANADA

This List of Prisoners of War is on record at Ottawa, Canada. It was copied (5 copies being made) by the National Society and a copy filed with the War Department in Washington. An Index was made from this copy and names listed in alphabetical order. This Abstract of those from Tennessee was made from the News Letters, March 1938--Dec 1939, and gives name and number of prisoner.

#1395 - - ARCHER, ISAAC	#1552 - - MOORE, JOSHUA
#1396 - - ARCHER, ROBT	#1647 - - MORRISETT, JOSHUA
#1346 - - BOYD, WM	#1219 - - PEIRCE, THOS
	#1414 - - PRUITT, GABREAL
#1401 - - CHEEK, WM	#1340 - - RAY, JOSHUA
#1413 - - CLARK, CHARLES	#1439 - - RAY, ROBT
#1261 - - COATES, ELIJAH	
#1420 - - COLE, THOS	#1390 - - SHUT, HY
#1363 - - EWINGS, JAMES	#1220 - - TROOP, JAMES
#1277 - - GIFFORD, FRAS	# 246 - - WINCHESTER, JAMES
#1651 - - GOWEN, THOS	#1249 - - WOOD, GEORGE W
#1409 - - KEMMEDY, WM	
#1470 - - LAND, JOSHUA	

WADDLE, JACOB - 24th U S Inf, from Sullivan Co, Tenn, captured at Ft Niagara, 2400 Pensioners, Armstrong

COLONEL DAVID HENLEY'S "WASTE BOOK"[1]

Col David Henley was appointed as Agent of the War Department in the Southwest Territory in 1793 while Gov Blount was on an official visit to Philadelphia.[2] He had already had a varied experience in public service. He was a veteran of the American Revolution and had been acquitted by Court Martial of insulting a British officer. Col Henley had also served as one of the Commissioners for settling the claims arising in the Northwest Territory.

The work of the new Agent for the Southwest Territory was broad in scope and strictly business, as may be gleaned from examination of the "Waste Book" covering the period from January 1797 to December 1798.[3] This volume is still in possession of Henley descendants. Col Henley was at times Superintendent of Indian Affairs, Quartermaster General, Commissary General of purchases and Paymaster General for both the Militia and the Regular Troops. During the years from 1793 to 1801, he had many assistants and clerks. Lieut Silas Dinsmore, who had been appointed in 1794 to live among the Cherokees, was Clerk and was active during the Treaty of Tellico in 1797 & 1798. Stephen Hillis served as Scribe. Each item as paid out was entered consecutively under its appropriate heading in the "Waste Book" and reports were later compiled from this record.

The 1793 Campaign was the only one of the many frontier expeditions against the Indians for which the Militia was paid.[4] Attorneys received payment for entire companies, but enough men were paid individually to make a listing of these men extremely valuable to a student of this period of history. The "Waste Book" has been abstracted for both Regular Army and Militia personnel because they particularly belong to the 1812 period. Sundry items have been included because of their peculiar interest. Every entry is of interest for some reason, and is fascinating to read.

June 15, 1959
Maryville, Tennessee

Inez E Burns

NOTES:

1 - Waste Book, as defined in the Oxford Dictionary gives: A rough account book (now little used in ordinary business) in which entries are made of all transaction (purchases, sales, receipts, payments, etc) at the time of their occurences, to be posted afterwards into more formal books of the set.

NOTES (Contd):

2 - His Commission reads: To David Henley, Esq-
Sir--
   You are hereby with the approbation of the President of the United States appointed temporally an Agent for the Dept of War in the Territory South of the River Ohio; your pay will be at the rate of $1,000.00 per annum and 2 rations of forage per day, and in case of your being with the Troops in the field 3 rations per day.
   Your pay and your emoluments to commence on the 6th ultimo, when you entered on the preparative parts of your duties.

            Given at the War Office of the U S,
               This 31st of August, 1793

                           H Knox,
                           Sec of War
<u>East Tenn Hist Publications</u>, No 18, 1946, pp-3-24

3 - There were, no doubt, other Waste Books, covering the entire period Henley was in office, but to date, no other volume has been found.

4 - "This sum, ($22,816.95) forwarded by the Accountant of the War Department to pay Gen Sevier and his Command for services in 1793, which money heretofore unauthorized. Appropriation was passed last Session of Congress to discharge the claims. July 10, 1797." <u>Waste Book</u>, <u>Ramsey Annals</u>, pp-558-589

GEN JOHN SEVIER'S ETOWAH CAMPAIGN

1793

Capt John Beard's Company 9-26 to 10-27-1793
- Garon, Solomon
- Hankins, Ens William
- Hinds, Joseph
- Lane, Samuel
- Lowry, Henry
- Potter, John
- Sharp, Corp Moses
- Woods, Sgt John

Capt   Blair's Company 9-29 to 10-29-1793
- Henley, James
- Vaugh, Obediah

Capt David Campbell's Company 6-14 to 7-14-1793
- Drake, William
- Ervin, Francis

Capt Robert Carson's Company 9-27 to 10-27-1793
- Cameron, Duncan
- Deaderick, David-Atty for the Company
- King, Peter
- McClanahan, David
- Robertson, Joseph

Col Landon Carter 1-4 to 10-14-1793

Capt   Carey's Company 9-1 to 12-3-1793
- Kidwell, Josiah
- Ross, Edward

Col Gilbert Christian's Regt
- McDougall, John-Surgeon's Mate

Col William Christian's Regt
- Brown, Thomas-Drum Major
- Cowan, William

Capt Thomas Cox 12-9 to 12-31-1793
- Jack, John
- Pope, John Adam
- Purviance, William

Col George Doherty's Regt 9-27 to 10-27-1793
- Copeland, Stephen, Adj

Capt Nathaniel Evans' Company
- Anderson, James
- Blair, James
- Botkins, Hugh
- Buckingham, Sgt William
- Cochran, James
- Cochran, John
- Coffield, Dempsey
- Cunningham, James
- Ferguson, Joseph
- Flenniken, William
- Franklin, John
- Huston, Richard
- Kelly, Alex
- Kerr, William
- Lovever, Andrew
- Lowry, Sgt John
- McClelland, Abraham
- McClelland, Sgt Samuel
- McGinley, James
- McNutt, William
- Murphy, David
- Swisher, Michael
- Tipton, Benjamin
- Wear, Hugh
- Williams, Richard

1793 (Contd)

Capt Samuel Flenniken
    Fields, Lt Robert
    Gilliam, Charles   Walker, Joseph

Capt Thomas Gillespie
    White, Henry   White, Moses

Capt Joseph Gist 9-30 to 10-29-1793
    Bryan, Andrew

Capt Samuel Gregg 1-14 to 11-25-1793
    Barrett, Michael   Kindall, William
    Browry, Francis   Morgan, Lewis
    Hughes, Richard   Sharp, Sgt William
                                      Spencer, Neal

Capt Michael Harrison
    Armstrong, John   Kerr, James
    Cameron, James   Leaman, Cornet Samuel
    Caldwell, Andrew   Lumpkin, William
    Conoley, David   McMahan, James
    Gamble, John   Milligan, Thomas
    Gollther, Thomas   Montgomery, Alexander
    Hannah, Joseph   Montgomery, James
    Harrison, Jesse   Pride, Burton
    Kelso, Hugh   Sims, Littlepage

Capt William Henderson's Company
    Carlock, Jacob   Mires, Benjamin
    Hendrix, Cornet Luke   Watson, John
    McSpadden, Moses

Capt Samuel Henley's Company
    Carriger, Godfrey   Ervin, Samuel
    Carriger, Henry   Lockard, William
    Colyer, Charles   Price, Solomon
                                    Smith, Thomas

Capt William Job's Company
    Job, David   Lusk, Thomas

Major Hugh Kelso 9-27 to 10-27-1793

Capt Robert King's Company July to October 1793
    Bird, John   Roads, George
    King, Sgt Edmond   Sunderland, William

Ensign John Lane 10-1 to 10-27-1793

Capt   McCormick's Company
    Feagan, John   McMurry, Samuel

Lt John McClelland 7-12 to 8-20-1793
    DeArmond, David   Hitchcock, William

Major Robert McFarland

1793 (Contd)

Capt Samuel McGaughey 9-27 to 10-27-1793
    Bogle, Sgt Samuel   Montgomery, Humphrey
    Ewing, George   Pollock, John
    Gillespie, John   Tipton, William
    Henry, Samuel   McLaughlin, Ens Alex
    Martin, John   Thomas, Henry

Capt John Markham 8-20 to 11-20-1793
    Bogle, Jonathan   Heavens, John
    Ervin, Samuel   Watkins, Isaac
    Doggett, Isaac   Wilcox, Abram
    Hankins, Thomas

Capt Joseph Mecklerath's Company
    Ore, James-Atty for the company

Lt Robert Rhea 8-9 to 9-16-1793
    Houston, John   Oats, David (scalped by
                                       Indians in 1794)

Capt James Richardson's Company
    Earnest, Henry   Rankin, Robert

Major George Rutledge 7-22 to 12-3-1793

Capt John Scott 7-22 to 12-3-1793
    Fegan, John   Garland, Samuel

Gen John Sevier

Capt John Singleton
    Cunningham, James   Potter, John
    Huston, James   White, David

Lt William Snodgrass 10-5 to 10-30-1793
    Beatty, William

Major Leroy Taylor
    Christain, George, Adj

Capt Parmenas Taylor 9-27 to 10-27-1793
    Blackburn, William   Manning, Joseph
    Cunningham, Sgt James   Moore, Elijah
    Dickerson, James   Ritchey, Alexander
    Ferguson, James   Wilson, Adam
    Hubbard, James   Wilson, Robert
    Jared, William   Wilson, Samuel

Lt James Tedford 4-5 to 4-27-1793
    McGaughey, William

Capt Anderson Watkins' Company
    Brooks, Sgt Thomas   Johnston, Pleasant
    Cunningham, Miles

1793 (Contd)

Capt Moses Webb's Company 10-5 to 10-30-1793
    Anderson, John   Carey, Samuel

Capt   Williams

Capt   Young's Company
    Haynes, William

Those paid directly for own services without information about company or regiment

- Ahee, Joseph
- Buchanan, Ezekiel
- Dean, Thomas
- Duncan, Stephen
- Franklin, John
- Green, Thomas
- Houston, Robert
- Husk, William
- Hutton, Josiah
- Ore, James
- Selvidge, Jeremiah
- Shelton, Thomas
- Tedford, George
- Tee, Edward
- Tench, William
- Wallis, John

Men who served in Sevier's 1793 Campaign who were living in Mero District when paid in 1798 by Robert Hayes Muster-Master

Lt Amos Bird
    Chote, John
    Glazier, Francis
    Snider, Charles
    Smith, Thomas
    Tittsworth, John

Capt George Blackmore
    Wilson, James

Capt William Blackmore
    Ford, John
    Shule, Sgt John
    Turney, John

Lt William Cage
    Crockett, John

Capt Stephen Cantrell
    Harrison, Nathaniel

Capt Joseph Frazier
    Walter, Joseph

Capt Thomas Johnson
    Cower, David
    Desha, David
    Desha, Joseph
    Glasgow, Jesse
    Jennings, Edmond

Capt Richard King's Company
    Blythe, Andrew
    Hamilton, George
    Hayes, James
    Hines, William
    McDonnell, John
    Stewart, William
    Taylor, Perry
    Tracy, Stephen
    Wilson, James

Capt Joseph Macklerath's Company
    George, Corp Thomas
    Haddishale, Henry
    Lattimore, Nathaniel
    Shute, William
    Teel, Nathaniel

Capt Richard Miles' Company
    Wells, Robert

Capt John Mushall's Company
    Blair, Samuel
    Turnbull, William
    White, William

Capt John Parks' Company
    Costtey, John
    Morgan, Lt Joseph
    Shute, Thomas-Drummer

1793 (Contd)

Capt Thomas' Company
    Taylor, Perry

Capt John Rains' Company
    Baker, Zachariah
    Donahoe, John
    Donahoe, John (Was he Jr?)
    Goen, John
    Lattimore, Joseph
    Norris, William
    Pillow, William
    Pillow, William (Was he Jr?)

Capt John Shannon
    Howdeshale, Jacob
    Lattimore, Nathaniel
    Shannon, David
    Young, Adam
    Young, David

Capt Joseph Shaw
    Cash, William
    Land, Jesse

Attorneys named who collected pay for services in Gen John Sevier 1793 Campaign in 1798

    Charter, James
    Chisolm, Ignatius
    Cowan, Samuel
    Cowan, Nathaniel & Samuel
    Conway, John Jr
    Crozier, John
    Deaderick, David
    Dunlap, Hugh
    Gammon, Richard
    Greer, John
    Greer, Joseph
    Huston, Robert

    King & Crozier
    McClung, Charles
    Miller, Robert
    Ore, James
    Ray, John
    Rhea, John
    Sevier, John Jr
    Shaw, Nathaniel
    Shelby, John
    Tatum, Judge
    Williams, John
    Wylie, Robert

1794

Bird, Abraham (wounded)
Blackburn, William (killed 8-14-1794) Capt Rickard's Co
Blackwell, David
Bowman, Elias
 -Capt Samuel Henry's Co
Buchanan, Ezekiel, Wagoner
Camel, Hugh
 -Ens James Henry's detach
Carr, William -Prisoner from Capt Read's Co
Chandler, Ens Richard Paymaster
Chisolm, Ignatius
 -Capt Menefee's Co
Cox, Sgt Thomas
Craig, James
 -Lt Nath Veitche's detach
Greer, Joseph
Guest, Thomas
 -Capt Menefee's Co
Henry, Lt James
Henry, Capt Samuel

Kenney, Ens James
Long, John
 (Joseph Anderson, exec)
Long, Lt Joseph
McGaughey, Capt Samuel
McLaughlin, Ens Alexander
Menefee, Capt
Pollock, John -Capts McGaughey & Tedford
Read, Capt
Rickard, Capt William
Serratt, Joseph
 -Lt Abraham Stover
Sloan, John -Capt Samuel Henry
Stover, Lt Abraham
Taylor, Cornet
Tedford, Capt Joseph
Thomas, Henry
 -Ens Alex McLaughlin
Veitche, Lt Nathaniel
Walker, Daniel -Lt Nath Veitche
Wellington, Lt
Williams, Ralph -Cornet Taylor

1795

Blair, Lt Robert	Johnston, Aquilla
Brown, Joseph -Cornet Hendrix	Low, Aquilla
Burns, Walter -Capt Henderson	McClelland, Sgt Samuel
Dunham, Harden -Cornet Hendrix	Menefee, Capt
Frost, Thomas	Menefee, Thomas
Greer, Phillip -Lt Mitchell	Mitchell, Lt
Harrison, Jesse -Capt Harrison	Nicholas, George -Lt Blair
Harrison, Capt Michael	Nicholas, William -Lt Blair
Henderson, Capt William	Rhea, Capt Robert
Hendrix, Cornet Luke	Rice, Step -Lt Blair
Houston, John -Capt Rhea	Smith, John
Ivy, Verdunt -Capt Henderson	

The following is a copy of the Muster Roll of the 12th Company of the 3rd sub-legion of the U.S. Army as of May 31, 1795. This company was sent to White's Blockhouse, which was located where the present Knox County Courthouse now stands. The company was commanded by Capt William Carr and Lt (later Capt) William Rickard. This Muster Roll was found by the late W E Parham of Maryville, Tennessee among the papers of David McKamey (War of 1812). This company was sent to Tellico Blockhouse as soon as the barracks were built, and in 1797 to Southwest Point. At this time lieutenants received $26, ensigns $20, corporals $6, drummers $5, and privates $4 per month. The payroll was signed by David Henley, Agent to the War Department.

Lt William Rickard	Corp Joseph Ferguson
Ens Samuel Davidson	Corp John Goldman
Sgt William Brent	Drummer James Henderson
Corp William Miller	Fifer George Dixon

Privates

Aldridge, Benjamin	Gosslip, John	Payne, Thomas
Aldridge, John	Harrool, John	Phillips, George
Barber, David	Henderson, James	Rickenberger, William
Barry, John	Henry, Jacob	Sedgwick, John
Berkly, Benj E	Hughes, Theopolis	Shaw, Abraham
Brummitt, William	Larkins, Edward	Shaw, Michael
Bryan, James	Markham, James	Sneed, Allen
Buck, Dennis	Marlow, David	Townsley, James
Coleman, James	McDonald, John	Trayman, John
Cosby, James	McKamey, Joseph	Turner, John
Dixon, William	Meminy, William	Vaught, Gasper
Donathan, Frederick	Moore, Alexander	Veal, Edward
Dudley, William	Morgan, John	Walsh, George
Edmonds, Abel	Moses, John	Washburn, Sherrill
Farrell, John	Murphy, Barnett	Watkins, Benjamin
Ferguson, Benjamin	Newman, Benjamin	Wilson, James
Fryar, Charles	Nickerson, John	Wood, John

(Nearly all of these men were Revolutionary soldiers.) These troops under Lt Col Thomas Butler had been ordered by Gen Henry Knox to Tellico Blockhouse. One of their stated duties was to remove the white people who were living over the Indian line. The Barracks and Blockhouse at Tellico were finished in Aug 1794.

1796

- Bridges, Joseph -Capt Rickard
- Brown, Capt Morgan
- Butler, Zachariah -Capt Rickard
- Brummitt, Corp
- Carr, William (Prisoner)
- Coffield, Dempsey -Capt Moses Webb
- Davidson, Lt Samuel
- Dunning, Lt Robert
- Fournier, Dr N H S
- Henderson, Capt Wm -Mtd Mil
- Johnston, Moses -Capt Parks
- King, Thomas (Deserter)
- Manley, Armsted -Capt Sparks
- Mitchell, Capt Thomas
- Morgan, Lt Joseph
- Parks, Capt John
- Phillips, George
- Preston, Wm -Capt Sparks
- Rickard, Capt Wm -3rd Regt
- Schote, Isaac -Capt Parks
- Sparks, Capt Richard -3rd Reg
- Tunnell, John (Deserter)
- Wade, Capt John -3rd Regt
- Webb, Capt Moses

1797

- Allison, Capt
- Bird, Abraham
- Bird, Capt Ross -4th Regt
- Bowman, Joseph Q M
- Bridges, Joseph (Disch)
- Brooks, Capt Joseph
- Brown, David
- Brown, John (Fifer) -Capt Sparks
- Browning, Amaziah (Died) -Capt Gregg
- Browning, Roger -Pd as heir of above (Father)
- Brummitte, Corp
- Bryant, William (Writer) -Capt Jos Brooks
- Butler, Capt Ed -4th Regt
- Butler, Zachariah (Disch)
- Campbell, Ensign
- Carr, Richard (Disch) -Capt Sparks
- Carter, Srgt
- Chisolm, Capt John (Tellico)
- Claiborne, Dr Thomas
- Cole, Capt Joseph
- Coody, Arthur (Interpreter)
- Crozier, John (P M at Knoxville)
- Davidson, Andrew
- Day, David
- Devin, Lieut
- Dickinson, Ensign
- Dodson, Corp James
- Doherty, Col George
- Dougherty, Wm (Deserter)
- Dunlap, Hugh -Secret mission to ascertain Coxe's forces
- Duvale, Srgt James
- Farragut, George -Asst storekeeper
- Fournier, Dr N H S
- Frier, Jeremiah (Deserter)
- Frier, Richard (Deserter)
- Gillespie, John
- Gillespie, Capt Thomas
- Gordon, George
- Gordon, John -Secret mission
- Grant, Maj James
- Grant, John
- Gregg, Capt James
- Haversham, Joseph (P M Gen)
- Hawkins, Benjamin -Agent to Creeks
- Hendrix, Cornet Luke
- Henderson, James (Disch)
- Hitherington, Capt John
- Hoffman, Michael (Deserter)
- Houston, Samuel
- Jack, Jeremiah
- Johnstone, Wm (Deserter) -Paymaster
- Kersey, Maj William
- King, Capt
- Klotz, Isaac
- Knap, Samuel (Musician)
- Latrop, Isaac -Capt Hitherington
- Lewis, Capt Thomas
- Lovely, Wm L -Clerk to Factor
- Love, Robert
- McColley, John (Drummer) -Capt Sparks
- McCoy, Annanias
- McLeod, Srgt Malcolm
- McDermott, Lieut
- McDermott, Cornet Paul -Dragoons
- McDonald, Daniel -Eng Strother

1797 (Contd)

McIntyre, Peter -Capt Sparks
McKenzie, Joseph (Disch)
McLin, Zachfield -Asst to Hawkins
McNimmee, Wm -Capt Richard
McTeer, James
Manley, Armstead
Marks, Lieut
Martin, David -Capt Richard
Mitchell, Capt Thomas
Montgomery, Srgt Maj William
Nash, John -Capt Sparks
Neal, Thomas -Capt King
Neville, George
Parry, Srgt Nelson
Patterson, Robert
  (Pd for cleaning rifles)
Peery, J
Phillipps, George
Pitchlynn, John (Interpreter)
Preston, William
Rawlins, Nathaniel -Capt Allison
Rickard, Capt William -3rd Regt
  (Paymaster for 1793 claims)
Riggs, Clotsby
Rose, Hugh -Capt Wade
Russell, Andrew -Capt Joe Cole's Co
Sharp, Anthony
Sharp, Danile -Capt Sparks Co
Sparks, Capt Richard
  -In command at Tellico

Strother, Ensign George
  -3rd Regt
Swain, Ensign Thomas
  -Recruiting Off
Taylor, Mr
Taylor, Jonathan
  -Recruiting Off
Tharp, Srgt Dodson
Thompson, Capt Robert
Tiner, Lewis
  -Clerk to Factor
Tittleton, James
  -Deserter from 4th Regt
Trimble, Ichabod
Turner, John Fothergill
  -Capt Rickard
Upton, James
Van Ranseleer
  -Capt of Dragoons
Wallace, James
Wade, Capt John (3rd Regt)
  -To Southwest Point in March
Wallington, Lieut of 4th Regt
Waters, Jonah Q M
Weaver, Christian -3rd Regt
Webb, John (Pack Horseman)
  -Capt Richard Sparks
Williams, Thomas H
  -Clerk to Silas Dinsmore
Wright, Lieut Charles
  -Sent to Knox from Phila

1798

Capt Richard Sparks' Company - 3rd Regt at Tellico Blockhouse

  Albright, Capt John
  Armstrong, William
  Brown, John (Fifer)
  Campbell, Ensign
  Carr, Richard (Disch)
  Claiborne, Dr Thomas A
  Dunlap, George
  Easton, Sgt Maj John
    (Pursuing deserters)
  Evans, Robert
  Flynn, William
  Haines, John
    -Storekeeper of Mil supplies
  Leadon, Corp Patrick
  Leitheiser, Lt
  Lockwood, Capt Benjamin

  McColley, John (Drummer)
    -Stationed at Tellico
  McDermott, Cornet Paul
  McLean, Lt George
  McLeod, John
  Nash, John
  Overshire, Corp
  Parry, Sgt Nelson
  Perry, Martin
  Salmon, Ensign
  Strother, Ens George
  Swain, Ensign
  Taylor, Lt Jonathan
    -Q M of Regt
  Thomas, Ensign
  Weaver, Christian
  Whaland, Patrick
  Wright, Lt Charles -Paymaster

1798 (Contd)

4th Regt, Blockhouse - Recruited in 1797

   Balls, Lt under Capt Robt Thompson
   Bird, Capt Ross
   Butler, Capt Edward
   Butler, Lt Col Commandant
   Chandler, Ens Richard -Paymaster for dischargees
   Gordon, George -Deserter from Capt Preston's Co
   Preston, Capt William
   Purdy, Lt under Capt Thompson
   Swain, Lt under Capt Thompson
   Thompson, Richard
   Thompson, Capt Robert
   Tinsman, Joseph -Deserter from Capt Butler's Co
   Wright, Edward -Dep Paymaster & Storekeeper

TELLICO BLOCKHOUSE

The Blockhouse was built in 1794 by Gov William Blount, with J W Hooker serving as the first Factor, and in 1797 and 1798 James Byers. John McKee was temporary Indian Agent. It was planned as a Fort and Trading Post, and until 1797 had only a token garrison. In 1794 we find that Barclay McGhee, John Lowry, Matthew Wallace, Robert Wilson, David Craig and James Greenaway were licensed to trade with the Cherokees at Tellico (Blount Journal). Major John Strother entertained the three sons of the Duke of Orleans there and introduced them to wild turkey, while the fort was in the process of being rebuilt. In 1797 the Barracks were built and the Blockhouse moved. Federal troops were then stationed there, with Lieut Col Thomas Butler as Commandant. The 3rd U S Regt with Captains John Wade, Richard Sparks and William Rickard and Ensign George Strother, and the 4th U S Regt with Captains Robert Thompson, Ross Bird, Edward Butler and William Preston, comprised the garrison. (The 4th was recruited in 1797.) Storekeepers there included James Ore, George Farragut, John Harris, Edward Wright and John Tiner.

Expense items found in the Waste Book mention:

Jacob Lavander, James Cunningham & 5 others Pd for moving Blockhouse to barrack yard	$ 54.00
James Hay (3-29-1797) - shingles for barracks	47.25
Hugh Beard - lumber delivered at the barracks	2.10
Stephen Hillis for going to Nicholas Bartlett's to get planks to case up the arms and muskets	4.42
Thomas H Williams, salary as Clerk & $1.50 for registering the deed for land the barracks is on	80.61
Silas Dinsmore, Agent to the Cherokees (Stationed at Tellico) - a quarter's salary	250.00
Gasper Vaught - Artist to the Cherokees & subsistence	69.00
His wife, as Spinster " " " "	57.50
Francis Jones, in charge of Quartermaster Dept	
Thomas Hope, double walnut desk for Silas Dinsmore (Desk now in Blount Mansion)	30.00
desk	25.00
table board to write at	6.00
Charles McCormick - 273½ yds linsey to be del by Barclay McGhee for use of public store at Tellico	159.55
John Hammer - 2 grindstones	2.50
Christopher Haynes - axes, mattocks & ploughs	557.14
Edmond Casteel - for getting down a flat from Knoxville to Tellico	7.00
Gen James White - for the magazine rent 9-15-1796--5-31-1797	37.50
Robert Morrow - a press to keep the public papers in	28.29
Oliver Cromwell - 7 trays for drying powder	3.00
John Hildebrand - 5 bu meal del at sundry times	2.50
Mary Robertson - 65 lbs hard soap	6.33
Robert Pearce - 6 spinning wheels	18.00
Negro - bottoming 6 chairs	1.00

Stephen Hillis, Clerk	$
Ludwell Grimes, clerk to Mr Hillis (3 mos)	90.49
Bernard Webb, Ditto	59.51
Sallie Owens & Mrs Hindman - baking bread for Capt Webb's troops	3.50
Joseph Habersham, P M Gen for Knoxville P O, by John Crozier, P M for the year 1797	274.11
Wm Baldic for making coffin, & carpenter work for Dr Claiborne	10.50
Alexander Cunningham, Ferryman across Holston River	
James Roddy & James Neely, Ferrymen over Holston at Knoxville	
John Sharkey, Ferrymen across Clinch River	
Dr Thomas A Claiborne - services 7 mos, 1797	219.64
Dr Claiborne - medicines & case of drawers for same	55.00
Dr N H S Fournier for attending Chickasaw Indians	31.00
Olive Pippin, Peggy Beard & Katherine Coody, matrons of hospital (2 mos each)	85.68
George Roulstone - advertising & blank receipts for Mr Hillis	9.50
- 100 orders & 200 permits for Col Butler	25.00
- public paper for Sec of Treas	1.50
- 200 copies address of Sec of State	25.00
- ad re horse del up by Cherokees	12.00
Roulstone & Parrington - adv for deserters in 4th Regt	55.00
James Grant - blank receipts for Sevier's Expd	20.00

Indian Department:
  Interpreters (usually paid $25 per mo) -

Carey, James - for the Cherokees (15 mos)	375.00
Coody, Arthur - for the Cherokees (4-1--6-30-1797)	75.00
Dinsmore, Silas - Temporary Agent to Cherokees (3 mos)	250.00
Hicks, Charles - for the Cherokees (7-1--9-30-1797)	75.00
McGhee, Malcolm - for the Chickasaws (3 mos)	75.00
McLish, William - for the Chickasaws (3 mos)	75.00
- for the Cherokees (6 mos)	150.00
Mitchell, Samuel - Temporary Agent to Choctaws (3 mos)	200.00
Pitchlynn, John - for the Choctaws (4-1--6-30-1797)	75.00
Riley, Samuel - for the Cherokees (1 yr)	198.74
- Ditto (3 mos)	62.52
Rogers, John - for the Creeks	
Robertson, Gen James - Temporary Agent to Chickasaws & Choctaws (8 mos)	282.42
Lieut Hartman Leithesur - for expenses of Wolfe's Friend & 4 other Chickasaw Indians going to Philadelphia to visit the President	500.00
Thomas Hudiburg - house for Chickasaws on way to Phila	
Barclay McGhee - horse & large wagon for carrying Opiomingo to Phila when wounded	400.00
Joseph Greer - for Negroes agreeable to direction of the Chiefs	300.00
John Rogers - expenses of 11 Creeks, Phila to Knox	446.90
James Carey - his & Cherokees expenses, Phila to Knox	923.08
21¼ gal & 2 kegs whiskey for Opiomingo, by his request & sent by George Colbert in boat Col John Steele went to the Natchez in	27.56

Opiomingo's wife - needles, pins & 2 lbs brn sugar $	1.56
John Rogers - furnishing 9 pack horses to carry Creek presents from Lookout Mt to his house	100.00
Robert Houston - for rent of a house for Opiomingo & family 8-26--11-26-1796	7.50
Opiomingo & his party - 5 bu meal to prepare them for journey to Phila	2.50
Samuel Henry - entertaining Malcolm McGhee & 8 Chickasaws & John Rogers & 11 Creeks (1796)	12.12
Benjamin White - canoe for John Watts	10.00
Mrs Jean Woods - for boarding Betsy McKee & Nancy Martin who came to Knox for surgical operations	
Capt John Wade - expenses of Opiomingo, traveling from Phila to Knoxville	204.22

Wagoners:

Beard, John (Indian) - bringing public goods to the Treaty at Tellico	160.00
Dunwoody, John & Buchanan, David - Knoxville to Tellico (1798)	8.00
Hambleton, William (1797) - bringing medicine & hospital stores & the Cherokee presents	
Kelly, John	
Klotz, Isaac - hauling Capt Wade's baggage to Southwest Point	
Miller, John (1795) & Moore, Solomon	
Silver, John (Indian) - bringing public goods to Treaty at Tellico	160.08
White, Moses - hauling goods from Knox to Treaty	
Wolfe, Morton (Indian) - bringing goods to Treaty	

Post Riders:

David Deaderick - carrying vouchers from Jonesboro to Baltimore	3.27
Srgt Malcolm McCloud - riding express to the Cumberland with dispatches from Silas Dinsmore to Gen Winchester, Commissioner for running the Indian line	5.00
Jesse Roach - riding express from Knoxville to Nashville, with dispatches from Sec of War to Commanding Officer at Walnut Hills & Natchez	10.00
George Strother - money advanced for express from Tellico to Estaunaula for Silas Dinsmore	1.50
Henry Quirk - bring down dispatches from the Chickasaw Bluff & return (76 days)	76.00
David Perkins - riding express from the Choctaw Nation to Nashville, Feb to Aug 1798	200.00
Sampson Williams - riding express with letters from Gen Robertson to Gov Blount	50.00
Charles Wright - riding express from Phila to Knox with dispatches from Sec of War to Commanding Officer Capt Richard Sparks at Tellico & subsistence (Approx 1 yr)	426.28

THE TREATY AT TELLICO

The Treaty at Tellico was entered into between the Federal Government and the Cherokee Indians on October 2, 1798.

The original Commission was: Alfred Moore of North Carolina, Fisher Ames of Massachusetts and Bushrod Washington of Virginia. The latter two did not serve and their places were filled by George Walton of Georgia and Col John Steele of Virginia. Gen James Robertson of Mero District, James Stuart, Speaker of the House of Representatives, and Major Lachlan McIntosh of Knoxville were the Agents for Tennessee. Stuart did not serve because of ill health and was replaced by Gen James White of Knoxville. Elisha J Hall served as Secretary for the Commission. Col Thomas Butler was the Commandant at Tellico Blockhouse and Silas Dinsmore was Agent to the Cherokees, with Stephen Hillis serving as scribe.

The Commissioners met with the Cherokees in July 1798 but failed to come to any agreement. They met again in September without McIntosh, Steele and Robertson. Finally George Walton and Thomas Butler signed the Treaty for the Federal Government on Oct 2, 1798.

Expense items re the Treaty include:

Benjamin Hawkins (Supt of Indian Affairs) Commissioner for running the Indian line	$1,000.00
Col David Henley (Agent of War under Sec Henry Knox) Commissioner for running the Indian line	1,000.00
Zachfield Maclin, Asst to Hawkins, salary	333.66
Expenses returning to Creek Nation	40.00
Mrs Patty Chisolm for keeping William McLish & Major George Colbert while visiting Col Hawkins	19.82
Gen James Winchester - re Cherokee line	309.67
Judge George Walton, salary as Commissioner at Treaty of Tellico	1,000.00
Also for services & expenses for holding & concluding Treaty of Tellico	2,012.50
Judge Walton by Col Steele	300.00
Col John Steele, salary as Commissioner	1,376.00
Daniel Ross by John Steele	68.00
Alfred Moore - attendance & travel as Commissioner	848.00
Expenses of Walton, Moore & Steele - Tellico (June 25)	1,150.00
Lt Col Thomas Butler, salary as Commissioner	988.00
Elisha J Hall, Secretary to Commission	100.00
Going to Phila with dispatches	200.00
7 Chain carriers & 2 markers & services of surveyor in running Cherokee line	392.00
Bloody Fellow as Commissioner	57.00
Wm L Lovely - rent of house for Commissioners & Agents	160.00
Nicholas Byers, ditto plus bed & pr of sheets	120.00
James Jones, Agent for James O'Hara & Co (Phila) - Provisions for the Treaty	1,000.00
Amos Bird, Agent for James O'Hara & Co - Provisions for the Treaty	1,000.00

King & Crozier (Knoxville) - supplies for Treaty	$4,022.83
Francis Preston - Ditto	630.00
James Ore, for Edward Carrington, Supt of Va, transportation of Cherokee goods from Richmond to this place (Tellico)	1,046.12
John Overton, counsel & pleadings in suit - Judge David Campbell vs Col Thomas Butler for removing him off the Indian lands	20.00
Thomas Gray, for same (4-1798) in Superior Ct	12.50
Hugh Dunlap - riding express, carrying Col Butler's proclamation to the Frontiers (9-22-1797)	15.00
Expenses for Judge McNairy, Mr Hawkins, the Dragoons ferriage, Mr Dinsmore & myself (Col David Henley) going to Tellico to examine the proofs relative to the intercepted letter of Gov Wm Blount	4.00
John Rogers - to bear expenses being ordered to Phila, by the Sec of War & Committee for investigating Gov Blount's criminal plot	100.00
Mrs Patty Chisolm - boarding John Rogers enroute to Phila (9-5-1797)	16.50
Maj James Grant, Capt Thomas Lewis & James Carey's expenses from Knoxville to Philadelphia by Special Act of Congress (8-18-1797)	130.00
Hugh Dunlap - for services (secret) performed for Col Butler at Nolachucky "Note- it was to ascertain the situation & force of Coxe" (8-29-97)	15.00
Agents expenses, going to Greeneville - to get information of Coxe (9-20-1797)	6.00
John Gordon - services on secret mission	100.00
Russell Bean's expenses to the Natchez	20.00
King & Crozier (1-13-1798) set of Laws of U S - 3 bks	7.00

PETITION FROM OVERTON COUNTY, TENNESSEE

Oct 26, 1813

TO THE HONOURABLE THE GENERAL ASSEMBLY OF THE STATE OF TENNESSEE NOW IN SESSION THE PETITION OF THE SUBSCRIBERS, INHABITANTS OF THE COUNTY OF OVERTON, HUMBLY SHEWETH THAT THEY FEEL DISPOSED TO HAVE A PART IN THE PRESENT WAR WITH HIS BRITANIE MAJESTY'S SAVAGE ALLIES, VIZ, THE CREEK NATION OF INDIANS AND CONCEIVING THEY CAN RENDER GREATER SERVICES TO THE UNITED STATE AS MOUNTED MEN THAN THEY COULD POSSIBLY DO ON FOOT DO HUMBLY REQUEST THAT YOUR HONOURABLE BODY WOULD PASS A LAW AUTHORIZING COLLONAL STEPHEN COPELAND OF SAID COUNTY TO RAISE BY VOLUNTARY INLISTMENT A FORCE OF 500 MOUNTED MEN OUT OF THE 3d JUDICIAL CIRCUIT IN SAID STATE TO MARCH AGAINST THE SAID NATION OF INDIANS OR OTHER TRIBES OF THE SAVAGE FOE AND FIGHT THEM IN THEIR OWN SAVAGE WAY AND ACT AS RANGERS ETC SO LONG AS IT MAY APPEAR NECESSARY AND THAT THE SAID VOLUNTARY FORCES WHEN SO RAISED MAY BE PAID AND ALLOWED THE SAME PAY FOR THEIR SERVISES AS OTHER MOUNTED MEN ARE ALLOWED IN THE SERVISE OF THE UNITED STATES ON SIMULAR OCCASIONS - AND THAT THE SENATORS AND REPRESENTATIVES IN THE CONGRESS OF THE UNITED STATES BE INSTRUCTED TO CAUSE THE SAID ACT WHEN PASSED BY YOUR HONOURABLE BODY TO BE SANCTIONED BY THE NATIONAL LEGISLATOR ETC. AN YOUR PETITIONERS SHALL EVER PRAY ETC.

Robt Adkinson, Wm Allen, Sever Alley, Solomon Alred, Wm Alred, Peter Arnet, Jesse Ashland; Arthur Babb, Philip W Bever, Peter Bilyew, James Boswell, Wm Boswell, James Bradshaw, Benj Brown, Sam Brown, Thos Burford; Samuel Callihan, Joseph Campbell, Cornelos Cannady, Thos Chamberlain, Francis Chaney, John Cisco, Wm Cooksey, James Copeland, Stephen Copeland, Wm Copeland, Larkin Cox, Edmon Crafford, Isaac Cunningham; Matthew Dale, Robt Dale, Wm Dale, Jacob Davie, Hall Dilling, Henry Dillon, Lard Dillon; John Eldridge, Sampson Eldridge, Zachariah Eldridge, Wm Evans; Alexr Fensler, James Finley, Wm Fleming; Thos Gallion, Thompson Gardenshire, Jesse Gentry, Henry Gillmore, Henery Gore; John Hamoc, Wm Harlow, Jos Harris, W Harrison, Hollel Herren, Isaac Hooser, Isaac W Hooser, John Horn, Stephen Horn, Wilie Hudleston, John Hughes, Isac Hurst; Mason Kelly, John Kennedy, James Key; Quillow Lamb, James Lee, John Lee, Thos Levington, Merel Littel; Moore Matlock, Charles Matney, James Mayfield, Stephen Mayfield, James Maxwell, John Maxwell, John Miller, Samuel Miller, Arthur Mitchell, Richard Mittens (?), Joshua Morrison; James McBotts, James McCampbell, Wm McCarney, Thomas McDaniel; John R Nelson; James Officer; Joel Paris, James Parks, Benjm Parrott, Richard Postton; Joseph Raney, Nelson Ray, Isa Roe, Eliga Rogers, Pattrik Roof, Isiah Ruckman; Robert Sersay, Simon Sims, William Sims, Birtton Smith, James Smith, Isaac M Smith, Hershel Speck, William Stark, John Stockton, David Stuart, Andrew Swallows, Jacob Swallows; B Tatten, Isaac Taylor, Wm Taylor; Filep Upton, William Upton, Wm Upton; Emstort Walker, John Walker, Jos H Windle, Benj M Workman, John Workman, Ephraim Wykoff; John Thomas Young -

The above names were wrote by me Jos H Windle at a Genl Muster by their requests.

Hiram Allen; Arthur Babb, Henry Bailey, Robt Boyd, Allen Brock, Joel Brock; Joel Cain, Daniel Cannon, John Cannon, John Cargile, Sterling Collier; Carter Dalton, John Davies, Elijah Davis, John Davise, Walter Disk, William Dobbs; Solomon Eaves, John Erwin, Madison Fisk, John Flat, Arthur Flowers, Benj Flowers; Joseph Garrott, George Gilpatrick, John Goode, Abraham Goodpasture, Arthur Goodpasture, John Goodpasture, Joseph Grammer, John Grayham, John Grimsley, Martin Grimsley, Wm Gunnells; Greenwood Harison, Tiry Harp, John Harris, Joseph Harris, Samuel Harris, Thos R Harris, Benjamin Harrison, Eli Harrison, W Harrison, Jeremiah Holeman, Isaac Holiman, Wm Holiman, John Huddleston, Jesse Hull; Isom Johnson; Vardiman Lee, Daniel Liles, David Liles; James Mabry, Jesse Masters, Thomas Masters, Arthur Mitchell, George Moore, John W Moore, James Murray, Randal Murray; Fras McConnell, James McConnell, John McCord, James McRoberts; Wm Officer; John Partrick, Wm Prat; John Rolls, Jacob Rook, Isaiah Row, Stephen Row; John Savage, Stephen Sewel, Isaac Shell, John Smart, Charles Staples, Archilles Stephens; Gideon Thomas; James Willard, William Willard, Reubin Witt, Henry Wood, James Woods; James Zachray

(Copied from original legislative petition on file for year 1813, Tennessee State Archives, Tennessee State Library, Nashville, Tennessee)

ACCOUNT BOOK OF THE FIRM OF HENDERSON & McGHEE, STOREKEEPERS
Maryville, Tenn   Oct 24, 1814 - Dec 16, 1815
(Book in possession of Mrs Gus Hunt, Madisonville, Tenn -
 Data copied by Nancy Jones Stickley in 1940 re 1812 Soldiers
 for Mary Hardin McCown, Johnson City, Tenn)

No of Acct	Customer	Remarks
164	Anderson, Wm	Waggoner
105	Biggs, Capt A	
51	Bovais, Maj	
166	Boyd, Capt Robt	
31	Cowan, Capt Samuel	
	Cusick, John B	Was Capt of the Militia with Gen Sam Houston, then a Lieut
193	Davis, ---	By discharge
193	Devine, ---	By discharge
16	Gardner, Capt James	
26	Gray, Maj William	
205	Harris, Samuel	By discharge
135	Harris, Maj Wm	
2	Henderson, Capt Thomas	
166	Henderson, Thomas	April 16, 1815 By part of John Gold's dis
193	Henderson, Thomas	Oct 1, 1815 By Davis' discharge
185	Houston, John	Waggoner (Aug 2, 1815)
6	Houston, Maj James	
130	Houston, Lieut Samuel	(June 10, 1815) (n: The Raven)
193	Hunter, David W	
187	Jack, Capt Wm	(Aug 1815)
35	Lett, Col James	May, 1818 - goods to wife
193	McCallylon,	By discharge of
160	McClemmons, Samuel	By his discharge
176	McKemy, Capt David	
59	McKee, Capt Alexander	
125	McKee, Capt Alex	
196	Martin, Moses	By bal of his discharge
121	Logan, Capt Wm	
48	Reagan, Capt John	
48	Ragan, Capt John	For his daughter
36	Rider, John Jr	By Alex Rider's discharge By his own By Alex Rider's back rations
125	Tedford, James	(May 1815) By a wagon discharge
125	Tedford, Capt James	
85	Thompson, Capt Samuel	
27	Thornburg, Col John	
27	Trimble, Capt John	
179	Wallace, William (Of Horse)	By a horseman's discharge 6 Lb- 15
16	Wallace, Capt Wm	
169	Wear, John	Waggoner
74	Woods, Capt John Esq	

ADDENDA

Additional names of Soldiers of the War of 1812 Buried in Tennessee obtained after the list was compiled.

ALLEN, WILLIAM (--liv 1828 List Sumner Co); Md ( ); served Tenn Mil; P D & 2400 Pensioners, Armstrong; likely Sumner Co; Unkn.

ALLCORN, Col JOHN (--3-9-1829 aged 62 yrs, Wilson Co); Md Prudence (c 1779--8-5-1854); Lieut Col, under Col John Coffee's Regt T V Cav, 9-24-1813--10-29-1813 & promoted to Col, Regt T V Cav, 10-30-1813--12-10-1813; W D & T S A & Tenn Soldiers in War of 1812, Vol 1- Allen; Allcorn Fam Cem 10th Distr, E Hunter's Pt Pike, 1½ m N Lebanon, Wilson Co; Pvt mkr.

BEASLEY, MAJOR A (--liv 1883 Rome, Smith Co); Md ( ); War of 1812; P D #5936; likely Rome, Smith Co; Unkn.

BLEDSOE, ANTHONY (--killed 7-20-1788 Bledsoe's Station, Davidson Co); Md ( ); Early Indian Wars, killed; Ramsey's Annals of Tenn & Acklen Records; Davidson Co; Unkn.

BLEDSOE, ISAAC (--killed 1793 Davidson Co); Md ( ); Early Indian Wars; Ramsey's Annals & Acklen Records; Davidson Co; Unkn.

BOSTON, GEORGE (--liv 1883 List Pleasant Shade, Smith Co); Md ( ); War of 1812; P D #7756; likely Pleasant Shade, Smith Co; Unkn.

BOYTE, LEMUEL (--liv 1883 List Dover, Stewart Co); Md ( ); War of 1812; P D #3736; likely Stewart Co; Unkn.

BRADFUTE, ROBERT (--aft 1860 Nashville, Davidson Co); Md 1- (--d 1827), 2- ( ); Pvt, Capt Nelson Brunt or Capt Wilson Bryan's Co; W D & B L Wt; likely in Nashville, Davidson Co; Unkn. (His first wife is bur in Old City Cem, Nashville)

BRADLEY, SAMUEL (--liv 1883 List Hartsville, Trousdale Co); Md ( ); War of 1812; P D #11,977; likely Hartsville, Trousdale Co; Unkn.

CATRON, Judge JOHN (c 1786--5-30-1865 Nashville, Davidson Co); Md ( ); War of 1812 under Jackson; T S A; Nashville, Davidson Co; Unkn. (Judge Catron was first Chief Justice of Tenn, 1831, later on Supreme Court of U S, 1837)

CONNER, ISAAC (--d 5-14-1814 in service); Md ( ); heirs were Kitty, Nancy, Lucinda, Viney, Ann & Thomas Conner of Knox Co; served 7th Regt U S Inf; P D & 2400 Pensioners, Armstrong; likely where died; Unkn.

CUNNINGHAM, ANDREW (--d 4-25-1815 in service); Md ( ); heirs were Andrew, James Robt & John Cunningham in Knox Co; served 20th Regt, U S Inf; P D & 2400 Pensioners, Armstrong; likely where died; Unkn.

DUNWOODY, PATRICK M (1-31-1789--d Jefferson Co); Md Esther Bare c 1815 (1-6-1793--); 1st Lieut, Capt John Brock's Co, Col Sam Bayless' 4th Regt Drftd Mil, 11-8-1814--5-18-1815; W D & T S A; likely in Jefferson Co; Unkn.

EATON, JOHN H (6-18-1790 N C --11-17-1856 Washington D C); Md 1-Myra Lewis (   ), 2-Peggy O'Neal (   ); Pvt, War of 1812; W D & T S A; Oak Hill Cem, Washington, D C; Pvt mkr. John H Eaton wrote Life of Andrew Jackson, pub 1817; served in U S Senate 1817)

EVANS, WILLIAM (--liv 1828 List Robertson Co); Md (   ); served T V; P D & 2400 Pensioners, Armstrong; likely Robertson Co; Unkn.

EVANS, CHARLES (--liv 5-18-1852 B L Wt, Hamilton Co); Md (   ); Pvt, Capt Hendrix' Co; P D #37,464 & B L Wt, Edwards Acct Bk, Leaves from Family Tree -Allen, 5-13-1934; likely in Hamilton Co; Unkn.

EFFLER, LAWRENCE (--liv 1883 Clear Branch, Unicoi Co); Md (   ); War of 1812; P D; likely in Unicoi Co; Unkn.

FIELDS, DAVID (--killed 3-27-1814 at Tohopeka, Ala); Md (   ); Pvt, Capt Joseph Everett's Co, Col Ewen Allison's Regt, E T Drftd Mil, 1-7-1814--3-27-1814 killed; W D & T S A & Tenn Soldiers in War of 1812, Vol 1 -Allen; likely in Ala; Unkn.

FORD, THOMAS (--d 2-14-1814 in service); Md (   ); Pvt, Capt John Hampton's Co, Col Ewen Allison's Regt E T Drftd Mil, 1-5-1814--2-14-1814 died; W D & T S A & Tenn Soldiers in War of 1812, Vol 1 -Allen; likely where died; Unkn.

RAGON, ELI (--liv 4-22-1852 Hamilton Co); Md (   ); Pvt, Capt Lewis' Co; B L Wt #47,645, Edwards Acct Bk, Leaves from Family Tree -Allen, 5-13-1934; likely Hamilton Co; Unkn.

www.ingramcontent.com/pod-product-compliance
Lightning Source LLC
Chambersburg PA
CBHW042352070526
44585CB00028B/2900